Authenticity in Nature

Making Choices about the Naturalness of Ecosystems

Nigel Dudley

earthscan

publishing for a sustainable future

London • New York

First published 2011
by Earthscan
2 Park Square, Milton Park, Abingdon, Oxon OX14 4RN

Simultaneously published in the USA and Canada
by Earthscan
711 Third Avenue, New York, NY 10017

Earthscan is an imprint of the Taylor & Francis Group, an informa business

Earthscan publishes in association with the International Institute for Environment and Development

British Library Cataloguing in Publication Data
A catalogue record for this book is available from the British Library

Library of Congress Cataloging-in-Publication Data
Dudley, Nigel.
    Authenticity in nature : making choices about the naturalness of ecosystems / Nigel Dudley.
    p. cm.
    Includes bibliographical references and index.
    1. Ecosystem management—Philosophy. 2. Nature conservation—Philosophy. 3. Naturalness (Environmental sciences) 4. Authenticity (Philosophy) I. Title.
    QH75.D83 2011
    577—dc23   2011013931

ISBN: 978-1-84407-835-6 (hbk)
ISBN: 978-1-84407-836-3 (pbk)

Typeset in Minion and Myriad
by Composition and Design Services
All photographs are by Nigel Dudley or Sue Stolton
Cover design by Clifford Hayes

MIX
Paper from
responsible sources
FSC® C004839
www.fsc.org

Printed and bound in Great Britain by
CPI Antony Rowe, Chippenham, Wiltshire

To Sue

Contents

List of Figures, Tables and Boxes

Figures

Tables

Boxes

List of Acronyms and Abbreviations

CBD	Convention on Biological Diversity
CI	Conservation International
CIFOR	Center for International Forestry Research
CWR	crop wild relatives
ESS	ecosystem services
FAO	UN Food and Agricultural Organization
FSC	Forest Stewardship Council
GIS	geographic information system
GFW	Global Forest Watch
HCVF	High Conservation Value Forest
IBI	Index of Biological Integrity
ICCA	indigenous and community conserved area
IPCC	Intergovernmental Panel on Climate Change
ISDR	International Strategy for Disaster Reduction
ITTO	International Tropical Timber Organisation
IUCN	International Union for Conservation of Nature
MCPFE	Ministerial Conference for the Protection of Forests in Europe
NBSAP	National Biodiversity Strategies and Action Plan
NTFP	non-timber forest product
PAGE	Pilot Analysis of Global Ecosystems
PES	Payment for Ecosystem Services
REDD	Reduced Impact from Deforestation and Degradation
SNS	sacred natural site(s)
TBFRA	Temperate and Boreal Forest Resource Assessment
TEEB	The Economics of Ecosystems and Biodiversity (programme)
UNECE	UN Economic Commission for Europe
UNDP	United Nations Development Programme
UNEP	United Nations Environment Programme
UNESCO	United Nations Educational, Scientific and Cultural Organization
UNFCCC	United Nations Framework Convention on Climate Change
UNHSP	UN Human Settlement Programme
WRI	World Resources Institute
WMO	World Meteorological Organization
WWF	World Wide Fund for Nature

Acknowledgements

One of the undervalued benefits of working in the fields of conservation and development is the chance to meet, work with and become friends with an exceptionally fine and inspiring group of people around the world. I've had that privilege now for several decades and the list of people who have contributed ideas, passion and experience that have gone into this book is far too long to be given here in full. They all have my thanks.

More explicitly, I would like to thank Judith Alfrey, Stuart Allison, Adrian Phillips, Kent Redford and Sue Stolton, who all commented on some or all of the text. Their criticisms encouraged me to rewrite and improve several sections, in one case substantially, and they picked up mistakes: remaining errors are my own responsibility. I'd also like to thank Tim Hardwick, Nick Ascroft, Laura Briggs, Jonathan Sinclair Wilson and others at Earthscan for both their help and their patience. Most of all I would like to thank my partner in life and work, Sue Stolton, who has shouldered far more than her fair share of our projects while I struggled to finish this text. This year is our 20th anniversary of working together as Equilibrium Research and it remains an enormous pleasure.

Introduction

A ttenborough Nature Reserve covers a few square miles of abandoned gravel workings bordering the River Trent near Nottingham, England, surrounded on the other three sides by suburban sprawl. Originally part of the flood plain of the Trent, the area was drained hundreds or perhaps even thousands of years ago and for centuries was used as grassland for cattle grazing, before gravel digging began in 1929. The remains of fishponds belonging to one of the local monasteries can be seen nearby. Today gravel is still being dug just beyond the borders of the reserve and barges pass through all day to the processing works on the edge of the village. The quarry company owns the site and leases it to the Nottinghamshire Wildlife Trust, which operates a popular nature centre and café in a solar-heated building on an island in one of the lagoons. Most of the reserve is open water with a few small islands, but there is also a network of paths and causeways and over the last 40 years mud flats, willow and alder scrub and grassland have regenerated. The Trust has created reed beds and birds like the bittern (*Botaurus stellaris*) have returned for the first time in living memory. Around 240 species of birds have been recorded (Carter et al, 2005) and from a conservation perspective the site is most significant for its over-wintering waterfowl.

As a boy I used to cycle to Attenborough Nature Reserve almost every day during the school holidays, content to wander for hours alone in what was still then a rather solitary place, weighed down with binoculars and collecting jars and identification books. Any skills as a field naturalist I have were accumulated slowly and painfully in that tiny area of abandoned workings. In time, I moved beyond identification to starting to understand a little bit about behaviour and ecology and visited frequently enough to get a feeling for the slow cycling of nature through the seasons. My experience must be similar to the majority of people working actively in conservation today; most of us don't get the opportunity to visit truly wild landscapes, or at least not on our own as teenagers, by getting on our bicycles and peddling a couple of miles down the road. Wastelands, abandoned lands, agricultural lands and other basically damaged ecosystems are where most modern naturalists get their first and perhaps their most intense experiences of wild nature. Even in the world's poorest and least developed countries, the proportion of people who have direct experience of natural ecosystems is falling all the time. Altered, managed and degraded areas are also the only places left for nature in a growing part of the planet. So these

FIGURE I.1 Attenborough Nature Reserve, a series of lagoons left behind by gravel digging, with power station in the background and a barge taking gravel from more recent excavations to the gravel works in the village

rather *unnatural* ecosystems are becoming increasingly important from both an ecological and cultural perspective.

The example is pertinent here because it represents one extreme of what I will be examining throughout the book: how our attitudes to naturalness need to change to keep pace with the rapid changes occurring in ecosystems throughout the world. In fact, Attenborough Nature Reserve started with very little biodiversity at all, being simply a succession of holes dug into a gravel bed. According to a simple interpretation of theories of island biogeography it should be virtually useless as an ecosystem: it is too small, too isolated and under far too much pressure to do anything except maintain a minimum of highly tolerant species. The area is also heavily polluted with sulphur dioxide and other pollutants, being downwind of a series of coal-burning power stations scattered along the Trent Valley. In the 1960s the River Trent was one of Britain's most polluted waterways, where the infamous 'detergent swans' became well known – large floating shapes made up of bubbles formed by the cocktail of chemicals in the water. Even today the area is hardly pristine. Local fishermen have illegally introduced a voracious alien crayfish into Attenborough's lagoons in an attempt to provide food for fish and there are also invasive zebra mussels (*Dreissena polymorpha*) from eastern Europe. Today the presence of the nature centre and café at the edge of the site has contributed to soaring numbers of visitors, who walk, exercise their dogs, cycle and run around the paths, many fairly oblivious to the wildlife around

FIGURE I.2 For many local children, a visit to the nature reserve is their first experience of 'natural ecosystems', even though this one is strictly speaking very unnatural

them. Yet the ecology is becoming steadily more diverse. When I first used to visit only four dragonfly species had been recorded, now there are 18, with new species gradually being blown to the site or migrating along the river. A few birds have gone over the last few decades – the barn owl (*Tyto alba*), tree pipit (*Anthus trivialis*), whinchat (*Saxicola rubetra*) and corn bunting (*Miliaria calandra*) – but more have taken their place or increased in numbers. Variety of butterflies and moths both seem to be increasing. The site has been adopted by an increasing number of migratory birds and has for them probably replaced wetlands that have disappeared elsewhere.

Just as significant in a different way is that this abandoned industrial site has become of enormous cultural importance for the area. For many local kids it is their first (maybe their only) introduction to nature 'in the raw'; schools run day trips and the Trust organizes popular pond-dipping birthday parties, thus forming the first important connection between wildlife seen on television and peoples' own experience. In the 1960s and 1970s visitors would be overwhelmingly white, now I see people from a wide range of ethnic groups. Coots and moorhens nest directly under the bridge leading to the café so anyone can see eggs and chicks, which is a totally new experience for many children and probably many adults as well.

The book in a nutshell

This book looks critically at what we understand as a 'natural ecosystem' and argues that these have been changed far more fundamentally than most of us like to admit. This does not mean that naturalness is irrelevant but rather it is still a critical component of human society, both from ethical and cultural standpoints and because of the many goods and services that natural ecosystems provide. Our concepts of naturalness have undergone some fundamental changes in history, from us being an unthinking part of nature, to a separation and conscious rejection of the natural and now a gradual and hesitant re-engagement. Attitudes to naturalness are not value free and attract strong levels of emotion. All existing ideas about what constitutes naturalness may need to be overhauled, particularly in light of climate change. Or to put it more simply: I criticize many of the myths of naturalness and wilderness but then rebuild concepts of naturalness in a slightly different and what might hopefully be a more usable form for conditions in the 21st century.

As ecosystems buckle under the weight of human pressures, we need a realistic set of measures to understand what is happening and to plan our responses. While we have some excellent criteria for assessing more-or-less natural systems, we are still struggling in many cases to understand and measure the importance of cultural systems, regenerating systems and damaged systems. My response to this entails, among other things, proposing a new definition of *authenticity* that can reflect elements of naturalness in both fairly pristine and radically altered ecosystems. This is increasingly relevant as ecosystems react quickly to climate change and old baselines disappear or become irrelevant. Authenticity focuses more on broad ecological function, resilience and persistence than on the minutiae of species composition and ecological history and also recognizes the likelihood of rapid change within ecosystems. The concept of authenticity breaks naturalness down into its constituent parts to help our understanding and thus our ability to manage these different elements.

Whenever we attempt to manage ecosystems we are making choices, often unconsciously, about levels and types of authenticity: in most cases there will not be a single 'authentic' ecosystem but a large number of alternatives. Although many conservationists will afford a higher value to more natural ecosystems, this is by no means always the case and debates about types and levels of naturalness are likely to grow. We should be making choices about naturalness much more consciously, and with more information, than has been the case until now. At the end of the book a 'manifesto for authenticity' is proposed: some steps to ensure that these issues are given higher priority in the future.

Text and examples focus primarily on terrestrial ecosystems, both because my own experience is mainly on land and also because debates about naturalness are far less advanced in marine environments. But the issue is also highly relevant to marine ecosystems and some of the important steps already taken to understanding marine conditions are summarized.

Some more background

This is a deliberately personal book and the large majority of examples cited are places I know and have worked in myself. I draw on over 30 years of working in the environment field: all but the first two or three self-employed, giving me free rein to indulge a butterfly mind. Over this period I have worked on renewable energy systems, air and water pollution, farming practices, then a long spell of forest conservation and restoration before focusing on the myriad social and ecological issues surrounding protected areas and their planning and management. My partner Sue Stolton and I have had the enormous good fortune to work all over the world, in all biomes, and in countries with dramatically different politics, cultures and religions. We have worked for UN agencies, governments, international bodies, non-governmental organizations (NGOs), companies and community groups: and from international policy to site-level conservation. What would normally be regarded as a hopelessly unprofessional mishmash actually works quite well for this kind of synthesis – or at least I hope it does.

Anyone with the curiosity to pick up a book of this sort already knows that we are living in a time of environmental crisis; a string of depressing statistics from governments, inter-governmental bodies and NGOs have emphasized this again and again (e.g. Butchart et al, 2010). It is not my intention to labour this point, but instead to look at the opportunities that we still retain. But research and personal experience over many years makes me recognize the likelihood that we will have to make a number of hard choices about ecosystems in the coming few decades and that we will have neither the resources nor the ability to keep everything as it was. The world is becoming less comfortable, more volatile and a lot less predictable.

The pressures are likely to increase. It has become popular to talk about 'biome shift' under climate change but this rather cosy picture of whole ecosystems moving quietly uphill or inland is not going to happen; instead at best new ecosystems will emerge and many of the signs are that these novel ecosystems will be poorer in species than the ones they replace. We already make a lot more cultural choices about the types of 'wild' ecosystems we want than most people realize; these choices are going to become more difficult and the level of intervention required to maintain functioning ecosystems is likely to increase. Paradoxically, this makes the concept of naturalness even more important: we need tools to help understand what is happening and why; to plan the extent to which we intervene and to measure the impacts of what we do.

Thinking about naturalness is necessarily a work in progress and I offer the following as a set of proposals rather than a definitive statement. My ideas have changed even while writing this book, largely due to a refreshed involvement in the climate change debate. When I started thinking seriously about the naturalness of forests systems, back in the early 1990s, scientists still mainly assumed that while ecosystems might be constantly changing at a site level (itself then a relatively new idea) they were relatively stable at the scale of a whole landscape, at least from the perspective of a human timescale. Like many other people I have had to revise my thinking fundamentally over the last decade.

Facts and emotion

Debates about conservation and naturalness are not just or even primarily about science; there is a lot of emotion mixed in as well. Many of the cultural and philosophical issues surrounding naturalness or authenticity are highly controversial. It would be fair to say that conservation is to some extent divided into two camps: those who focus primarily on wilderness or some similar concept and the need to preserve what is left of mainly natural habitats, and those predominantly interested in nature as an aspect of culture, whose focus is primarily in places where humans and nature coexist. The very word 'wilderness' has become a battleground between people who regard it as a positive or negative term. Many indigenous people resent hearing their traditional lands described as 'wilderness' because they believe it undervalues their own management and occupation of these areas. We will examine these issues in detail but for now it is worth noting that feelings run surprisingly deep.

I sit somewhat uncomfortably in the middle of this discussion. The example that opens this introduction shows fairly clearly that I give value to

FIGURE I.3 The massive waterfall in Nahanni National Park, a remote and inaccessible area of northern Canada, which marks the opposite extreme of naturalness from a suburban nature reserve in a long-settled country

what we might call artificial nature (or at least artificially formed ecosystems). But at the same time I recognize the huge importance – practically, culturally and ethically – of large ecosystems functioning without human interference. As a professional working in the conservation field I have had the privilege of visiting many such places and their values and benefits are becoming more and more apparent every day.

So let's finish the introduction with an example from the other end of the naturalness spectrum. Halfway through writing this book Sue and I were privileged to be invited to join a trip down the Nahanni River in northern Canada and onto the Ram Plateau, to celebrate the recent expansion of the Nahanni National Park. The Nahanni is an extraordinary wild river, remote from centres of population, with a waterfall twice the height of Niagara and cliffs higher than the Grand Canyon, flowing through one of the largest and most spectacular karst limestone landscapes on the planet, which features on the cover of this book. There are perhaps a hundred people living inside its borders. The First Nation people living around the edge have no stories of visiting the highest areas of the mountains. Large parts of the protected area are therefore among the very few places in the world that might truly merit being called 'wilderness' in terms of the simple, modernist concept of an untouched landscape; we were walking on mountains that few if any people have visited before.

Trying to make sense of how Attenborough Nature Reserve and Nahanni National Park fit together into an overall global conservation strategy is one of the challenges that we'll be addressing in the pages to come.

CHAPTER 1

The Myths of Wilderness – Myth 1: Unmodified, Wholly Natural Landscapes and Seascapes Still Exist over Large Areas

Key messages

- *There are no places left on Earth wholly uninfluenced by human activity.*
- *Many changes took place thousands of years ago, others are new.*
- *Apart from conversion, we influence ecosystems by removing species, moving species and by otherwise changing ecosystem processes including by pollution and climate change.*
- *By overemphasizing habitat loss, conservationists risk missing the significance of less obvious changes to 'natural' systems.*

The Serengeti plains are recognized as a natural wonder of the world, with one of the last three huge mammal migrations remaining (under threat as I write from a road improvement scheme). There are vast, breathtaking areas of savannah littered with rock outcrops or *kopjes*, patches of dense woodland and the Mara River flows free. A million wildebeest and zebra trot purposefully towards thunder and lightning on the horizon, where they know that rains will bring lush new grass. There is still a delicious hint of the wild: once the sun goes down we've several times been housebound because families of lions are roaming through the kopje where the Parks authority has its accommodation. Serengeti is also one of the best studied natural tropical savannah ecosystems, home to a permanent field station from the Frankfurt Zoological Society, a magnet for professional ecologists and subject to monitoring over many decades by Tony Sinclair, working with staff at the Tanzania Wildlife Research Institute. In three hefty volumes, Sinclair and his collaborators have collected information on the dynamics of the ecosystem (Sinclair and Norton-Griffiths, 1979; Sinclair and Arcese, 1995; Sinclair et al, 2008). But dig at all deeply into these texts about one of the world's great 'wild places' and the human hand quickly becomes evident, most clearly through the use of fire, which creeps in mainly from surrounding farmland, shaping the ecosystem in concert with browsing and grazing (Norton-Griffiths, 1979). More fundamentally, tropical dry ecosystems like Serengeti are inherently unstable, shifting in composition, dominant species and ecological interactions over time. By putting a metaphorical fence around one piece we attempt to freeze something that would naturally change and develop, creating an immediate tension for managers. Towards the end of the last century, for instance, elephant numbers rose high enough that mature woodland started to disappear, which coupled with increasing fire frequency looked set to alter the entire ecosystem; it seems increasingly likely that Serengeti is subject to long-term vegetation cycles or transitions between stable states following occasional major disturbances (Dublin, 1995). And, throughout its history as a protected area, Serengeti National Park managers have been consciously attempting to manipulate the ecosystem to keep it in as steady a state as possible, for example to 'bring under control and minimise the damage caused by wildfires and to promote the use of prescribed fires for management purposes' (SENAPA, 2005). Fire had, it is almost certain, already been used as a management tool by people in the area for centuries. Serengeti *appears* to be wild, and has many important *components* of the wild, but its relationship with naturalness is actually much more complex than the average tourist recognizes. While most working ecologists will be aware of the complexities involved this thinking has not yet reached most of the general public and politicians, nor to a significant extent is it always recognized by conservation departments or non-governmental organizations (NGOs).

FIGURE 1.1 Serengeti National Park in Tanzania gives the impression of a vast wilderness, but the ecology has been influenced by humans for centuries, particularly through the use of fire to encourage grasslands and thus favoured species for hunting

The title of this chapter may annoy a few readers, but please stick with me. The word 'wilderness' means different things to different people and we'll get into that in Chapter 3. For now, to set the groundwork for the rest of the book, I want to concentrate on one quite particular 20th and 21st century interpretation of the word: wilderness as defined by conservation biologists to describe particular aspects of naturalness and ecosystem integrity – 'untamed nature' or 'nature in the raw'. There are various definitions; for example one from the IUCN Wilderness Task Force to describe protected areas categorized as wilderness: '… large unmodified or slightly modified areas, retaining their natural character and influence, and without permanent or significant human habitation' (Dudley, 2008). Note the definition is nuanced – '*slightly modified*', '*significant habitation*' – which is critical but often overlooked.

The two populist myths discussed below and in the next chapter are that **large areas of completely unmodified habitat still exist** and, conversely, that **there is no such thing as 'wild nature' and the whole concept of naturalness in ecosystems has become redundant.** I will argue that both have the potential to be equally damaging in terms of their influence on the way that we approach conservation.

Media portrayals of nature usually give the impression that there are still large areas of the world where species and ecosystems continue to exist in a natural state. This is what we see in countless television programmes, read about in nature books and colour supplements, visit online through webcams and, increasingly, enter through the virtual world of video games. Most nature films concentrate on animals and plants in their natural setting and keep people well away from the camera lens. Virtually everyone with the most elementary education knows that such places are under threat but their existence into the 21st century is generally assumed: in the Amazon, in the vast boreal forests of Russia and Canada, in Borneo and similar places. Natural ecosystems are portrayed as the 'other' that we need to journey to and enter. People who go on wildlife holidays expect to be leaving civilization behind and to come into contact with nature unaffected by humans in a way that is generally not possible in their home countries. Ecotourism companies, wildlife safaris and national park managers collude in creating a particular impression and visitors are often upset if this worldview is challenged or undermined. Tour boats in the Galapagos carefully avoid settled areas. Footpaths in national parks skirt around settlements. In Serengeti, ecologist Ephraim Mwangomo told us that many visitors are upset by the radio collars attached to some of the lions as part of the research programme, as this does not fit with their preconceived ideas of the area remaining in some primeval, pristine state. (The same tourists are quite happy to sit in their comfortable lodges sipping a gin and tonic in the evening.) The belief in a wild and untouched 'out there' remains powerful.

This misunderstanding is dangerous. It distorts our ideas of what is possible or desirable under the auspices of conservation, both by raising false hopes about what might be 'saved' but at the same time underestimating some of the options open in terms of restoration and good management. It also ignores some critically important social issues, compounding a mistaken view of wilderness as being made up of empty, untouched landscapes and undermining its cultural significance. I will be arguing that if more-or-less natural ecosystems are going to continue to flourish we need to make some radical changes in the ways in which we perceive them, in our management priorities and in the governance of such areas. To do this we need to understand clearly where we are starting from. The next section of this chapter summarizes what has changed and why.

Distorted views of humans and nature

Everyone knows that huge parts of the planet have been radically modified by agriculture, urbanization, intensive forestry, mining and overfishing (e.g. Foley et al, 2005). Less well understood, at least in terms of the scale and severity of the changes involved, is the extent to which apparently natural areas have also been impacted, intentionally or accidentally, by humans.

As we will see in Chapter 8, roughly a third to half of the world's land surface still has strong natural characteristics; that is, it remains covered with natural vegetation and harbours native species. This is the focus for the current chapter, which attempts to answer questions like: How natural? What exactly does natural mean nowadays? What has changed and what is likely to change?

Some – in fact quite a lot – of the remaining natural areas consist of rock and ice: while these have a complex ecology of their own, they don't particularly concern us here. Part of the rest will be secondary vegetation that has regrown following past clearance. In practice these areas will also be treated as natural although there are distinctions between the two. Several of the world's best known 'natural forests' are found around the sites of former civilizations, such as in Central America, south-east Asia and the Amazon. Throughout much of Central and South America, for instance, 'natural forest' grows over the ruins of earlier Mayan, Aztec, Toltec and Inca civilizations that at one time had cleared huge swathes of land. Visitors to the globally famous Chichen Itza pyramid in Yucatan, Mexico can look out at other pyramids, now lost in what appears to be natural, ancient forest. But if the recovery of the Maya forests in Central America shows us that once-settled areas can revert to more-or-less natural ecosystems, they also demonstrate that such recovery is seldom final, or absolute. Terborgh (1992) shows that forests growing on sites cleared by Mayan civilizations 1200 years ago still show markedly different, and less diverse, tree composition than older forests. Ecologists in Europe have developed sophisticated keys to determine how long ago particular vegetation types have been disturbed (e.g. Goldberg et al, 2007).

Other natural ecosystems have a much longer history. But even these have undergone a variety of human influence. It has become received wisdom to link environmental destruction to modernism, to the 'dark satanic mills' that William Blake railed against at the dawn of the Industrial Revolution, and more recently to the wave of destruction that accompanies industrialization in the 21st century. There is a tacit acceptance that the blame lies firmly with expansionist policies in Europe and its satellites: that as soon as we have trampled over a landscape in our big boots, with our guns over our shoulders and our axes in our hands, things can never be as good again. While I'm certainly not denying the catastrophic impact that we can and have had, this is not the whole story.

When was nature changed?

It is possible to find ecological histories that follow this model to an uncomfortable degree. Most poignantly these are recorded from small islands with a distinctive and fragile ecosystem, poorly adapted to the arrival of sailors and settlers who had little understanding of local ecology. The catastrophic ecological impact of European settlers on islands such as Madeira and the Canaries is now well known (Crosby, 1986) and the rapid destruction of the flightless dodo (*Raphus cucullatus*) on Mauritius has become symbolic of the worst of Western colonist expansion (Fuller, 2003), the bird finally disappearing little more than 60 or 70 years after first being 'discovered' by Europeans (Roberts and Solow, 2003). Around 85 per cent of the 190 or so bird species that have become extinct since 1500 lived on isolated islands, including large isolated land masses like Australia and New Zealand, although most losses took place on small islands and extinctions from the Pacific, the Mascarenes and Hawaii have all been extraordinarily high.

Colonial expansion undoubtedly and dramatically increased the rate of change in many other countries as well. The new rulers arrived without knowledge of how to manage complex tropical ecosystems, without long-term emotional links to the landscape, harbouring fantasies about the inexhaustibility of the new lands and arriving at a time when economic expansion and industrialization had created shortages of many natural resources of Europe. In India, for example, the British Raj stripped forests to build ships, railroads, harbour piles and other infrastructure with favoured species like teak virtually disappearing in the wild; the tonnage of British merchant ships alone reached almost 5 million tonnes in 1860 and the consequent timber grab permanently changed the ecology of the subcontinent (Gadgil and Guha, 1993). The Spanish did much the same in the delicate grassland ecosystems of the Southern Cone of South America. In an astonishing orgy of destruction, early European settlers reduced herds of North American bison (*B. bison*) from tens of millions to near extinction in the course of a few years (Brodie, 2008).

But the theory of Europeans single-handedly destroying a series of ecological paradises assumes that the world encountered by soldiers and colonists was still essentially empty; that the 'natives' were huddled together in a few tiny enclave settlements and left the rest untouched. Research by archae-ologists, anthropologists, biologists and historians has chipped away at this fallacy until very little of it remains. While there are some areas that have prob-ably never been settled or significantly visited by humans – a lot of Antarctica for instance, some mountain-tops, a few inland forest areas and some of the most remote islands – they are now known to constitute a tiny minority of the total land area. The large majority of the land surface has been influ-enced by humans for millennia; European explorers generally encountered civilizations much older than their own. Many of today's 'empty landscapes' only lost their human inhabitants through some specific act of chance or politics and are often mute witness to past tragedies: imported diseases, land grabs and genocide.

In the Americas and Australia, ecologists often used the date of white settlement as a baseline on the assumption that nothing much had changed before, but this theory has comprehensively been demolished by historians. By 1492 much of the land in the Americas had already been humanized, with grasslands created, forests modified and wildlife disrupted (Denevan, 1992). While the extent to which this happened is still subject to debate (e.g. Vale, 1998), the fact that massive ecological changes occurred is no longer seriously questioned (e.g. Flannery, 2001). When early white pioneers pushed their way into empty landscapes in the West they were often following in the wake of imported diseases that had already wiped out whole communities; human pressure was probably less in 1750 than in 1492 (Denevan, 1992).

And not just in the newly acquired European colonies: during the Highland Clearances in Scotland, the majority of Highlanders, sold out and betrayed by their clan chiefs, were evicted to make way for sheep farming in the 18th and 19th centuries (Prebble, 1963); I have walked many days through the beautiful landscapes of Scotland without seeing another person, but the opportunity for me to enjoy some solitude was bought at a wickedly high price.

Indeed, one of the criticisms of the western ideal of wilderness comes from indigenous peoples who are frustrated that their own, sometimes more subtle forms of management are unnoticed or ignored. This is a hot topic which attracts strong feelings. However, increasing recognition of the extent to which areas of land and coastal waters have been settled and manipulated, and a general backlash against colonial fantasies about 'empty wilderness', has led to some counter-myths, which suggest that early, pre-European settlers were invariably sensitive to the rhythms of the planet and maintained a delicate harmony with nature. While such models exist, many of the earlier human communities also caused dramatic changes to ecology and a diminishing diversity of life in much the same way as the Europeans did hundreds or thou-sands of years later: the demise of the ecology of Easter Island is a particu-larly poignant example (Diamond, 2005). Rates of extinctions of birds in the central Pacific islands were even greater during Polynesian settlement than in the European invasion that followed (Pimm et al, 1994).

Even where hunting does not result in extinctions, it has helped to shape the ecology of ecosystems for millennia. Kent Redford (2000), a zoologist with a deep knowledge of hunter–gatherer societies in the neotropics, identified a number of commonalities about the impact of hunting on mammal populations in the region: that human hunting has caused both local and global extinctions; that we preferentially hunt the largest animals available but will switch to smaller ones in times of shortage; that at least in the neotropics most hunted animals are fruit eaters; and in consequence humans and their prey eat much the same food. Over-hunting, due either to human population increase or to supply a growing bushmeat trade, is now recognized as a critical factor in threatening the extinction or extirpation of many species (Nasi et al, 2008), but earlier forms of hunting have long ago already helped to shape their ecology.

Settlers, whether part of the European colonial expansion or earlier diasporas, also tend to cause the most damage when they are new to the ecosystem and have not yet learned its rhythms. Pre-modern communities developed over time so that their influence over ecology also changed. In New Zealand, the Maori almost certainly caused major ecological changes and a series of extinctions when they arrived, but in the hundreds of years following had evolved ways of managing the natural resources. When Captain Cook arrived, although they still cultivated a few Polynesian species most of their food came from indigenous plants. In particular, the lowland forests, with their slow-growing, rich fruit trees, were often far more productive than the agricultural lands and were kept intact for that purpose – an aspect lost on the Europeans who viewed natural looking forests as so much waste land to be replaced (Park, 1995).

Similarly, researchers identify increased hunting efficiency among Australian Aboriginal communities around 4000 years ago as coincident with the loss of species such as Tasmanian tiger (*Thylacinus cynocephalus*) and Tasmanian devil (*Sarcophilus harrisii*) from the mainland, although the arrival of the dingo (*Canis lupus dingo*) may have also played a role (Johnson and Wroe, 2003). Modern humans may have refined and accelerated the art of destruction but did not necessarily invent it.

Pre-European communities consciously shaped ecology, most prominently through the use of fire, by altering hydrological systems and by planting, sometimes moving species of plants and animals to radically different parts of the world. The use of fire in Africa was touched upon in the introductory section. In North America as well, burning was widely used to create ideal habitat for game (Beinart and Coates, 1995), although the resulting habitat appeared 'natural' to the new arrivals from Europe.

The idea that humans *ever* moved into a stable, existing 'primary' ecosystem is also at odds with the facts in many cases; changing climatic conditions and other environmental factors mean that many of today's 'natural' ecosystems developed after *Homo sapiens* was already on the scene. By the time forests spread back into Western Europe following the last ice age humans were already present, migrating northwards as the ice retreated

FIGURE 1.2 The giant Saguaro cacti of the Sonoran desert are icons of the wild in America, yet the typical cactus-dominated ecosystem developed well after humans were already present in the landscape

(Mithen, 2008) and they doubtless affected the ecology of the forest ecosystem even as it was developing. Similarly, the giant saguaro cactus habitats of the Sonoran desert, iconic of American ideal of desert wilderness, did not develop until long after human groups were living in the region (Philips and Comus, 2000). The forests of Central America are also now thought to have developed in the presence of humans (Redford, 2000). In the following text I will sometimes refer to *original ecosystems* or similar as a shorthand way of describing balanced, functioning ecosystems with all expected component species, but the limitations of the use of 'original' should be remembered and many of these ecosystems will never have existed in the absence of humans.

Humans dominating ecology over much of the planet's land surface

So what has happened? The impacts of human settlement and manipulation are neither simple nor the same from one place to another. Some changes are obvious, others far more subtle.

In the most highly modified or intensively managed ecosystems, there has been a radical loss of species richness and the curtailment of many ecological processes and interactions: compare a wheat field to a natural meadow, or an oil palm plantation to a tropical moist forest. Typically, a few species adapt well to such simplified, human dominated landscapes and seascapes, including some fast-growing plant species that act as pioneers after major disturbance (weeds) and a small number of highly adaptable animal species. The commonest weeds, like stinging nettle (*Urtica dioica*), chickweed (*Stellaria media*) and knotgrass (*Polygonum aviculare*), now occur on all five continents (Mabey, 2010). These are the types of plants and animals that can be found in suburban gardens; a rich and important group of species in themselves but in most cases only a tiny minority of the total.

This human-adapted fraction of the original population can often flourish in the absence of competition, but where by tradition or necessity people rely on wild birds and animals for food even the numbers of these species can be severely depressed. I have driven for many hours through rural parts of Vietnam and China for instance without seeing a single bird; when I try the same exercise in journeys through England and Wales I can often spot a thousand or more birds in an hour. But whether or not the total *number* of remaining individuals is high or low in modern urban, agricultural or industrial areas, the *variety* is likely to be far lower than in the original ecosystem. This is not always the case in managed forests; disturbances such as clear-cutting can create a sudden influx of pioneer species so for instance the total number of flowering plant species can increase for a few years. But this is deceptive; the incomers will likely be common weed species or invasive species replacing less common, more specialized species of mature forests including non-vascular plants (e.g. Haeussler et al, 2002). Other groups like fungi and invertebrates will also usually have undergone major losses when forests are cleared. And the diversity in tree plantations, particularly those using exotic species, is almost always lower than a natural forest on the same site, sometimes to a dramatic extent: an overview published in 2007 found that 94 per cent of studies reported lower biodiversity in plantations than in native forests (Stephens and Wagner, 2007).

However, management intervention does not invariably mean loss of diversity. In some cases highly managed ecosystems can have similar or even higher diversity than the original ecosystem. Studies of changes in bird populations over 50 years in Michigan found that despite substantial land-use changes, bird diversity had remained fairly constant, although the composition of the bird community had changed dramatically (Parody et al, 2001). Traditional agriculture in the Mediterranean, where human influence has one of the longest histories on earth (Grove and Rackham, 2001) is often cited as a classic example of biodiversity rich, human dominated landscapes; this will be discussed in greater detail in later chapters.

In a minority of these rich cultural systems, the ecology can even closely resemble the original ecosystem. The tembawang gardens of West Kalimantan in Indonesian Borneo are planted as sacred sites and for the fruit they contain but over time can develop a species mix and structure very similar to the native forests of the region (Marjokorpi and Ruokolainen, 2003). In the heavily modified landscapes they stand out like tiny oases of naturalness but they have been entirely created. Some apparently natural ecosystems may be quite heavily managed by local people in ways that it is hard to detect from casual observation

But the general trend over the last few centuries has been to reduce the diversity of ecosystems strongly affected by human cultures; this process is currently accelerating. Rich culturally managed areas such as the examples given above are becoming rare in many parts of the world and are increasingly threatened, for example High Nature Value Farming hotspots identified in the European Union are under severe pressure and some of the species they conserve are in decline (EEA, 2004). As our approaches to land management become more intensive, the space for nature in cultural landscapes is increasingly swept aside, except when conscious efforts are made to alter management patterns to favour other species.

How we impact even apparently natural ecosystems: Additions, subtractions and other interferences

Many analyses of ecosystem change confine themselves to obvious habitat change, such as the conversion of forest to farmland. But the world's remaining wild lands have also undergone radical changes, although here they are more subtle and harder to spot. Changes occur in ecosystems that would, to anyone but a trained ecologist or someone who had a deep and long-term knowledge of the area, appear to be more-or-less natural. Our influences are complex, but can be divided up into a number of broadly defined groups. Apparently natural ecosystems can be altered, and their functioning distorted, in four main ways: (i) as a result of the selective *removal of key species and removal or changes to habitats*; (ii) or through the *addition of new elements* into the ecosystem; (iii) by *changes in natural disturbance patterns*; and finally (iv) as a result of *changes in climate* that occur through human activities. Each of these will be looked at in more detail and its implications discussed.

The selective removal of key species and habitats

This has temporarily or permanently disrupted many otherwise fairly natural ecosystems. The word 'key' is critical. Species come and go and ecosystems can generally adapt fairly quickly to the presence or absence of a particular plant or animal without major changes in functioning; some closely associated species may be affected but the ecological ripples soon die away. More consequential changes occur when the species or group of species that has been removed fulfilled a critical ecological role that cannot easily be replaced by other species. Perhaps the commonest examples are the loss or decline in predators at the top of the food chain, usually large carnivores, which are often selectively removed because of the threats they pose to humans or livestock and the loss of populations of economically valuable species such as particular fish. A collapse in population of wild dog and cat species has led to a boom in herbivores throughout the developed world. For example loss of wolves (*Canis lupus*) and coyotes (*C. latrans*) has led to the massive growth of white-tailed deer (*Odocoileus virginianus*) populations throughout much of North America (e.g. Stout, 1982).

Such changes can impact even in places that appear to be functionally natural. Loss of dingoes (*Canis lupus dingo*), albeit they arrived relatively recently in Australia, has resulted in a similar expansion of red (*Macropus rufus*) and grey kangaroos (*M. giganteus and M. fuliginosus*). Earlier predator extinctions in Australia and a massive population decline among the Aboriginal people who hunted large numbers of kangaroos, further adds to the confusion. One result of this ecological distortion is that three million kangaroos are killed by professional hunters each year to keep populations stable and there is a huge but unmeasured illegal kill (Grigg, 1989). While much of the stimulus for this cull is to release grazing land for sheep, imbalance in predator–prey relationships is acknowledged to be a critical factor in the boom in these species (Caughley et al, 1980). The groups of kangaroos seen leaping spectacularly through native bush in the national parks might appear to be a vision of untamed nature but they are, in many places, a severely distorted population which is in turn altering vegetation patterns and succession.

In large parts of Western Europe, where hunting pressure has led to decline, extirpation or extinction of predator species, the problem is more intractable. In effect human hunters have replaced the wolf, lion, lynx and the extinct sabre-toothed tiger as the top predator of wild deer and goats.

Impacts snowball with the number of species removed. Local hunting of animals for food in many tropical countries has escalated as human populations increase and a growing urban middle class are willing to pay for highly prized wild game. The rapid expansion of the subsequent 'bushmeat trade' is leading to even more dramatic ecological changes (Roe et al, 2002): apparently healthy looking natural forests, which may nominally even be protected within national parks, but which are increasingly devoid of animal life. Many large animals are already functionally extinct in vast areas of neotropical forests for instance, even where vegetation still appears to be intact (Redford, 1992).

The bushmeat trade is particularly pervasive because it targets virtually everything; any drive through central Africa is likely to find people standing beside the road holding up the corpses of lizards, snakes, birds and small mammals for sale. Bushmeat makes up more than a fifth of animal protein in rural diets in over 60 countries (Bennett and Robinson, 2000) with annual consumption in Africa estimated at 1–3.4 million tonnes (Milner-Gulland and Bennett, 2003). A UK government study put annual global value of bushmeat sales at around US$7 billion (Elliott et al, 2002). Animals like pangolins are brought live to market: a seller pulled one from his pocket to show me in Yaoundé, Cameroon, uncoiling it neatly with a flick of his wrist like a child with a yoyo. A growing number of the natural forests of Africa, Asia and Latin America are what conservationists are calling 'cemetery forests'; the trees remain but the animals have disappeared or been dramatically reduced. These animals do more than simply use plants for food and shelter; they are often intimately involved in the spread and germination of seeds, maintenance of disturbance patterns and selective grazing. Their disappearance will create more profound changes in the structure of the ecosystem.

Loss of natural herbivores is also problematic: grazing keeps grassland ecosystems from being invaded by scrub and trees and often helps to maintain a diversity of plant species. If herbivores decline or are eliminated, habitat can change dramatically. In Uruguay, for example, cattle and sheep have almost completely replaced natural herbivores, which have also been heavily hunted, so that several are now endangered. Of the three Neotropical deer species in Uruguay, pampas deer (*Ozotoceros bezoarticus*) is reduced to two populations, the status of grey brocket deer (*Mazama goauzoubira*) is unknown (González, 2004) and no viable populations of marsh deer (*Blastocerus dichotomus*) has been found for 50 years. As a result, complete removal of grazing by domestic animals also now usually leads to a decline in plant species diversity (Altesor et al, 2005, 2005a) because there is nothing to replace them.

Similar and perhaps even more dramatic impacts are taking place in many of the world's oceans, with whole species being driven to virtual extinction by large-scale fishery operations, which have until now often had the political clout to fend off attempts to limit the catch. These changes are far more difficult for us to visualize but may in some cases be even harder to reverse. Around a fifth of the protein intake in developing countries comes from fish, predominantly wild caught (Béné at al, 2006). Booming human populations and a growing taste for fish in many developed countries have combined to create a devastating series of population crashes in the world's oceans. Unsustainable fishery has been identified as the single largest threat to marine ecosystems (Pauly et al, 2005) although the number of fisheries at risk is the subject of debate (e.g. Worm et al, 2009). (The possibility of ocean acidification may since have become even more significant.) Replacement of wild fisheries by aquaculture is proceeding apace but many fish farms rely on wild-caught fish for feed (Naylor et al, 2000), increasing overall pressure on natural populations. The role of recreational fishing has also been highlighted, with one estimate suggesting that it may be responsible for up to 12 per cent of the total catch in some areas (Cooke and Cowx, 2004).

Some impacts from removal of species may already have a long history, through prehistoric and historic influences by earlier human populations. The extent to which indigenous peoples impacted historically on ecology is still (sometimes bitterly) disputed. Tim Flannery (1994) caused a furore by claiming that aboriginal settlement had resulted in a wave of extinctions in Australia and New Zealand, accounting for the loss of 12 species of moa in the latter for example. Similar analyses have been carried out in North America where an 'aboriginal overkill' hypothesis was proposed by Charles Kay (1994), suggesting that the large human populations were severely limiting numbers of many mammals, such as the moose (Kay, 1997) through hunting pressure before European invasion and the impact of introduced diseases decimated numbers of Native Americans and allowed some species to recover their numbers.

The extent of human influence on the rapid extinctions of the Holocene has not yet been resolved and other researchers propose a much stronger role for changes in climate that occurred at around that period (e.g. Wroe et al, 2004). However, there is no doubt that humans have drastically altered some ecosystems through species removal: in Wales for instance the beaver, wolf, wild cat (*Felis catus*), brown bear (*Ursus arctos*), red deer, roe deer, wild boar (*Sus scrofa*) and possibly also the wild cattle (*Bos primigenius*) all became extinct during historic periods, mainly through over-hunting (Matheson, 1932). We inherited an impoverished fauna in many areas and unfortunately our generation has succeeded in further accelerating the trends in losses.

It is not only loss of big and spectacular species that has impacts on ecology. The selective loss of particular microhabitats can have huge knock-on effects and not all ecologically important species are large or obvious. In many parts of central and northern Europe for instance, centuries of forest management have selectively removed dead trees, both because they are an obvious source of fuel and because dead wood harbours diseases that can spread to living timber. A walk through mixed stand forests in countries like Slovenia or Switzerland can feel like a journey into a natural environment: a carpet of wild flowers, trees of mixed ages and birdsong from the canopy. But there will, generally speaking, be a lack of dead or dying trees, which are often deliberately removed by forest owners. This is now creating a crisis for the species that use dead wood for food and shelter: woodpeckers are well known victims for example but there are literally hundreds of beetles, fungi and micro-organisms that are entirely reliant on dead or dying timber. In many temperate forests deadwood supports up a 25 per cent of forest biodiversity. When forests are left alone to attain true old-growth status the proportion of deadwood usually increases dramatically. In Białowieza forest, on the border between Poland and Belarus, deadwood contributes almost a quarter of above-ground biomass, from 87 to 160 m^3 per hectare (Bobiec et al, 2000). In Tasmania, 350 beetle species have been collected from dead *Eucalyptus obliqua* logs in wet forests, along with many flies, earthworms, velvet worms and molluscs (Grove et al, 2002). Research in the Pacific Northwest of Canada found that 69 vertebrate species use cavities in dead timber (Boyland and Bunnell, 2002). The notion that old trees or dead wood should be avoided is built deep into the psyche of western foresters: it is far from uncommon to hear even conservation professionals in Europe talking about 'over-aged' forests and the need to intervene

FIGURE 1.3 A large proportion of endangered species in Finland are associated with dead wood, following decades of forest management, so in some Finnish protected areas healthy trees are being felled to recreate this critically endangered habitat

through management to 'maintain' biodiversity. The idea that deadwood is an important component of forest restoration is gradually being recognized (Dudley and Vallauri, 2005). In Finland for example, Metsähallitus, the Finnish Forest and Parks Service, has even taken to felling some healthy trees in key national parks such as Nuuksio, just outside Helsinki, in an emergency temporary measure to create dead wood habitat.

Other critically important species may be hidden from sight or obscure. Mycorrhizal fungi play a complex symbiotic role in ecosystems, including particularly facilitating uptake of nutrients by vascular plants (Finlay, 2008). Declines in these fungi, for example as a result of pesticide spray drift (Thorpe and Dudley, 1985), can be a significant factor in losses of diversity of above-ground plants (van de Heijden et al, 1998). Increasingly, the importance of multi-species interactions is being recognised (Strauss and Irwin, 2004), which increases our appreciation if not always our detailed understanding of likely knock-on effects from species losses within a functioning ecosystem.

Along with removing species and habitats, we also *change* habitats, sometimes dramatically. Throughout much of the world, the demands of transportation, flood control and access have combined to encourage the alteration of rivers and streams, building up banks, straightening, damming, creating fishing pools and preventing overspill, all of which also change freshwater ecology. Drainage of marshes and wetlands has caused dramatic biodiversity losses in many areas. But changes can be much more subtle as well and affect places that otherwise appear to be natural. I recently drove along the border zone between Kuwait and Iraq, where defences built since the 1990–1991 Gulf War include a three metre trench to stop vehicular access. In the flat landscape of the region, where microgeographic changes determine the location of temporary streams flow and wadis (often only discernible by changes in vegetation), the trench is having dramatic impacts on hydrology and sand movement, which in turn is changing the ecology of the region. For many situations we still have relatively little understanding of when ecosystems will be able to adapt fairly smoothly to a particular change to landscape or geomorphology or when such a change will cause impoverishment in species or ecology.

Unfortunately, some of these changes cannot be addressed quite as simply as replacing dead wood resources by felling a few trees. Extinctions are irreversible and in practice once top predators have disappeared from the landscape it is hard to persuade human communities to accept them back again even if they continue to exist in other areas. When a group of us were asked to carry out an analysis of South Korea's national park service in 2008 we were all impressed by the standard of management and the ambitious restoration projects for the Asian black bear (*Ursus thibetanus*) and Korean goral (*Nemorhaedus caudatus*), but there are no plans to reintroduce the tiger (KNPS, 2009). Other forms of restoration, while possible, are expensive, socially divisive and uncertain as to their result. We can never understand the full range of ecological interactions in any given ecosystem, so that it can be difficult to even work out what is missing. Although I will be arguing that restoration needs to play a far more central role in land and water management strategies, the chances of getting back everything that has been lost are remote; if climate or other conditions have changed, the original composition of species may no longer even be suitable for a particular location.

Additions into the ecosystem

Additions into the ecosystem can be equally disruptive. The best known examples are introduction of invasive species – what Jeff McNeely has called the 'great reshuffling' (McNeely, 2001) and the impacts of airborne or waterborne pollutants. Although these two are very different in form and cause, they both result in an overall loss of diversity: more quickly equals less.

Invasive species

Some ecologists believe that invasive species pose as significant a threat to natural ecosystems as habitat change, although they receive a fraction of the attention. Humans have moved species for millennia and some, like the

Polynesians, Incas and Romans, elevated this into a sophisticated science. Most introduced species cause no harm, being confined to cultivated areas or surviving in tiny populations, like the Bennett's wallabies (*Macropus rufogriseus rufogriseus*) that lived for a few decades far from home in the moors of the English Peak District (Yalden, 1988). But a small number find their new home unnaturally favourable, cut off from predators and in ultra-suitable living conditions. They boom, sweeping native species aside. Invasive species bring a high cost, both through ecological disruption and also in economic terms. In the United States around 50,000 foreign species cause an estimated $120 billion worth of damage each year and are the primary threat to 42 per cent of native species on the Threatened or Endangered listings (Pimintel et al, 2005).

Many early introductions were useful food plants, later species were moved for trade, hunting or because they were considered sacred. Introductions may also be for aesthetic reasons, research, biological control and even fraud. Some key examples are listed in Table 1.1. Globalization has increased the mixing – in ships and aircraft, on the mud sticking to travellers' boots and inside people as parasites and diseases.

Marine ecosystems in particular are being transformed by invasive species. Around 10,000 species are known to have been transported and transferred through ship ballast: a proportion of these have become highly invasive. Others move attached to ships' hulls, on drilling platforms, in nets, with diving equipment and through canals. Nicholas Bax and his colleagues provide an unnerving overview (2003); some examples give a flavour of the changes. A study of six ports in Australia, New Zealand and the United States found new marine or estuarine species establishing at a rate of once every 32 to 85 weeks. In Port Phillip Bay, south Victoria, the population of the invasive north Pacific seastar (*Asteria amurensis*) has risen to an estimated 100 million individuals, with a biomass greater than all the harvested fish in the region. In Europe, the green algae *Caulerpa taxifolia* was first seen in Monaco and has spread to 97 per cent of suitable surfaces between Toulon and Genoa. Further east, an invasive comb jelly, *Mnemiopsis leidyi*, has caused the collapse of a multi-million dollar a year fishery in the Black Sea. The list goes on. Many ocean habitats have been transformed as profoundly as cultural landscapes onshore.

Back on land, most countries already have a huge number of non-native plant species growing alongside their native flora. A quick analysis of the list of 'wild' flora around my home city of Nottingham (Shepherd, 1998), shows that of 700–800 flowering plants and grasses at least 170 are introduced. Only a handful of these, like Japanese knotweed (*Fallopia japonica*) and Himalayan balsam (*Impatiens glandulifera*) are invasive. Such mixing is not confined to cities or obvious centres of population; on the Orkney Islands off the coast of northern Scotland over 130 of the vascular plant species are escapes (analysed from Bullard, 1979).

The influence of invasive plant species is often proportionately larger in areas that have been long-isolated from major land masses and have evolved

TABLE 1.1 Some of the motivations for moving plant and animal species

Motive	Examples
Terrestrial food supply	Most of the world's major crops have been moved extensively (Diamond, 1998), for example bananas (*Musa*) from south-east Asia; sugar cane (*Saccharum*) from Asia; and cocoa (*Theobroma cacao*) from Latin America. Most of these crops have been drastically altered by breeding and are confined to cultivated areas. Fruit and nut trees like the olive, apricot, coconut and walnut were moved so long ago and so often that the locations of their original wild populations are not known for certain.
Aquatic food supply	Fish introduced to act as food sources or that escape from fish farms have devastated native fish populations in many countries. The spread of Nile Tilapia in Africa is well known.
Materials	Plants and animals used as sources of materials have been translocated: examples include cotton (*Gossypium hirsutum* and others) from Mexico, Australia, Africa and Asia and rubber (*Hevea brasiliensis*) from South America.
Sport hunting	Various deer such as the red deer and sika deer (*Sika nippon*); wild boar; many game birds such as the pheasant (*Phasianus colchicus*) and red-legged partridge (*Alectoris rufa*) have been introduced wherever conditions are suitable.
Sport fishing	Several species of trout (e.g. *Salmo trutta, S. gairdneri*) have been introduced throughout the world, replacing native fish species and disrupting freshwater ecology (Flecker and Townsend, 1994). Anglers also sometimes introduce alien species as food supply for fish.
Aquarium trade	Accidental or deliberate releases of pet fish are causing major ecological impacts in some regions – this has been identified as a potential problem in the Laurentian Great Lakes for example (Rixon et al, 2005).
Aesthetics	Some of the most aggressively invasive plant species have been introduced because they look attractive in parks and gardens. *Rhododendron ponticum*, originally from the Himalayas, has become invasive in many upland areas of the UK. Plants like the giant hogweed (*Heracleum mantegazzianum*) originally from the Caucasus (Nielsen et al, 2005), are now subject to expensive control policies.
Biological control	Species introduced to control pests sometimes become pests themselves. The cane toad (*Bufo marinus*), introduced against scientific advice into Australia to control a population of a beetle that attacks sugar cane, is highly toxic and can kill snakes that eat it. The toad is spreading, and is predicted to continue massively to expand its range around the country (Urban et al, 2007) and one analysis suggests it threatens populations of 30% of native snake species (Phillips et al, 2003).
Scientific fraud	Populations of several rare Arctic-alpine plant species 'discovered' on the island of Rum off the coast of Scotland are believed to have been introduced by their supposed discoverer to add to his scientific renown (Sabbagh, 1999).

many endemic species. The impacts of non-native flora in Australia and New Zealand are notorious (see Box 1.1) but far from unique. Nor are such whole-sale alterations confined to obviously cultural landscapes: I recall seeing a surprising number of European plant species on the lower slopes of the mountains in Torres del Paine National Park in Chile, one of the great natural areas of that country; they apparently sneaked in when the area was a cattle ranch. Much of the pasture in Europe and North America is dominated by exotic, often specially bred grasses and non-native grasses now cover huge stretches of Africa and Latin America.

Exotic plants are found deep in habitats that most people assume are natural. Even before European settlers produced a huge mixing in the Americas, the indigenous groups of Latin America had moved species around the continent and some of the most remote tribes in the Amazon harvest 'wild' plants originally from hundreds or thousands of miles away. The domestication of the potato has been traced back 7000 years to the banks of Lake Titicaca in Peru (Spooner et al, 2005). Following this the Incas collected potato varieties from all the people they contacted and conquered, leading to a large but unnatural concentration of species in their stronghold in Peru. The Peruvian Potato Park has been set up by local communities (Colchester and Argumedo, 2003) to preserve what they now regard as natural biodiversity (National Research Council, 1989).

When invasive species get a grip, results can be dramatic. A few species have altered entire ecosystems and cost millions of dollars through impacts on agriculture, fisheries, shipping and tourism and in (frequently ineffective) control programmes. The common water hyacinth (*Eichhornia crassipes*) is native to the Amazon basin, where it flourishes in lagoons and slow-flowing tributaries. Its beautiful flowers encouraged people to introduce it around the world, where it developed into one of the most invasive species on record, forming dense mats that disrupt river traffic, for example on the Nile, clog lakes including Lake Victoria and undermine irrigation schemes. Its rapid growth and ecological tolerance has made it invasive virtually anywhere, although it is most dangerous in tropical and subtropical countries. Among the many places I have seen it are Djoudj wildlife sanctuary in the Senegal delta in West Africa, the Kinabatangang River in Sabah, Borneo and the wetlands of Keoladeo National Park in India. I've singled these three out because they are all protected areas with active management, set up to maintain critically important ecosystems, yet efforts to control the hyacinth are apparently at best holding the line.

Introduced animals can also dramatically change ecosystems, by changing grazing pressure or predation, altering the species mix or 'locking' a vegetation type that would otherwise develop into something else – for instance preventing grassland from developing into forest. I mentioned the impact of loss of deer in Uruguay. Most of the country is assumed to be natural grassland, but by the end of the glacial period humans were already present. It may be (and we don't yet know for sure) that deliberate use of fire slowed

BOX 1.1 Acclimatization societies

Much of the historical mingling of species did not happen by accident; for every brown rat swimming ashore from a merchant ship there was a deliberate introduction. Nor were these all for utilitarian reasons. During European colonization, efforts were made to establish them in radically different climate and ecosystems, often for no other reason than curiosity. This created a suite of problems that we are still struggling to overcome today.

Until then, with a few exceptions, most introduced 'foreign' species were kept in captivity. The first zoos are known from Egypt around 1400 BCE. Later, menageries also became popular in other countries. For example the UK Royal Menagerie was housed in the Tower Of London for around 600 years, before being presented to the new Zoological Society of London in 1860.

In the 18th century a new movement emerged, particularly in the empire-building countries of Europe and in some of the new colonies: the introduction of species for no other reason than scientific interest, cultural aesthetics and, in the case of the new colonies, to make the local ecology more like home. In 1854, Geoffroy Saint-Hilaire formed La Societé Zoologique d'Acclimation in France and a few years later Frank Buckland followed suit with the Acclimatisation Society of the UK. Similar societies soon sprung up in Scotland, the Channel Isles, Russia, the United States, Hawaii, Australia and New Zealand and 54 such societies have been identified in the French and English-speaking worlds (Lever, 1992).

The UK society started as it meant to go on, with a launch dinner of eland (*Taurotragus oryx*) at the Aldersgate Tavern and the aim of '*introduction, acclimatisation and domestication of all innoxious animals, birds, fishes, insects, and vegetables, whether useful or ornamental*' (sic, my emphasis). Significantly, the third objective of the society was '*The spread of indigenous animals, &c., from parts of the United Kingdom where they are already known, to other localities where they are not known.*' (All quotes from Lever, 1992.)

Acclimatization in New Zealand and Australia

Anyone passing through immigration in Australia and New Zealand today will be aware of the care taken to discourage accidental introduction of alien plants and animals: rigorous controls food, soil and plant and animal matter, sniffer dogs, tough questioning by customs officials and random searches. But to quote a cliché, this is like bolting the stable door after the horse has fled. Quite literally in Australia, where millions of feral horses known as 'brumbies' devastate native ecosystems. (Not unexpectedly there are societies aimed at the protection of the brumby.) Deliberate introduction of non-native flora and fauna has caused the extinction of several native species; millions of dollars worth of damage to agriculture and forestry every year and a vast bill in control attempts.

Similarly, as part of a deliberate recreation of conditions in the UK, the New Zealand Acclimatisation Society introduced many plants, birds and mammals. An Acclimatisation Act was passed, first by the council of Nelson and later by the colonial parliament, 'to encourage the importation of those animals and birds, not native to New Zealand, which would contribute to the pleasure and profit of the inhabitants'.

Like most European naturalists visiting New Zealand, I am struck by both the similarities and the differences: a native flora so alien that I am confused even with field guides in my hand, but at the same time over much of the island almost exactly the same mixture of birds and wild flowers that I would expect in any farming area of Britain. The commonest bird is believed to be the chaffinch (*Fringilla coelebs*), also among the commonest in the UK, and other common species include the blackbird (*Terdus merula*), song thrush (*T. philomelos*), greenfinch (*Carduelis chloris*), gold-finches (*C. carduelis*), redpolls (*C. flammea*), yellowhammers (*Emberiza citrinella*), skylarks (*Alauda aervensis*), starlings (*Sturnus vulgaris*) and dunnocks (*Prunella modularis*), along with the near ubiquitous house sparrow (*Passer domesticus*). None of these should occur within many thousand miles of New Zealand, yet many appear to be doing better there than in their native territories (McLeod et al, 2007), where agricultural intensification has caused dramatic falls in populations of skylarks and yellowhammers for example (Anon, 2009). Over-wintering populations of skylarks are around three times higher in New Zealand than England (Wakenham-Dawson and Aebischer, 1998). The species listed above, in contrast with the game birds that have also been introduced, were brought purely to give colonists a sensation of 'home'.

or stopped expansion of the forests and retained a predominantly grassland ecosystem (Behling et al, 2005). When European settlers arrived and intro-duced horses and cattle they would have found large areas of grass (*campos*) albeit with many more shrubs than in the rolling fields of rural Uruguay today; these shrubs still spring up on roadside verges and wherever livestock are excluded. European farming led to dramatic ecological changes (Panario and Bidegain, 1997). Even these altered natural grasslands are being replaced by exotic species; for instance 'artificial grasslands' increased by 32 per cent between 1980 and 1990 and there is increasing use of fertilizers and pesticides (Republica Oriental del Uruguay et al, 1992).

Unnaturally high populations of domestic grazing animals have a dramatic impact on grasslands and former forests throughout the world: subsidized sheep farming of upland Europe; goats grazing drylands in the Middle East; the denuded pastures of New Zealand and Tasmania and so on. In Dana Reserve, in Jordan, negotiations with local farmers to halve numbers of livestock resulted in a dramatic regrowth of vegetation compared with the desert-like conditions found all around. Changing grazing levels in arid environments can tip fragile ecosystems over into desertification. In Kuwait, a country still coming to terms with the huge environmental damage caused 20 years ago during the first Gulf War (Omar et al, 2005), overgrazing has shat-tered many ecosystems, replacing complex desert floras with bare sand and contributing to mounting problems of sand dune movement and dust storms (Al-Awadi et al, 2005).

Management choices can also change population levels of wild animals, so that these effectively become 'invasive' in their own habitats. In Scotland, loss of predators and conservation for the hunting industry means that red deer (*Cervus elaphus*) populations were estimated to be at least twice their natural maximum by the 1980s (Tompkins, 1986) contributing to virtually zero forest

FIGURE 1.4 Water hyacinth is spreading throughout the tropics, seen here in Djoudj Reserve, on the border between Senegal and Mauritania

recovery over much of the country. The bare uplands are far from natural, in many cases the original tree stumps can be seen preserved in the peat, and Scotland has one of the highest losses of natural forest in the world, yet to many visitors it appear to be the epitome of a wild landscape.

Predatory animals can also dramatically alter the ecology of entire ecosystems. Introduction of the brown rat (*Rattus norvegicus*) onto islands has devastated bird populations and changed species from being predominantly ground nesting to denizens of steep cliffs and offshore rocks. The introduced American mink has had a similar impact in Europe, for example crossing the ice of the Baltic during the winter to islands in the Finnish Archipelago National Park, attacking the nests of velvet scoter (*Melanitta fusca*) ducks among others (Vaisenen, pers. comm.). In Britain it has added to the pressures of overhunting (Lovegrove, 2007) to drive the once-abundant water vole (*Arvicola amphibius*) to the edge of extinction (Barreto et al, 2006). Ironically, the spread of the mink has been aided by deliberate releases from mink farms orchestrated by animal rights groups. In the Pacific, vertebrates on Guam have been devastated by the introduced brown tree snake (*Boiga irregularis*) (Savidge, 1987). Seventeen of the 18 native bird species have been severely affected, with 12 likely extirpated on the main island and most other populations reduced by around 90 per cent (Wiles et al, 2003). The snake's ability to climb to high nests

FIGURE 1.5 Uruguay's original grassland vegetation springs up whenever it is protected from grazing pressure, such as along roadside verges

is a major factor in its impact (Conry, 1988). Bats and reptiles have also been affected and by 1990 only three vertebrate species, all small lizards, were still found in most forested areas (Fritts and Rodda, 1998).

The wave of invasions shows no signs of diminishing. Climate change may further increase the risk by changing competitive advantages between species, altering their ranges; facilitating movement through extreme weather events (e.g. species literally being blown to new sites in typhoons); and by creating conditions in which native species can themselves become invasive (Burgiel and Muir, 2010).

Pollutants

The other additions that can reach even remote and otherwise natural ecosystems are the various forms of pollution transported in the atmosphere and in rivers or oceans. Back in 1989 Bill McKibben published a short, punchy polemic called *The End of Nature* in which he mourned the loss of naturalness and identified the emerging impacts of climate change as what we would now call the tipping point, when he finally realized that natural didn't exist any more. McKibben's book has a lot to recommend it but I think he was being a bit too optimistic in his thesis; for me the final end of the 'untouched' came quite some time before that. In fact if I had to choose one single event that clinched the issue it would be a piece of rather elegant research carried out in Antarctica over 20 years before.

In 1966, when public concern about pesticide pollution had first been heightened by Rachel Carson's groundbreaking book *Silent Spring* (1962) scientists designed an experiment to test the extent that the commonly used organochlorine insecticide DDT had spread around the world. One problem then current was in proving that the chemical residues left by DDT did not occur naturally in the bodies of animals – an argument that was being advanced by the pesticide industry. Someone remembered that the Antarctic explorer Captain Robert Scott had written about a dead Adelie penguin (*Pygoscelis adeliae*) lying outside the hut where he and his fellow-explorers had been trapped and eventually died. In the frozen polar conditions the penguin body had not decomposed; the bird was found and specimens taken so that its DDT levels could be compared with those of an Adelie penguin then living (George and Frear, 1966). No residues were found in the bird dead 50 years or more, before the pesticide had been developed, while there were measurable levels in the contemporary penguin, despite there being no use of such pesticides in Antarctica. This proved that DDT had been artificially introduced into the ecosystem, moving hundreds or thousands of miles, probably transported along the food chain and eventually ingested by the penguin along with the fish it eats.

This simple experiment, with its links to the last great unexplored continent and the glamorous but doomed polar explorers, marks a watershed in our understanding of naturalness. If pesticides are found in these conditions we can be reasonably certain they will exist everywhere else as well, the question then is to what extent they affect the ecosystems in which they are found.

Concern about agricultural pollutants has waxed and waned ever since the great industrialization of agriculture kicked off in earnest following the Second World War, with ecologists focusing at various times at biocides, fertilizers, run-off from animal wastes and methane releases from cattle (Conway and Pretty, 1991). In the late 1970s the UK Royal Commission on Environmental Pollution produced one of the first reports on environmental hazards related to nitrate fertilizers (Kornberg, 1979) and raised a storm in the agricultural industry. Nitrate in water provides high levels of nutrients that can create eutrophication: a population explosion of green algae that, when they die and decompose, take so much dissolved oxygen that other aquatic life is suffocated. In the mid 1980s, when the short-lived London Food Commission asked me to assess the impacts of nitrate fertilizers on human health and the environment in the UK (Dudley, 1986), most European governments were still denying that there were any significant problems. But the European Union introduced limits on maximum nitrate levels in drinking water to prevent risks of infant methaemoglobinaemia or blue baby syndrome. Attitudes changed dramatically. Civil servants who had been dismissive suddenly started asking for meetings and looking at alternatives. But while welcome reductions have been seen in some countries since this scare, the incidence of nitrate pollution has continued to spread around the world. There is growing evidence that what was until recently considered a problem limited to agricultural areas is becoming a major threat to inland and coastal waters, including the Great Barrier Reef (Devlin and Brodie, 2005). This is not, as yet, a global problem since excess nitrate is concentrated in those countries with modern, intensive agriculture (UNEP and WHRC, 2007) but its impact is mounting and looks likely to increase dramatically in Asia for instance. A parallel set of issues relates to phosphorus, also increasing rapidly in many areas due to spillage from farming systems. The phenomenon of Harmful Algal Blooms has been linked to the presence of increased nutrients from sewage, agriculture, aquaculture and atmospheric deposition, with phosphorus levels particularly significant in freshwater systems and nitrate pollution in coastal and marine waters (Anderson et al, 2002).

The impact of pesticides on bird populations is too well known to need a lot of repeating here (see papers as far back as Moore, 1962), but some statistics are still truly shocking. In the county of Essex, England, populations of the sparrowhawk (*Accipiter nissus*) fell from an estimated 400–500 pairs to just one pair in the course of a few years as a result of pesticides such as DDT causing thinning of eggshells and consequent failure to reproduce. Peregrine falcons (*Falco peregrinus*) essentially disappeared from North America east of the Great Plains and populations collapsed in other parts of the continent (Brown et al, 2007). Here losses did not only affect bird populations but also had huge knock-on effects on other species, particularly of prey species such as voles, which in some cases boomed in the absence of predators. Despite the banning of some of the most toxic chemicals and recovery of some raptor populations in Europe and North America, in other regions damage is continuing and intensifying. India is currently undergoing a catastrophic decline in vultures as a result of pesticide pollution (Shultz et al, 2004). Less well recognized, but probably larger in scale overall, has been massive losses among reptiles and amphibians, invertebrates and plants as a result of pesticide use, with long-term pollutants and the role of spray drift (Thorpe and Dudley, 1985; Hurst et al, 1991) being particularly significant. Even when species do not completely disappear, their numbers may fall dramatically.

The effects of pesticides took time to identify, in part because of the way in which they occurred: in birds for instance mainly by causing thinning of eggshells and poor chick survival rates. Similar 'hidden' impacts hampered identification of one of the other great air pollution events of the 20th century. In the early 1980s, lake fishermen in wild areas of southern Scandinavia started to report a strange phenomenon; for a few years they were catching unusually large fish, but then populations abruptly crashed and in many cases species disappeared altogether. At the same time, unexplained fish kills were occurring, particularly during the spring snow melt. Frantic research by the state authorities showed that fish in many lakes had stopped breeding; in the absence of competing young the remaining adults grew large on the abundant food available but there was no replacement population. Increased levels of acidity were quickly identified as the cause of both impacts (Wright et al, 1976; Overrein et al, 1980). Sulphur and nitrogen oxides were being released from power stations, converted to wet acids in the atmosphere and reaching the ground again, sometimes hundreds of miles from the source, in the form of mist, rain and snow – the term *acid rain* was quickly coined by the media. In lakes, addition of acid gradually replaced base materials without any measurable change in overall pH, until all base materials were used up and then acidity rose very quickly: the so-called *titration effect*. In rivers, melting snow caused a sudden pulse of acidity that could kill fish in the spring. Similar impacts started to be reported from parts of North America (Sub-Committee on Acid Rain, 1981).

Tracking down the causes of acid rain, and particularly the sources of the pollution, created an intensely political debate where science and opinion became inextricably mixed (Dudley, 1986a): the UK government fought a rearguard action against evidence that pollution from British stacks was impacting ecosystems an ocean away in northern Europe. I worked as a researcher on the Friends of the Earth acid rain campaign and visited Sweden and Norway to see impacts at first hand and talk with the young activists who had made long-range air pollution into an international political issue. I travelled the UK interviewing scientists and fisheries officers for a book (Dudley et al, 1984) and to prepare evidence to the UK Parliamentary Select Committee considering a response to what rapidly became a tense political issue. (Feelings ran high: it was about this issue that the Norwegian Minister of Environment described the UK Minister of Environment as 'the biggest *drittsekk* [shitbag] I have ever met'.) Unlike the more controversial issue of the effects that air pollutants have on trees, freshwater impacts are now almost universally accepted and were, among other things, the spur for additional protocols to the European Convention on Long-Range Transboundary Air Pollution. Impacts included a reduction in freshwater diversity as sensitive fish and other aquatic creatures disappeared, with a corresponding boom in numbers of the few acid-tolerant species that remained (Drabløs and Tollan, 1980). Because the impacts of acidifying pollutants are often simplified, even in the scientific literature, to issues related to a few upland lakes and forests in highly polluted areas, I have summarized the range of effects in Box 1.2 below.

A critical issue from our perspective here is that these effects can extend way into areas that are otherwise considered natural: some of the most serious acidification problems were found in remote areas of southern Scandinavia and in the uplands of the Adirondack Mountains of the USA, including within areas set aside to maintain a natural ecology. (This was also a reason why the psychological and cultural impacts were so severe: I remember Norwegian ecologists and anglers describing their feeling of frustration and impotence as invisible pollutants arrived from hundreds of

---

BOX 1.2 Impacts on the environment from sulphur and nitrogen atmospheric pollution

Air pollution from dry deposition of sulphur dioxide and nitrogen oxides and wet deposition of sulphur and nitric acids, distorts and reduces biodiversity, often far from the source of pollution and in otherwise fairly pristine environments. A variety of trends are summarized below (Dudley and Stolton, 1995).

- **Lower life forms are usually more affected by air pollution than higher life forms:** in particular, lichens, bryophytes, fungi and soft-bodied aquatic invertebrates. Sulphur and nitrogen pollution has affected literally hundreds of lichen species in Europe and extirpated many from industrial areas (Looney and James, 1988). Yet years of research have found only two birds whose range has been affected: the house martin (*Delichon urbica*) by sulphur dioxide (Newman et al, 1985) and the dipper (*Cinclus cinclus*) by the impacts of freshwater acidification on its food species (Ormerod et al, 1985); neither has shown a dramatic decline.
- **In general, plants are more affected than animals on land, but not in freshwater:** a literature survey found reference to declines in three times as many terrestrial plants as animals (Tickle et al, 1995). Studies of benthic fauna in Sweden found that diversity among animal species declined by 40 per cent for a pH reduction of 1 unit, while plant species declined by only 25 per cent (Engblom and Lingdell, 1991).
- **Most affected species decline but a minority increase:** a few species thrive in polluted conditions. Some appear to be stimulated; for example many aphids grow faster in high sulphur dioxide and nitrogen oxides (Whittaker, 1994) and some pollution resistant species expand to fill gaps left by the disappearance of sensitive species.
- **Air pollution has played a key role in changing the distribution and ecology of many plant species:** including particularly lichens (During and Willens, 1986) and bryophytes (Rose and Wallace, 1974), but also flowering plants (van Dobben et al, 1983) including trees (Clesla and Donaubauer, 1994). Impacts include direct toxicity, sometimes from pollutant combinations (Turk and Wirth, 1975); effects on reproduction (Cox, 1992); changes in soil fertility and pH (Berdén et al, 1987); changed competitive ability; and increased aphid predation (Whittaker 1994). In Epping Forest, near London, lichen diversity declined from 150 species to 36 following the Industrial Revolution (Rose and James, 1974).
- **Impacts on invertebrates appear to be wide-ranging:** both in freshwater where soft-bodied animals are most at risk (Herrmann et al, 1993) and among various terrestrial groups (Gärdenfors, 1989). In acidified freshwaters phytoplankton diversity can halve (Eriksson et al, 1983); crustaceans decline in diversity (Fryer, 1980); and molluscs virtually or completely disappear (Økland, 1992). A few acid-resistant species flourish: in Europe these include phantom midge (*Chaoborus* spp.), alder fly (*Sialis* spp.), water boatmen (Corixidae and Gyrinidae), caddis fly (Trichoptera), some stonefly (Plecoptera), dragonfly and damselfly (Odonata) (Fry and Cooke, 1984).
- **Impacts on higher animals are most commonly linked with food loss and reproductive effects, rather than to direct toxic effects on adults:** for example the distribution of the osprey was believed to have been affected by loss of fish in acid lakes in Sweden during the 1980s (Eriksson, 1984).
- **Many larger animals have proved reasonably adaptable to air pollution:** for example fish-eating birds such as divers (*Gavia* spp.) and the goosander (*Mergus serrator*) have adapted to reduced biomass in partly acidified lakes in Scandinavia, possibly through increased hunting success in clearer water (Eriksson, 1985).

- Different air pollutants have a range of effects on a single species: combinations can sometimes produce a joint effect greater than the sum of individual effects (synergism or the 'cocktail effect') and on other occasions cancel each other out. Some lichens are more sensitive to gaseous sulphur dioxide than to wet acid deposition, while in other species the reverse is true (Looney and James, 1988).
- Some environments are particularly susceptible to sulphur and nitrogen pollution damage: including: environments with a low buffering capacity (Flower and Battarbee, 1983); environments open to regular or occasional episodes of intense pollution, such as normally basic rivers following an acid snow melt (Leivestadd and Muniz, 1976); environments containing particularly sensitive keystone species.

miles away and altered the ecology of areas they had regarded as set aside to retain a natural ecosystem in perpetuity.)

This history is not entirely one of gloom and doom however. Research more recently has shown that the effects of reducing sulphur and nitrogen emissions from power stations as a result of the Convention on Long Range Transport of Air Pollution in Europe and similar controls in North America has resulted in partial and accelerating recovery of many aquatic ecosystems, with decreasing sulphate levels in freshwaters (Stoddard et al, 1999). Some of these impacts can, with political determination, enforcement and time, be at least partially reversed.

There is no space here to review every pollutant. Others with particular impacts on otherwise natural environments include those associated with legal and illegal mining, particularly through use of chemicals such as cyanide and mercury by artisan miners (Lacerda, 1997), already a huge problem with small-scale gold mines in Asia and the Amazon basin (Palheta and Taylor, 1995). Fossil fuel extraction causes a regular and occasionally catastrophic pollution load; events in the Gulf of Mexico during 2010 drew worldwide attention because they occurred in the full light of the US media but other pollution, such as the huge impacts offshore in Nigeria (Rowell et al, 2005), may in reality be more pervasive. A cocktail of metals, radioactive materials and industrial, agricultural and military chemical pollutants are altering ecosystems in ways that we can hardly begin to describe.

Changes in the ways that ecosystems regenerate over time

Next and perhaps most often missed, many apparently natural ecosystems are being altered by subtle but highly important impacts on the way in which they change and regenerate over time. We have already touched on the almost universal tendency of foresters to remove the old-growth component of forest ecosystems. In some ecosystems, modification is so widespread that we no longer see natural regeneration processes at a scale to make general assessments.

One of the unforeseen side effects of the collapse of the Soviet Union was that for the first time in decades Finnish scientists had access to forests within the same boreal ecosystem as their own but where natural disturbance patterns had been allowed to continue unchecked. In consequence previously held ideas about the predominant role of wind in knocking down old trees had to be reconsidered and the impacts of heavy snow were found to be far greater than thought: the Finns had literally not had enough natural reference forests to understand what was going on.

More generally and less often acknowledged, many of today's 'wilderness areas' have been managed for centuries, sometimes for millennia, by humans, most frequently through the deliberate use of fire. This is known, for example in the case of aboriginals throughout Australia, in the European Mediterranean, in the grasslands of Latin America, in many tropical forests through swidden ('slash and burn') agriculture and in the savannahs of Africa. Fire use by Aboriginal peoples in Australia took place on a huge scale, was all pervasive and mentioned by virtually every early explorer: James Cooke referred to 'This continent of smoke' and there is growing evidence that this has caused gradual but profound changes, over thousands of years, to the make-up of forests and scrub (Flannery 1994). There is now also good evidence that the huge herds of antelope, wildebeest and zebra in the African plains have been artificially increased by maintaining larger than natural areas as grassland with occasional trees rather than dense forests. Nearly every forest stand in Finland has been burnt at least once in the past 400–500 years and from 1700 until the 1920s slash and burn agriculture was practised on half to three quarters of forests (Parviainen, 1995). Anthropogenic use of fire in Switzerland over thousands of years has changed forest composition and researchers have suggested that in its absence silver fir (*Abies alba*) would still form lowland forests there (Tinner et al, 1999). Fire is popularly considered to be an essential part of ecosystem processes in Mediterranean regions, although recent research challenges the perceived wisdom that plants are particularly fire-adapted in these ecosystems and cautions against deliberate increase in fire frequencies if ecosystem degradation and plant extinctions are to be averted (Bradshaw et al, 2011).

Deliberate grassland burning continues in many African national parks today. It is also the case in many forests, where prescribed burning is used as a way of reducing fuel loads in an attempt to prevent more catastrophic fires; following huge fires in national parks such as Kosiosko in Australia in 2003, national park authorities there are under political pressure to burn more regularly. Although the ecological implications are increasingly being recognized, managers are expected to continue to use fire for safety reasons. Fire-prone landscapes are thus, throughout most of the world, being deliberately kept in a state where huge, intense fires are minimized, by the deliberate use of smaller fires (known as cool fires) to burn off potential fuel without necessarily killing mature trees. It is only in a few more remote areas, such as the huge boreal

FIGURE 1.6 Climate change and human disturbance are changing fire ecology throughout the world. While fire is a natural part of ecosystems such as the dry eucalypt forests of Australia, pictured here, it is now affecting many non-fire dominant ecosystems, resulting in major changes to ecology

forests of the north or remote parts of Australia, that the decision has been taken to let wildfires burn free. Elsewhere, managers aim to impose limits on the extremes of fire, maintaining more stable vegetation mosaics and smaller patch sizes. Conversely, throughout populated, fire-prone areas the tendency is for increased fires through arson and accident: humanity's propensity for smoking cigarettes has changed a huge number of forest and grassland ecosystems. Throughout most of the areas where humans have influence, the net tendency is to prevent many apparently natural ecosystems from attaining their expected level of maturity.

Fire is not the only factor altering regeneration patterns: selective logging, removal of economically or socially important plant species, over-fishing, grazing by domestic livestock and disproportionate hunting pressure all truncate natural ecological patterns. In general, semi-natural ecosystems are growing younger as the oldest individuals, which may be trees, or fish, or the largest deer in the pack, are selectively targeted. At the same time, regeneration *processes* are increasingly manipulated, such as by the suppression of the hottest fires or selective removal of certain species. These changes are hard to measure and their long-term ecological impacts still imperfectly understood. They are also by no means complete: attempts to suppress the hottest forest fires are for instance being undermined by changes in weather patterns which conversely encourage fire. As natural ecosystems become increasingly truncated, fenced in and limited in size, the temptation to manage them to retain a 'steady state' grows stronger, but in most cases we still do not understand the long-term ecological consequences of such decisions.

Climate change

The last group of impacts is also perhaps in the long-term the most important and still the least understood. Despite the efforts of hackers, bloggers, genuine sceptics and industry-supported disinformation campaigns, there is no longer any serious scientific debate about the fact that climate is changing. There is however still a lot of uncertainty about the precise causes, rate, magnitude and direction of these changes and even more to be learned about their likely effects. We already know that from an ecological perspective the changes are likely to be profound. Climate change, like a far more pervasive version of acid rain and agricultural pollution, is a human impact that routinely affects ecosystems far from its source, being no respecter of the boundaries of either nations or protected areas, with the result that many traditional conservation strategies will simply fail to be effective.

We don't need to look at computer models to know that climate change can have dramatic impacts on ecology and society; historians and archaeologists can already provide compelling evidence. Brian Fagan, a professor of anthropology in California, has provided a gripping account of how the periodic El Niño climatic phenomenon, which made the headlines at the turn of the millennium, has been creating ecological havoc for at least 5000 years. Fagan's book (1999), one of a series he has written about historical climate change, looks at the impact that climate fluctuations had on a range of historical cultures, including the Moche warrior priests of Peru, the Maya of Central America and the Egyptian pharaoh culture. These types of impacts continue today and are likely to be exacerbated by climate change. The bums hanging around the docks in Monterey, California in John Steinbeck's 1945 novel *Cannery Row* were victims of a collapse in the sardine industry caused by an El Niño event in the 1940s. A 1997–98 'event' caused well over US$10 billion worth of damage around the world.

Relic ecosystems also provide evidence of past changes. When I visited my friend Alun Williams, who was nursing in a remote Aboriginal community, he took me deep into the Australian desert. We slept one night in a huge meteorite crater and, in the relative cool of the early morning, walked through an extraordinary valley of palm trees, the last remnant of a vast tropical forest that existed when the climate was wetter, stretching across an area that has today has been changed to desert. There were similar forests in the Sahara when the Pharaohs ruled Egypt.

In 1993, WWF International commissioned Sue Stolton and I to research and co-author *Some Like it Hot*, a book on the predicted impacts of human-induced climate change on biodiversity (Markham et al, 1993). We synthesized information from many of the leading climate change ecologists of the day. At that time our overview was almost wholly speculative – a compendium of possibilities drawn from modelling studies, applying predicted climate changes to known species and ecosystems and relying on the opinions of experts about what might happen as a result. A decade later, WWF asked us to revisit the issue and write a paper updating the book in time for the 2003 World Parks Conference; by then we could start to see how the projections and guesswork of the early 1990s was starting to be measured in reality (Dudley and Stolton, 2003a).

The bad news has been further quantified in the years since; in preparation for this book I have once again revisited the opinions and proposals drawn together in *Some Like it Hot* and tried to see how they stack up against what is being said today by the (far larger) group of climate change scientists now operating. When Camille Parmesan (2006) surveyed peer-reviewed studies of observed changes believed to be linked to climate change, she found 866 published between 1899 and 2006, with 40 per cent of those appearing from 2003 and 2006; numbers have continued to rocket up in the years since. Studies of the impacts of climate change on distribution of species focus mainly on animals, while phenological (timing) studies are mainly of plants, although there are plenty of exceptions. A summary comparison of what scientists were saying around 1990 and what has emerged since is given in Table 1.2: many are by now measurements of what has happened; some are refined predictions.

In broad terms, most of the predictions that scientists were making two decades ago now have considerable evidence backing them from field observations and measurements; the models and predictions have proved accurate as far as they go. But although the impacts are manifest, we still don't know very much about the implications.

Overviews by McCarty (2001), Walther et al (2002) and Parmesan (2006) describe a range of types of impact: changes in geographic range (typically movement polewards as temperatures rise); elevational range; breeding range; flowering date; flight period; emergence date; spawning date; breeding migration; breeding date; migration date; first song; end of hibernation; and growing season. Broadly speaking, these are all an issue of either timing or location: as average temperatures increase, plants and animals move along with optimal conditions, either polewards or upwards, and they also emerge, reproduce and if necessary migrate measurably earlier in the season.

The science of phenology – 'the study of the times of recurring natural phenomena especially in relation to climatic conditions' was until modern interest in climate change mainly the preserve of amateur naturalists and often looked down on as rather a joke by professional ecologists; today it has gained a critical new lease of life as one of the key quantifiable indicators of change. Scientists have measured the influence of fluctuating climate on wild species for many decades; the critical question in this context is whether or not current

TABLE 1.2 Comparing prediction and measurements of climate change

Biome/group	Predicted impacts	Examples of observed impacts
Oceans	Impacts on phytoplankton and thus productivity	Major changes seen (Hays et al, 2005) with mismatch between trophic levels and functional groups (Edwards and Richardson, 2004) and reduced calcification (Riebesell et al, 2000).
	Fish species move to high latitudes	Two thirds of fish in the North Sea in the Atlantic have shifted latitude or depth over 25 years (Perry et al, 2005).
	Changes in abundance in warmer waters	Changes in fish abundance have been strongly correlated with temperature changes in seawater (Brander, 2007).
Coastal zones	Inundation of coastal marshes	Rapid loss of the Blackwater National Wildlife Refuge in Chesapeake Bay is thought to be due to both direct human pressure and sea-level rise (Leatherman et al, 1995).
	Inundation of dunes and flora changes	
Mangroves	Inundation	Forest loss and sea-level rise could destroy 96% of tiger habitat in the Sundarbans in India and Bangladesh in 50 years (Loucks et al, 2010), but overall deforestation is a probably a greater threat than sea level (Alongi, 2008).
	Changes in salinity altering species mix	
Coral reefs	Bleaching	Recent research suggests that up to a third of corals face increased extinction threat under climate change (Carpenter et al, 2008). Changes do not affect all species equally; some are more resistant (Hughes et al, 2003). More recently, threats of ocean acidification have further increased pressure on corals (Hoegh-Guldberg et al, 2007).
Wetlands	Loss of shallow/temporary wetlands	
	Optimal conditions for species change, some extinctions possible	

(continued)

TABLE 1.2 *(Cont.)*

Biome/group	Predicted impacts	Examples of observed impacts
Grasslands	Changes in rainfall and increased fire	
	Drying out favouring scrub invasion	Scrub invasion is taking place although it is not yet certain how much this is caused by climate change or factors like over-grazing by livestock (van Auken, 2000); too much and too little fire can both suppress trees (Briggs et al, 2002).
Tropical moist forest	Major changes due to less moisture in some areas	Evidence of large-scale and dramatic changes in biomass of old-growth forests, risks of exceeding temperature and drought thresholds leading to major damage (Malhi and Phillips, 2004).
	Increase in fire	Fire has increased dramatically in forests, e.g. in Borneo (Leighton and Wirawan, 1986) but separating climate change from other human influences is hard (Dudley et al, 1997).
	Key threats to tropical mountain cloud forest	
	Loss of forests at edge of their range	Many changes observed including shifts in and losses among species (Pounds et al, 1999).
	Loss of susceptible species	Many examples, e.g. crashes in amphibian populations in Costa Rican forests have been linked to climate-related changes in dry-season mist frequency (Pounds et al, 1999).
Temperate/ boreal forests	Shifts in optimal conditions to high altitudes and latitudes	Consistent evidence of shifts in optimal conditions in meta-study within northern hemisphere (Parmesan and Yohe, 2003).
	Decline in boreal forest	
Mountains	Glacier loss and associated impacts	Loss of volume in glaciers has been globally consistent (Dyurgerov and Meier, 2000; Oerlemans, 2005) although there are exceptions. There is still a debate about the role of climate change in these changes.
	Radically altered hydrological conditions	Changes in permafrost and hydrology are being widely recorded, for example in Alaska (Hinzman et al, 2005), while snowpack is declining throughout western North America (Mote et al, 2005).
	Loss or shrinkage of high alpine zones/species	Observations in Austria found 70% of mountains had richer flora than in 19th century, consistent with climate change (Pauli et al, 1986).

Arctic	Reduction in sea ice and impact on food web	Sea ice has continued to decline since the 1950s, with the rate of shrinkage accelerating more quickly than expected (Stroeve et al, 2007). Decreased sea ice and a consequent two week loss of hunting has been blamed for weight decrease in polar bears in the Hudson Bay area of Canada (Stirling et al, 1999).
	Caribou and reindeer food supply affected	Measured declines in many caribou and reindeer populations across their range are consistent with predicted results of climate change (Vors and Boyce, 2009).
	Tundra shrinkage	Forest and shrub has expanded into grass tundra in Alaska and elsewhere since the 1940s, consistent with predicted models (Hinzman et al, 2005).
Antarctic	Shifts in flora population	Changes have been observed in flora, for example plants expanding their range and colonizing new areas (Smith, 1994). In addition there have been major impacts on animals. The sea-ice dependent Adélie and emperor penguins (*Pygoscelis adeliae* and *Aptenodytes forsteri*) have almost gone from northern sites in Antarctica since 1970. Emperors had declined from 300 breeding pairs to just 9 in the western Antarctic Peninsula by 2005. Krill has also declined dramatically in losses linked to disappearance of sea ice (Gross, 2005).
Pests and diseases	Increase in invasive species and emergence of new pests	There is growing evidence that climate change will favour many invasive animal species (e.g. Chown et al, 2007), including in marine environments (Occhipinti-Ambrogi, 2007). Additionally, some weed species have been shown to grow better under increased CO_2 concentrations (Dukes and Mooney, 1999); e.g. an invasive grass grew proportionately faster than native species in the Mojave Desert (Smith et al, 2000).
Species and genetic diversity	Net decrease in diversity	Modelling has added detail to projections; for example one study of biodiversity hotspots predicted an average of 11.6% extinction rates for endemic species (range 1–43%) (Malcolm et al, 2006).
	Problems for migratory birds	Earlier migration among birds is recorded for most continents; annual migration of marine species is measured as changing with temperature; some species are changing migration routes due to changed conditions (Parmesan, 2006).
	Range and boundary changes	A meta-analysis over >1700 species in the Northern hemisphere found average changes of 6.1km/decade north and 6.1m/decade upwards (Parmesan and Yohe, 2003).
	Phenology changes	A meta-analysis found average advance in phenology of 2.3 days/decade in Northern hemisphere (Parmesan and Yohe, 2003).
	Species getting out of step with ecosystem	Analysis of the small number of studies of phenology changes as compared to food as a yardstick found most were mistimed due to climate change (Vissier and Both, 2005).

changes match those expected under climate models: that is, whether climate-related changes are linked to *climate change* as the phrase is currently under-stood or are instead just a reflection of more random or short-term fluctuations.

Climate scientists are often hampered by lack of long-term data, but some exists for those prepared to think outside the box. The Japanese have kept records for hundreds of years of the emergence of cherry blossom (*Prunus jamasakura*), an event of huge cultural significance: Nobel prize-winning author Yasunari Kawabata made it the centre point of his novel *The Old Capital*. Records show that changes in flowering time showed no signifi-cant trend from 1400 to 1900 then underwent a statistically significant shift towards earlier flowering, and flowering time has moved forward even faster since 1952 (Menzel and Dose, 2005). Similarly, comparison of the timing of grape harvests in Europe have also shown a trend towards grapes maturing earlier in the season, with 2003 having the earliest harvest recorded in 500 years (Menzel, 2005). In the UK, a collection of key phenological data was started by the pioneer scientist Robert Marsham in 1736 and continued by his family for two hundred years, providing dramatic evidence of earlier flow-ering and arrival of migrants (Sparks and Menzel, 2002).

Such long-term data sets are rare and mined assiduously by researchers. There are doubtless a few more to be turned up – records kept by religious institutions perhaps or festivals linked to key biological events. But given the evidence for a speeding up of climate change, much shorter term records can also be illustrative. Trends towards earlier occurrence have been recorded for ecological events as diverse as timing of frog calling; egg laying in birds; arrival time for migrants; flowering time; first appearances of butterflies and emer-gence of phytoplankton blooms (collated in Parmesan, 2006).

Evidence is also starting to emerge for species moving to keep up with a changing climate. In Europe, for example, the processionary moth (*Thaumetopoea pityocampa*) has moved northwards 87km in 23 years in what is believed to be a response to changing temperatures (Battisti et al, 2005). In the UK, 23 out of 24 temperate dragonfly species have moved their ranges northwards (Hickling et al, 2005), while in Florida five new tropical dragonfly species were recorded in 2000 alone, presumably migrating from Cuba or further south (Paulson, 2001). In the Netherlands, 77 new epiphytic lichens have been recorded colonizing from the south (van Herk et al, 2002). Range shifts have also been recorded for butterflies such as the Edith's checkerspot (*E. editha*) in North America (Parmesan, 1996) and the Apollo (*Parnassius apollo*) in France (Descimon et al, 2006); indeed two thirds of 35 butterflies assessed in Europe had shifted their ranges northwards 35–240km (Parmesan et al, 1999). Numerous other studies look at distribution of birds (e.g. Crick, 2004) and fish, again showing similar trends with patterns of distribution following patterns of air or water temperature.

However, although we have mounting evidence of changes, we still know less about what they will mean in practice: will species be able to adapt or will climate-related shifts upset whole ecosystems? One critical issue relates to *mistiming*: if for example a caterpillar emerges earlier because of warmer weather, will its food plant also have advanced to the same degree or will it be left to starve to death? Or will a few smart individuals learn to adapt to different food species? So far there have been relatively few studies although those that have been under-taken generally found some evidence of mistiming (Vissier and Both, 2005): its consequences have not been explored in detail. There are also some studies that show species are starting to adapt to changing conditions (Adger et al, 2005).

The fact that some species can adapt does not mean that all will be able to do so; species at the edge of their ranges, with specialized niches, those already under pressure or just with less genetic predisposition to adapt either physically or ecologically will remain at higher risk than adaptable species. Extinctions linked to climate change are already thought to have occurred, particularly in narrow ecological niches in mountain areas. The best known to date is the worldwide decline in amphibians (Balustein and Wake, 1995) including a catastrophic loss of 67 per cent of harlequin frogs over 20–30 years in Central and South America (Pounds et al, 2006). While the reasons for this loss are complex and probably multiple, many researchers now believe that changing climate plays a role.

There is, as mentioned above, an order of magnitude more information available today than there was even a decade ago. This hasn't necessarily made it easier to work out what is going on; there is a tendency to blame any ecological perturbation on climate change and it is worth treating some of these claims with a good deal of caution. Researchers point out that it is often difficult to be sure about how significant the role of climate change is compared with other environmental changes (Pyke, 2004). In some cases climate has become a convenient scapegoat for other impacts much closer at hand. Although we now have a lot of very useful data we are still a long way from working out exactly what it will all mean in terms of future ecosystem responses.

Conclusions: What have we lost and what are we still losing?

Some of the pressures described above have been altering ecosystems for thou-sands of years, others only emerged after the Industrial Revolution, or with the post-1945 intensification of agriculture, or as a result of globalization and the boom in foreign travel in the 1990s. Their influences ebb and flow over time; in combination they are the driving forces behind a profound and continuing transformation of the planet's ecology. All of them share in common that they can affect apparently natural ecosystems as well as places that have been obvi-ously modified or degraded. Yet in general, most analyses of species decline put the emphasis heavily on impacts of habitat loss.

Ignoring or playing down causes apart from habitat loss is not just a problem in terms of our understanding about the ways in which ecosystems function, but has direct impacts on how we implement conservation. While habitat change is generally acknowledged to be the primary cause of loss it is not the sole cause and this narrow focus has created a slightly perverse result of people assuming that if habitat remains all will be well. Yet when attempts are made to look quantitatively at causes and effects, the situation isn't so clear. Various pieces of research carried out in Germany as long ago as the 1980s demonstrate the complexity. A study of the specific reasons for decline of 581 plant species (Sukopp, 1981) found that alongside the expected villains, like habitat destruction, drainage and land-use change, 89 species declined due to herbicide use, 69 from river and lake management, 31 from water pollution, 56 from eutrophication, 172 from abandonment of management, and so on (species could be listed for more than one cause). Similarly a study of reasons for decline in threatened butterflies identified pesticides as a cause in almost a quarter of cases, herbicide use or similar in 12 per cent, changes in forest edges in over 20 per cent; again multiple causes were identified and habitat loss is the most important single cause (quoted in Bauer, 1985). In a thorough review, Bauer also identified specific threats to species of animals ranging from mammals to invertebrates, which included among others lowering of groundwater, agrochemicals, water pollution, eutrophication, changes in river banks, acidification and removal of dead wood. None of this should detract from the huge threats that major habitat change causes for conservation, but it suggests that many things can happen even in apparently more natural ecosystems that nonetheless alter conditions sufficiently to threaten or eliminate a proportion of species. Few other places have attempted such a thorough evaluation. It is only when changes become dramatic – empty forests or empty lakes – that we generally take notice.

Many of our wild lands are being altered, usually impoverished and consequently weakened. Some of these changes may for practical purposes be irreversible, others most certainly are not. Yet until recently there has been a marked reluctance for conservation organizations to afford these issues the importance that they deserve. Few of the larger conservation NGOs have worked seriously on pollution for instance, except for that which causes climate change.

Of course habitat change has been devastating to biodiversity and ecosystem services but it is not the only problem: a tendency to ignore the less obvious impacts on natural habitats risks losing much of what remains. There has not been a square inch of the planet's surface, on the ground or under the water, that has not been influenced to at least a small extent by human activity and for the large majority of the planet these changes are dramatic, even in many of the places that we like to consider as still 'wild'. We return to these issues in the last chapter, which suggests some practical responses to the analysis.

CHAPTER 2

The Myths of Wilderness – Myth 2: Naturalness Is Irrelevant

> **Key messages**
> - Disturbed or human-dominated ecosystems never support all potential biodiversity or ecosystem services.
> - Cultural landscapes that rely on human intervention are a useful management strategy in crowded, long-settled areas but the idea that biodiversity 'needs' humans is flawed.
> - Natural ecosystems are not just social constructs as some commentators suggest, they have existence and value distinct from human society.
> - In a changed and rapidly changing world, the concept of naturalness remains important but needs further elaboration and interpretation.

Six o'clock in the morning, somewhere in the English West Midlands, a landscape that has been shaped and sometimes almost overwhelmed by factories and large-scale manufacturing since the start of the Industrial Revolution. We've driven out to a tiny bit of wasteland between the massive cities of Birmingham and Wolverhampton; the skyline is full of chimneys. We are walking across a field, of sorts, with a canal running through one edge in an area surrounded by abandoned factories. Suddenly there is a weird clattering noise overhead and we look up to see a male snipe (*G. gallinago*) 'drumming' its display flight; diving so fast that its outer tail feathers make an unmistakeable rattling sound. Drumming mostly takes place at night and we are lucky to be watching it in the clear light of a spring morning. The canal, to our surprise, is crystal clear and home to a good population of miller's thumb (*Cottus gobio*), a fish confined to unpolluted water and also usually active at night; we're up early enough to be catching nocturnal animals just before they settle down for the day. There is a water spider as well (*Argyroneta aquatica*), Britain's only completely aquatic spider, and we can see its air-filled silken nest stuck among a mass of water plants a few inches below the surface. We take some photographs and notes. Leaving the site we are immediately back in the thick of the city, our van weaving among commuters on their way to work, while we look for a café to have breakfast.

If natural ecosystems no longer exist, at least in a pure form, doesn't that mean that naturalness is irrelevant? A growing numbers of commentators think so. Their arguments run along three main lines:

1   Naturalness has gone, therefore we'd better get used to living with a new kind of nature that is emerging as a result.
2   Humans are part of nature and in many parts of the world have long interacted with nature in a positive way: these 'cultural landscapes' *need* human intervention or their values will be lost.
3   Terms like 'naturalness' and 'wilderness' are just social constructs with no value outside those imposed by society and are one of many possible interpretations of a particular ecosystem, with no particular precedence over any other.

I think that these are all myths, as dangerous as the myth that absolute naturalness still exists in their potential to divert us along irrelevant pathways. All of them have some truth and of the three, I have most sympathy for the first; but this is also a simplification.

Naturalness has gone – Rejoice in the new mix

This message has emerged, not surprisingly, from places where changes to ecology have been most profound: rich countries with little of their land left unmodified; urban areas and the suburbs and hinterlands; areas of intensive agriculture and other heavily managed ecosystems. Many of the ideas are very good; it is their illogical extension into a global philosophy that I'm questioning.

The importance of nature in the margins of industrialized society was increasingly recognized during the 20th century as a consequence of a growing interest in natural history among societies that had very little chance to interact with nature in anything like the raw. Studies of wildlife living in major cities such as London (Fitter, 1949) and recognition of the 'unofficial countryside' that existed alongside farmland or urban areas (Mabey, 1973; Sinclair, 2010) helped to show that the natural world was not confined to the exotic and faraway. Richard Fitter (1945) reported 145 bird species in the London area, either resident or present for part of the year and a further 41 as passage migrants; the list has kept expanding and now stands at over 200 species for Regent's Park alone. (There were 592 species of bird on the British list as of September 2010 but many of these will be rare migrants and Regent's Park, right in the heart of London, must have seen most of the commonly occurring species.) During the summer of 2010 we joined thousands of other people in peering through the telescopes that the Royal Society for the Protection of Birds kept trained onto the top of the Tate Modern gallery by the side of the River Thames, where a pair of peregrine falcons (*Falco peregrinus*) was nesting. A proportion of bird species adapt very well to urban living. Among many other instances, I have watched extraordinary aerial displays by starlings (*Sturnus vulgaris*) in the evening in Rome, seen the famous red-tailed hawk (*Buteo jamaicensis*) in Central Park in New York and the pariah kites (*Milvus migrans govinda*) circling overhead a dozen Indian cities. Even more surprisingly, a proportion of migrating birds head straight through rather than around cities: I've seen flocks of warblers flash through inner city Bristol for instance and a friend sitting in his back garden in the east end of London was once surrounded by a flock of firecrests (*Regulus ignicapillus*) of all unlikely things.

Even in the most polluted cities – in fact often *especially* in the most polluted cities with their rich pickings on rubbish heaps – wild animals and plants flourish. Take Hanoi for instance. Hoan Kiem Lake is on the edge of the old quarter and home to an ancient turtle, relic of an old but virtually extinct species. All around the lakeside, motorcycles circle in a continuous stream, music thumps from karaoke bars and at night the Turtle Tower, perched on an islet, is floodlit and covered in sparkling lights. It is hard to imagine a more quintessentially urban scene. But wherever lights reflect in the water, nowadays there will be a constant rippling of fish. A few years ago the only living things I saw there were a few bats flickering low over the water at dusk, but lately I have begun to spot more young turtles again and there is a little heron that perches on a tree next to my favourite café. I have seen pond herons too, and bulbuls, and there are dozens of beautifully decorated butterflies. Hardly Arcadia yet, and quite a lot of the turtles are aliens abandoned by pet owners, but life is definitely creeping back to somewhere that a few years ago would have been written off as polluted and derelict beyond hope.

Natural history programmes on television started to show people what was going on literally outside their back doors. The importance of the commonplace in nature was proposed as a coherent philosophy by authors like Sue Clifford and Angela King through the organization Common Ground (King and Clifford, 1985), arguing that we respect and celebrate nature in our own home landscapes rather than always expecting it to be somewhere else. Common Ground also championed the role of arts in nature, regarding artists and writers as conduits for interpreting the local (e.g. King and Clifford, 2000). A 'city wildlife' movement sprang up in the 1970s and 1980s, characterized by a focus on nature gardening and urban natural history societies. I was part of this briefly at the beginning of the 1980s, working for Friends of the Earth in Birmingham in the UK, where an Urban Wildlife Group was set up to celebrate the nature of the West Midlands and create nature reserves in churchyards, canal banks and derelict ground. As the opening example in the chapter shows, this massive urban area still then contained rich patches of wildlife: it was possible to stand on the edge of an abandoned quarry and see hundreds

FIGURE 2.1 Many habitats in urban and suburban areas are now heavily influenced by human management or even, as in the case of Central Park in New York, entirely created

of sand martins nesting, find rare plants in hospital grounds (a couple of us sneaked into a local mental hospital one weekend and found rich swards of ancient woodland, saved from trespass by the irrational fears that such places create) and watch sparrow hawks swooping on pigeons in the heart of the city. An emphasis on urban nature was then considered radical and generally resisted by people involved in the established conservation bodies, who worried about loss of revenue and diverting attention from nature in rural areas. Friends of the Earth had some tense meetings with some of the county naturalists' trusts at the time, although it is hard to imagine given the popularity of urban nature today.

Some conservationists have taken the success of urban conservation a step further philosophically, proposing that wild plant and animal species are far more robust than we generally assume and that many are adapting well to humanized societies and cultural landscapes. Tim Low, based in Australia, wrote a trenchant critique of wilderness approaches to conservation and a description of the ability of many wild species to adapt to human-modified landscapes, pointing out that 'the barriers between people and wildlife are weakening as animals learn new tricks' (Low, 2002, p121).

The ability to adapt to what we might call artificial environments is not limited to urban areas. The merlin (*Falco columbarius*), a small raptor, had almost been written off as a resident species in Wales due to a combination of pesticide poisoning, upland improvement and, as the population plummeted, even predation by the larger peregrine falcon. But then it was discovered (Parr, 1991) that the merlin had started nesting in the spruce plantations that conservationists generally loathe for their low biodiversity; it is now estimated that there was a 50 per cent switch in breeding habitat between 1975 and 1985 (Parr, 1994). Similarly, in southern Brazil and Argentina, eucalyptus plantations can provide useful habitat for the puma (*Puma concolor*) (Mazzolli, 2010) and the greater rhea (*Rhea americana*), both of which need cover but are not particularly fussy about what it contains.

Sites that may not look particularly nice or fit in with our ideas of 'nature' can sometimes support high biodiversity; sewage farms are famously rich in birds for instance. Pollution levels may be lower in these artificial sites too. Although urban gardens can be subject to heavy use of agrochemicals (Dudley, 1986b) increasing interest in wildlife gardening is helping to create relatively pristine havens in many domestic gardens, parks, the edges of golf courses and in the waste areas that survive in large cities where invertebrates and amphibians may fare better than in pesticide-impacted areas of 'real' countryside. Garden ponds have become a major habitat for frogs and toads in the UK (Beebee, 1979).

There is much good sense in the philosophy of celebrating altered nature. Urban and suburban nature reserves can be important links in connectivity conservation for both migrant and resident species and they are also, critically, the places where children and their parents have a chance of interacting with nature on an everyday basis (Tryzna, 2005).

But this is not the whole story. Such areas might contain a rich wildlife in terms of *numbers* of individual plants and animals but seldom or ever will they support an equal *variety* to that found in natural ecosystems: a proportion of species are too specialized in their ecological requirements to survive in highly modified ecosystems. As a rule of thumb, the more we alter ecosystems the less species will be able to survive there. While I spent the last chapter arguing that there were no totally natural places left, there are plenty of *predominantly* natural areas surviving and to approach or manage these for biodiversity conservation in the same way as a bit of abandoned industrial ground would be the height of irresponsibility.

Take farming for instance; the continual biodiversity decline in Europe as agriculture intensifies is a clear indication of the implications of different land management strategies. We now know, due to comparative research in Denmark, Germany, the UK and elsewhere, that organic farms can significantly increase biodiversity levels as compared to conventional farms (Stolton et al, 2000). But we also know that the biodiversity of an organic farm, however sympathetically managed, is still lower than a comparable area of natural grassland or woods. Well-managed farms can support an important proportion of wildlife, provide sympathetic habitat to allow movement of species and they can also play a key role in maintaining population levels of common species, but a working farm can never be equivalent to a natural habitat. Nor can a timber plantation, despite the strenuous efforts of the industry to stress the biodiversity value of such sites. Plantations can support individual species, sometimes of high conservation importance, and can sometimes even support higher levels of biodiversity than the farmland that they replace, but when plantations replace natural forests the results are almost always negative for conservation, even when efforts are made to use wildlife-friendly approaches (Edwards et al, 2010). Logging in tropical forests and in temperate and boreal forests (Dudley, 1992) both change and usually impoverish biodiversity, even if the forests are afterwards left alone or if logging is carried out as sensitively as possible.

While all the types of habitat discussed above can be useful for conservation, and need to be integrated into conservation strategies, they are not the equivalent to, nor are they a replacement for, more natural habitats. So while we may indeed need to rejoice in the new mixes where they occur, this is no reason to turn our backs on the concept of wild nature in totality or assume that it is somehow no longer relevant.

Nature needs us – If we don't intervene important values will be lost

This argument goes as follows: in places where humans have a long history of ecosystem management, remaining species have become adapted to and now rely on conditions within the cultural landscape. Humans are now an integral part of the functioning ecosystem and removal of our influence will lead to a loss of biodiversity. This philosophy is embedded most deeply within the 'protected landscape and seascape' approach and given semi-official status by designation of a special management category of protected area by the International Union for Conservation of Nature (IUCN): 'category V protected landscapes and seascapes'. The definition states: 'A protected area where **the interaction of people and nature over time has produced an area of distinct character with significant ecological, biological, cultural and scenic value**: and where **safeguarding the integrity of this interaction** is vital to protecting and sustaining the area and its associated nature conservation and other values' (Dudley, 2008, my emphasis). It is also strongly reflected in the cultural landscape concept as interpreted under the World Heritage Convention. Because these two concepts are closely intertwined I will consider them together here.

Protected landscapes are found throughout the world but are particularly concentrated in Europe. Examples used as case studies in a survey by the World Commission on Protected Areas (Brown et al, 2005) include many of the national parks of Europe; landscape conservation initiatives in Nepal; land managed by pastoralists in eastern and southern Africa; cultural landscapes of the Andes; some offshore islands and coastal regions of Brazil; and long-settled landscapes in parts of the eastern United States. The recent Satoyama initiative launched in Japan also promotes 'lived in' landscapes for their conservation values (Bélair et al, 2010). All such areas mix long-term management and habitat alteration with remnants of fairly natural vegetation and all are characterized by the existence of land management practices that have evolved over time and can claim to be in some kind of balance with nature. Central to the protected landscapes concept is the idea that we need to intervene to maintain values. Tim Low (2002, p296) writes of Australia: 'Conservation is intervention. You can't save nature by letting it alone; management is a must.' The most enthusiastic proponents of cultural landscapes argue that virtually all ecosystems, being influenced by humans, require a human element in management.

The concept that humans play a critical and necessary role in the natural system is central to the conservation ethic in the Mediterranean countries of southern Europe. The French historian Fernand Braudel wrote: 'When you don't cultivate the land in the Mediterranean the land dies.' Many Mediterranean ecologists agree and argue strongly that the heterogeneous landscape mosaic of the region, shaped and modified by farming practices stretching back over thousands of years, allows a richer biodiversity than would otherwise be possible (Atauri and Lucio, 2001) and that abandonment of such systems will lead to losses (González Bernáldez, 1992). It is argued that this holds true for both animals (Pino et al, 2000) and plants (Rescia et al, 1994). The mixing took place so long ago that the original population centres of many tree species are now unknown. Moving back to an 'original' ecology is assumed to be impossible. Nor is it necessary to maintain wildlife. Assessment of protected areas in Catalonia, Spain, for example found iconic species like the bear and lynx surviving better in protected landscapes than in strictly protected reserves (Mallarach, 2006). Santos and Thorne (2010), in a study on management options in Mediterranean oak woodlands in California and Portugal, identify multiple-purpose use and keeping people on the land as important conservation strategies, to avoid 'overmaturity' and scrub invasion that will replace the 'original' woodlands.

Some Mediterranean countries have used the protected landscape approach to develop area-wide conservation policies. I have for instance been introduced to some of the Catalonian protected landscapes by Josep-Maria Mallarach and José Atauri, two of the specialists quoted above, and the region's carefully planned protected landscapes, including cork oak forests, vineyards, grazing areas and wetlands, are playing a critical role in slowing or halting biodiversity loss in Spain. I wish we had anything like as good in the UK.

The drivers for such approaches are as much cultural as ecological. Managers of cultural landscapes attempt to 'freeze' an ecosystem in a particular state rather than accept the natural changes and cycling over time; they are also sometimes charged with similarly attempting to freeze the economic system as a result. There may be good reasons for doing this, either because a particular landscape composition provides needed goods and services (fruit trees, grazing, water sources etc.) or because the remaining habitat is now too small and fragmented to support a more dynamic ecosystem that accommodates large-scale vegetation cycles over time. Such landscapes have important cultural, historical,

FIGURE 2.2 In Catalonia, Spain, planning authorities have cooperated with farmers, woodland managers and other landowners to create habitat for wild species in what is a predominantly cultural landscape

artistic and aesthetic values that people wish to preserve. Using traditional management approaches, they are often accepted by people more readily than 'new' approaches. At our human time-scale we also become used to certain habitats structures and tend to regard any change as a loss.

Protected landscapes thus provide an effective balancing of social and biological aims in what is already a crowded landscape. They work better than more strictly protected areas in the Mediterranean region for large carnivore conservation because they cover a much larger area; small, highly protected reserves are of limited use to animals with large ranges: the two approaches can sometimes be used very successfully together. But if, theoretically, all the protected landscapes became more strictly protected areas there seems to be no reason why the lynx and bear should decline. Similarly, restoration of a more natural ecosystem over large areas would certainly change the *composition* of biodiversity but we cannot as yet know if it would lead to an overall *reduction*, because the experiment has not been tried. Nor is it very likely to be, because of the high human population levels and because in some areas the key predators and large herbivores have declined to such an extent.

The best of the protected landscapes of Europe seem to be an excellent compromise solution in maintaining as much biodiversity as possible in a crowded, long-settled area. But the fact that natural values decline if traditional farming is replaced by more intensive farming for example (Donald et al, 2001), does not mean that traditional farming is necessarily or always the optimal strategy for conservation. And when it does appear to be essential, for instance when using livestock to ensure that chalk grassland is not encroached by woodland and thus loses all its rarest species, it is because livestock are acting as a replacement for native herbivores (or other disturbance systems) that have long disappeared or declined to such low levels that they are no longer useful management mechanisms.

We should also bear in mind that protected landscapes protecting something that is very much a human construction: we are aiming to conserve the mixture and numbers of species that are there at the moment, which is a choice made by society. When people argue that biodiversity will decline if managed landscapes are replaced by unmanaged landscapes they generally mean that some of the species that have flourished in an artificial landscape will decline, other past 'losers' might be expected to replace them. This may be a perfectly valid argument: conservation policy is driven by and paid for by people and therefore needs to respond to their priorities. It often means putting an emphasis on species that have iconic or traditional values rather than some pure or academic concept of 'biodiversity', which means very little to anyone but a few specialists. Proponents of protected landscapes stress their social and cultural values as well, which they argue are equally as important as any biological values from the area.

These ideas were challenged in an influential paper by Harvey Locke and Phil Dearden (2005), who argued that IUCN protected landscapes (and extractive reserves, IUCN protected area category VI) were not 'protected areas' at all in the sense meant by IUCN and should not be recognized as such on the World Database of Protected Areas. The criticism levelled at the less restrictive protected area approaches was quite specific. It was not questioning the legitimacy of landscape approaches, nor denying the importance of cultural landscapes, but was challenging the potential of such places to contribute significantly to biodiversity conservation. It was not saying 'get rid of them', but rather 'don't count them too heavily in conservation strategies' although many commentators assumed that the paper attacked the concept of cultural landscapes. Their perspective has, in turn, attracted some careful responses (see e.g. Mallarach et al, 2008) and a great deal of debate within international protected areas policy.

The questions go way beyond academic debate into the realms of passionate and deeply held belief. At the extremes of this debate I have seen the genuine anger and frustration in many conservation biologists at what they believe to be backsliding, obfuscation and weak tactics in promoting protected landscapes during the middle of a biodiversity extinction crisis. And I have been in protected area debates where 'biodiversity' is almost regarded as a dirty word, associated with an authoritarian approach of pushing people aside in favour of wild nature, without thought for the cultural and social implications of these actions. There are, fortunately, people in the middle of this debate trying to address more integrated approaches to landscape management.

I am a sceptical fan of protected landscapes. Sceptical because the protected landscape concept has been applied cynically in many places, so governments can give an impression of taking conservation seriously without investing much in either resources or political effort. With the exception of Mallarach's work in Spain (which looks at an exceptionally well-designed protected landscape programme) we know very little about whether or not protected landscapes really protect nature (or for that matter culture). Yet they now make up over half the protected areas, by area, in Europe and are growing fast throughout the world. In terms of biodiversity conservation, they remain a huge gamble.

I also feel uncomfortable with the tendency of proponents to assume that nature invariably needs humans to thrive. This has led to an over-emphasis on the importance of habitats associated with particular cultural systems and an undervaluing of systems that are allowed to develop naturally (Schnittzler et al, 2008). It also puts an emphasis on *numbers* rather than *naturalness*; a cultural landscape with artificially boosted species diversity is instinctively considered superior to a more natural ecosystem with lower diversity or with some previous species absent. (In fact I know of little work comparing overall diversity, as a cultural landscape is allowed to become more natural, although some studies do exist for particular groups like birds.) This tendency has also led some to claim that invasive species can play a more positive role in ecosystems than is often the case, such as a belief that the invasive sacred ibis (*Threskiornis aethiopicus*) in southern Europe encourages breeding in the native spoonbill (*Platalea leucorodia*) – a claim that recent careful comparisons has now brought into question (Clergeau et al, 2010).

But protected approaches are important because they do suggest a practical way of maintaining a proportion of natural species and ecological interactions in the many parts of the world where large natural or even semi-natural areas no longer exist. Cultural landscapes also provide a vehicle in which we can start to consider the question of choice in level of naturalness and the role of humans as part of natural systems. We'll return to all these issues later in the book.

It is now generally recognized that protected landscapes and cultural management have an important role in conservation, if they are planned and managed well, but not a complete role. Protected landscapes are not a panacea that should replace every other form of conservation management, nor are they a suitable strategy in every situation. As discussed in Chapter 8, most well-designed protected area systems will require a mixture of management strategies, from strict protection to much more open and fluid conservation strategies. At the same time there is increasing acceptance, or re-acceptance, of the view that some places should be left entirely without interference. I would go further; one of the aims of at least some forms of conservation should be to protect or recreate conditions in which ecosystem functioning needs little or no further interference from humans – that is, a return to naturalness should be one major aim of conservation strategy.

I'm aware that the arguments made above rest on rather shifting sands. Climate change increases the need for us to intervene in ecosystem management and we may indeed then have far fewer options for walking away and letting nature get on with it. But this will be due to an ongoing, human-created crisis rather than any mystical relationship between 'man and nature'.

Naturalness and wilderness as social constructs

The third reason commonly given for being wary of concepts like wilderness or naturalness is that they are only social constructs, which we have dreamed up ourselves, and as such have no more validity than any other social construct.

Once again, there is truth in this but not a whole truth. It can sound pretty cool in some circles to raise an eyebrow and dismiss nature as a cultural construct. Taken to a post-modern extreme, the same could be argued about almost anything; with the risk that reality slowly fades away. The Chinese sage Chuang Zhu made much the same point a long time ago when he wrote that a man dreaming that he was a butterfly might really be a butterfly dreaming that he was a man (Merton, 1960). Ideas like this are interesting and at one level impossible to disprove but they are also not much practical use in helping us live our lives. Eileen Crist (2004) is one of a number of analysts to kick back against the constructivist approach, pointing out that constructivists 'do not deconstruct their own rhetoric or assumptions' (p6). She points out that the constructivist approach has consistently failed to take the biodiversity crisis seriously, diverting attention to discourses about the meaning of the predicament rather than tackling the predicament itself, and argues that nature has a reality beyond that invented by humans. This is the perspective which is taken here and extended to the whole concept of naturalness.

History and culture certainly shape our perceptions of the natural world. As we'll see in Chapter 3, lots of people have their own ideas about what a 'wilderness' represents and concepts like 'landscape', 'seascape', 'ecoregion', 'ecosystem', 'biome' and virtually any other definitional or collective term used in ecology will have multiple interpretations. Even an apparently precise descriptor like 'protected area' has taken years to define.

This confusion is sometimes used as an excuse for dismissal; western conservationist definitions of 'wilderness' are dismissed as the fantasies of a few rich people who want to have exclusive access to aesthetically pleasing areas for adventure holidays and to follow quasi-mystical ideas about getting 'in touch' with nature. But while I have sympathy for the frustration felt at simplistic notions of empty landscapes, many of the concepts embraced by words like naturalness and wilderness have now been defined fairly precisely. They have been defined by human beings, with their own biases and cultural backgrounds, but then so is every other concept. There is no inherent reason why the views of wilderness held by city dwellers are less valid than the views of landscape held by indigenous peoples: both come laden with preconceptions but lose none of their cultural relevance in consequence. And to regard all other species as only having value when viewed through the lens of human experience is a huge act of arrogance. It is one of the reasons that global ecosystems are in such a mess.

Concepts like naturalness and wilderness also have important practical values; they are for instance useful for identifying places that have particular resonance to certain groups of people and also particular values for all human societies, as discussed in Chapter 4.

So in conclusion, in the same way that a belief in entirely natural ecosystems is simplistic, out of date and likely to confuse things, the complete dismissal of naturalness is also unhelpful. 'New nature' in towns, in the suburbs and on farmland and wasteland is important and should be celebrated but it is not a complete replacement for naturally functioning ecosystems and will only contain a fraction of the species and functions. Natural ecosystems don't 'need' people either; in long-managed cultural ecosystems and in damaged ecosystems there may be changes unless we intervene, but the extent to which we do so is a cultural choice. And finally naturalness is more than simply a social construct: a functioning ecosystem has an existence quite apart from whatever interpretation we put upon it. Dinosaurs lived quite happily for a very long time without the benefit of interpretation from ourselves. Trying to work out what naturalness really means, what its values are and how it might be addressed through management takes up the remainder of the book.

CHAPTER 3

How Our Attitudes to Natural Ecosystems Change with Time and Place

Key messages

- *Human attitudes to nature have changed from instinctively seeing ourselves as part of nature, to a conscious separation and rejection of nature and now a gradually rediscovery of our links.*
- *These stages are not always clear cut and all three can be found existing around the world.*
- *Attitudes are heavily influenced by faiths and philosophies and reflected in arts and culture.*
- *There is currently a confusion of different worldviews that need to be reconciled.*

I'm sitting in a mountain lodge in the Nepal Himalayas, reading *The Birds of Nepal*. The woman who has just cooked me supper comes and sits beside me. We have no language in common but she starts to point to illustrations of birds she recognizes. Her friend joins in and we gradually go through the whole book. I show them a few species I think should be there but which they have ignored; but they both shake their heads very confidently. They're good; there is no way a random group of people in a European village would know as much about wildlife and these two will not have had the advantages of binoculars, identification books or much spare time. We spend a great hour or so together in our wordless conversation and they clearly have a deep understanding of the nature around them. Yet when I get chatting to a couple of English-speaking men from the village who are guiding a large trekking group, they confess to being mystified as to why people come there at all; when I tell them that they're living in one of the most beautiful places I've ever seen they claim not to understand what I'm talking about.

Maybe they were just winding me up, but I've heard repeated stories of Nepali hill villagers oblivious to the aesthetics of their homeland. And sure enough there is no reason why they should be; the mountains may look nice in a tourist's photograph but they are a tough place to scrape a living, particularly when you're poor. Yet adding a further twist to this story, the same men were deeply disturbed by rumours that foreign climbers had scaled Machhapuchhre, the 'Fishtail Mountain' visible through the lodge window, which is sacred to Buddhists and off-limits to everyone by order of the Nepali government.

This reverence for the sacred in nature is prevalent throughout the region and takes precedence over simple aesthetics. Twenty or more years later, while I have been writing this book, I attended a workshop between the conservation organization WWF and a group of senior Buddhist monks and scholars in Thimphu, Bhutan, to discuss links between sacred natural sites and protected areas of the Eastern Himalayas. Among the recommendations that emerged was a strong call from the Buddhists for the government of Nepal to introduce a three month moratorium on mountain visitation in Nepal so that the spirits of the mountain might recover from the physical and emotional battering they have received from the thousands of visitors who come every year, many of whom are ignorant or careless of the landscape's sacred values. Khenpo Phuntsik Tashi of the National Museum in Bhutan wrote in a paper presented at the workshop (Khenpo, 2010):

> *By virtue of being in a pure mountain environment, spiritual beings, trees, and rocks are free from the contamination associated with mundane human activity. It is because of this lack of contact with impurities that mountains are considered a source of inspiration, and the ideal environs in which one can develop positive spiritual qualities ... The summiting of pristine sacred peaks would cause deep spiritual distress.*

Although Chapter 2 argued that concepts like naturalness and wilderness should not be dismissed as transient social constructs, human attitudes undoubtedly influence the ways in which we react to naturalness. Our views have also altered dramatically over time. Below I look at attitudes to natural ecosystems and discuss how this varies from place to place, culture to culture and with the attitudes and experiences of individual people. Alongside my own experience I draw on a range of scholarly studies; this is a rapidly growing field of interest and only a summary is given here. I consider how we react to nature by looking at history; how religious faiths view nature including sacred natural sites; and how the arts, including particularly painting and writing, have shaped and been shaped by the way that people are thinking about nature at a particular time.

There are two simplified and contradictory views about the way in which pre-modern or non-western societies view natural ecosystems. One assumes that people regard them simply as unexploited or underexploited land, or as dangerous places to be avoided; if conservationists hold this worldview they usually view people living in natural environments mainly as a 'threat'.

FIGURE 3.1 In Bhutan, Buddhist authorities recognize conservation as an aspect of their faith; one reason why most mountain tops are out of bounds to climbers in the country

Conversely, others believe that all less-industrialized societies, and particularly indigenous peoples, are likely to have a mystical and deep relationship with the natural world and a far more innate sense of nature than can ever be expected of consumerist western society. Within the conservation world this group often argues that if local communities are given control over their land, or given *back* control of their land, they will usually manage it well and conserve its natural values. Although it is possible to cite examples or case studies to back up either of these claims, on a broader scale both are over-simplistic. Or perhaps it would be better to say that the ways in which communities approach management will be influenced by a host of social, cultural and political issues and by the characters and aspirations of individuals; generalizations are likely to be wrong.

Things become even more complicated when modern, industrialized human societies are thrown into the mix and our own attitudes dissected. Not only that; different groups of people in society can have radically different perspectives: the attitudes toward nature of a rich person hunting in a private forest estate will tend to be different from that of a peasant scratching a living on a bare hillside. The millennia-old tensions between settled farmers, nomadic herders and hunter–gatherer societies also create different world-views of nature that spill over into modern society.

How the relationship between humans and nature has changed over time

Attitudes to nature have not been constant and have gone through some identifiable stages, although these have never been as abrupt or complete as a quick account suggests. A rather speculative and simplified thumbnail sketch of humans' changing relationship with the wider ecosystem, at least in the West, might go something like this: (i) emergence from and initially very close identification with rest of nature, followed by (ii) a conscious split and increasing sense of superiority over nature at the time when settled agriculture developed – a split that became more pronounced after the industrial revolution – followed in turn by (iii) a gradual and as still incomplete rekindling of the earlier feeling of unity, or at least recognition of the values of the rest of nature. By consciously separating itself from nature, civilization created the concept of wilderness (Nash, 2001). The extent to which a split has occurred differs between cultures. The stages outlined above are not as distinct as can be expressed in a single sentence, nor should they be interpreted too precisely, but they illustrate an important process.

Knowledge of older stages remains speculative. Because many early concepts of nature developed before the invention of writing, our understanding of what happened more than a few thousand years ago is based on the interpretation of archaeologists and specialists in myths and folklore. Enthusiasts can suggest their own theories with little fear of being disproved.

But most scholars agree that there was a definite change in attitudes towards the natural world, including a distinction of 'wilderness' from places where people lived, around the time that humans settled and started to practice agriculture. For many millennia, say 200,000 years, humans existed by hunting game animals and gathering wild plants, probably living a mainly nomadic lifestyle with limited possessions. While there is a large debate about our impact on ecology during this period, it is likely that, even after *Homo sapiens* emerged as a distinct species, people initially still saw themselves as *part* of nature rather than *distinct* from it. Hunters venerated the animals that they hunted and killing was often attended by ritual and recorded in pictures; the ones that survive were mainly executed on cave walls or in other suitable places. Cave paintings are found throughout the world and include many detailed pictures of wild animals and of people hunting them. Pictographs seem to have been abandoned as soon as hunting stopped being the primary lifestyle, and painting did not emerge again for thousands of years, pointing to its ritual rather than aesthetic significance for hunter–gatherer communities (Mithen, 2003). The earliest surviving artefacts appear to support the hypothesis that people regarded many animals as important and probably sacred.

Similar worldviews survive in human groups that continue hunter–gatherer lifestyles today or in places where such lifestyles have only recently disappeared. Critical to our perspective here, these people tend not to make the same distinction between humans and the rest of creation as we have done

FIGURE 3.2 Most cave painting, such as this in the Drakensberg Mountains of South Africa, has a ritual and spiritual association with the hunt

for so many centuries. The Dayak people of Borneo refer to themselves as Orang Ulu or 'upriver people' and the Orang Utan (*Pongo pygmaeus*) as 'forest people', and regard themselves as very much equal to, rather than superior to, this other primate species. The hunting of the bowhead whale (*Balaena mysticetus*) in Alaska by the Inuit has long been surrounded by complex beliefs and rituals (Lantis, 1938) and, at least until quite recently, by taboo, magic formulae and the use of amulets. Writing in 1978, the Mayor of the North Slope Borough said: 'The taking and sharing of the whale is our Eucharist and Passover ... the Arctic celebration of the mysteries of life' (Hopson, 1978). Many Inuit believe animals that are not hunted will decline. People have an obligation to both respect and to hunt animals (Brody, 1987) and in this case whalers believe that the bowhead only allows itself to be captured if it favours the hunter or the village. The whale skull is thrown back into the sea to allow its spirit to return (Lowenstein, 1980). The failure to land a whale by Barrow whalers on the North Slope of Alaska in the spring 1982 hunt was ascribed by some as due to strife in the village (Dudley and Gordon Clarke, 1983). We can speculate with confidence that this type of identification with nature was once near universal.

But hunter–gatherers have been declining in relative numbers for thousands of years and now make up only a small proportion of the world's population. Ten thousand years ago, with the domestication of crops and livestock, areas used by humans began to be distinguished in peoples' consciousness and we also started to see ourselves as distinct from and – importantly – *superior* to the rest of the living world. Max Oelschlaeger puts it like this: 'viewed retrospec-tively, the idea of wilderness represented a heightened awareness by the agrarian Neolithic mind, as farming and herding supplanted hunting and gathering, of distinctions between humankind and nature' (Oelschlaeger, 1991, p3).

So when we talk about loss of wilderness, this might be described as the loss of a society where people worked *with* nature in favour of a society where people seek to *dominate* nature. Modern concepts of wilderness being empty or untouched land have little historical precedence (and have caused a lot of unnecessary tension). But while these concepts are modern, they are also hugely powerful and inform much of the debate in western societies, so cannot simply be ignored.

This developing sense of alienation from nature can be traced out in changing myths and faiths, writing and illustrative arts. In the Mediterranean region, where settled agriculture originated, archaeologists and historians speculate about a philosophical development from belief in a mother goddess (although many archaeologists now reject the concept of a Neolithic mother goddess (Mithen, 2003)), who herself gradually transmuted to a more agri-culturally minded goddess of fertility, for instance among the Etruscans and Egyptians, to male gods such as Yahweh, who was 'not a nature god, but a god above nature' (Oelschlaeger, 1991, p43). Yahweh was also, possibly for the first time, a unique god ('thou shalt have no other gods before me', *Book of Exodus*, chapter 20, verse 3). Vogel (1999) argues that the choice of Mount Sinai in the desert as the place for God to make his covenant with the Jewish people was symbolic of the message that their relationship with God was now more important than their relationship with nature. Although this change in attitude was profound it was not universal and was certainly not followed by all cultures, as we'll see.

Tension between untamed nature and settled farmland appears in the earliest known written story, the Sumerian *Epic of Gilgamesh*. This is still being pieced together but is known best from 12 clay tablets found in a library in the ruins of the Assyrian city of Nineveh, now in Iraq, by Austen Henry Layard in the 1840s. In the story Gilgamesh and his friend, the wild man Enkidu, take a long series of journeys in the course of which they have to kill Humbaba, the giant defender of the forest, in a symbolic battle that is often interpreted as a defeat of 'wilderness' by 'civilization'. On a more mundane level it was also a story about access to natural resources, much as these conflicts still are today. Folklorists follow the key concepts (and even details of descriptions of the forest) down through the ages to much more recent tales such as those in the Welsh *Mabinogion* story cycle and the Arthurian story of Sir Gawain and the Green Knight (Sandars, 1960). Similarly, the old-English poem *Beowulf*, composed thousands of years after Gilgamesh, depicts nature as a terrible place that harbours destructive monsters; this theme runs down the centuries to writers like Shakespeare, who put the destructive witches in *Macbeth* on a 'blasted heath' rather than any tended and manicured landscape. Wilderness became associated with danger.

Dangers of this sort could sometimes be exciting. The popularity of hunting as a pastime, rather than a necessity, was partly due to the frisson of danger involved, in the same way as extreme sports like base jumping today. Some of the earliest 'protected areas' were natural ecosystems set aside for hunting (Schama, 1995). Rituals still actively followed in western hunting have antecedents that stretch back way beyond the reach of history. But the rich and powerful people who controlled the hunting estates were also content for the rest of nature to be set aside for more productive purposes; wilderness could be fenced in and isolated.

The concept that nature needed to be 'tamed' persisted through the centuries: it is still alive today in many sectors of society. For example, the massive transformation of the landscape undertaken in Germany, largely through hydrological engineering, drainage of wetlands and straightening of rivers, was overtly and approvingly regarded as a conquest of nature. Frederick the Great of Prussia, who drained more marshland and fen than any other contemporary ruler, is reported to have looked down on the newly drained Oder marshes and claimed 'Here I have conquered a province peacefully' (Blackbourn, 2006). The engineering of the German landscape remains a live issue today, with passionate disagreements about whether flooding in the Rhine and tributaries is best tackled by building more dykes or restoring natural flood patterns (e.g. Schwarz et al, 2006).

But confusingly there is also a persistent belief that the loss of Eden, which appears in stories of all the faiths of the Mediterranean, is a symbolic recounting of the switch from the innocence of hunter–gathering to the complexity and tensions of agrarian societies (Mabey, 2005). Such beliefs went well beyond myth-makers, Jean-Jacques Rousseau, for example (1754), appeared to view civilization as a 'fall' from nature. It would be an oversimplification to say that agricultural societies during this early period regarded the wild as something purely negative. Wilderness in the religious and philosophical writings of the Middle Eastern traditions often features as somewhere to go to work out ideas: many of the prophets in both the Judaic and Christian traditions went into the 'wilderness' either to meditate on a temporary basis or to live for long periods as hermits. Jesus Christ did this for a reported 40 days and Mohammed received his great revelation in a cave on a rocky mountainside. In desert regions in particular you don't have to go very far to reach wilderness, just a few steps beyond the edge of the oasis in many instances, so prophets and hermits might expect to get regular visits from people walking out from their own homes; in many cases hermits relied on gifts of food and drink from nearby villagers. Wilderness could be a testing ground – as it was for figures such as the Christian Saint Anthony – but it was also somewhere empty and peaceful enough to allow deep contemplation on issues of

FIGURE 3.3 Going into the wilderness to seek wisdom or undergo some personal test is a key feature of many faiths in desert areas. In these places the desert wilderness creeps right up to the edge of an oasis, as in this picture from the Tunisian Sahara

philosophy or faith. The early Christian desert hermits supported themselves by labour such as weaving baskets and mats out of palm leaves or rushes and selling these at nearby towns (Merton, 1960); Gustave Flaubert depicts St Anthony sitting cross-legged making rush mats at the start of his dramatic poem *The Temptation of St Anthony*. These sages deliberately chose solitude in the wilderness although not as a permanent or unbreakable state. There is still an active hermit tradition in many parts of the world today, including within some European national parks, and the traditional link between spiritual fulfillment and natural landscapes remains unbroken, as we shall see.

People have also now started looking at nature in different ways and consciously reconnecting: the whole of the conservation, wilderness and outdoor pursuits movements are testament to this as are a host of back-to-nature movements around the world. At the same time, others are still disconnecting. Some indigenous societies, where a generation ago people had high ecological knowledge, are filling up with youngsters who have never learned these skills. Ecological knowledge usually declines as communities become wealthier (Pilgrim et al, 2008). Here we will focus on the reconnection. But before we look at some of the people who spearheaded this philosophical revolution, we'll move on from the hermits in the desert to look more generally at how religious faiths have reacted to and shaped our attitudes towards naturalness.

The natural world in religious faiths

Attitudes to the natural world have been profoundly affected by regional faiths and philosophies. The nuanced relationship between nature and the sacred varies enormously between and within faiths and the general Mediterranean rejection of the natural did not occur everywhere in the same way. On the one hand nature is sometimes accepted as a central aspect of the sacred and a fitting subject for worship while in other cases any direct link between species and religious belief is regarded as little more than folklore and frowned upon by religious authorities, or even rejected as idolatry and heresy. Attitudes also change as faiths grow and develop.

At the risk of simplification, the mainstream faiths can be divided into two broad philosophical streams. What we might call the 'oriental' faiths (Buddhism, Daoism, Hinduism, Jainism, Shinto, Sikhism and Zoroastrianism), which are also generally the older of the surviving major faiths, all regard nature as a critical aspect of the divinity that should accordingly be treated with reverence. Adherents of most of these faiths deliberately seek out natural areas as places to worship and see themselves as part of rather than separate from the natural world in a way that has apparently survived unchanged since before settled agriculture. In these cases people have never made the kind of abrupt distinction between humans and nature described earlier, at least in philosophical terms. Sacred places are often important for the followers of more than one religion, all of whom react to the spiritual values inherent in particular landscapes or features. For example Mount Kailash, in the Tibetan Autonomous Region of China is sacred to Buddhism, Hinduism, Jainism and Bon, whose adherents regard any climbing to the summit as defilement (Prasad Oli, 2010). Groups such as the Jains and many sects of Hinduism and Buddhism regard all animal life as sacred and practice strict vegetarianism. The fearlessness of monkeys in many Indian towns and the proportionately large numbers of birds in the fields and forests of southern India bears witness to some of the practical implications of these beliefs. Other Asian societies do eat meat, and in fact some groups or nations have cleared whole areas of most wild birds and mammals, but still regard animals as fundamentally representational of the sacred in the same way as the hunting parties of the Inuit described above.

In contrast, there has been a more variable relationship with nature from the three monotheistic, 'occidental' faiths (Christianity, Judaism and Islam). The strong teaching against idolatry means that the concept of sacred species or sacred sites was rejected, in some cases quite violently and there was also for a long period, at least in the Judeo-Christian tradition, belief that the rest of nature had been created for humans to use as they will. What would now be regarded as appalling levels of cruelty against animals were, until quite recently, justified on theological grounds in many European countries (Roberts, 1983). The traditional Western view has seen humans with their immortal souls as something fundamentally distinct from the rest of nature. Simplistic interpretations of early Christian writings used to propose that nature had been created specifically to support humans (see White, 1967). Aldo Leopold writes that 'conservation is getting nowhere because it is incompatible with our Abrahamic concept of land' (Leopold, 1949, pviii). Traces of this perception were integrated, unconsciously for the most part, into the modern conservation movement that developed in the 19th and 20th centuries. Environmentalists retained the idea that humans were uniquely different but flipped the concept around to view humans as damaging outsiders – as alien invasive species if you like – entering an otherwise pristine and perfectly functioning ecosystem and triggering a wave of destruction. This isn't a new idea: in fact with variations it is one of our oldest stories and the Judaic version of the Garden of Eden is one manifestation of concepts that appear in the writings of many religions (Mabey, 2005). A quest to find the historic site of Eden was one of the reasons why some Europeans promoted geographical expansion at the time of the Renaissance, along with the better known economic and political incentives (Grove, 1995).

But despite the rhetoric of some religious leaders, in practice followers of all these faiths have developed close relationships with the natural world within their worship. For example, rags are tied to sacred trees in Israel even today for a number of reasons, including pacifying the trees' spirits (Dafni, 2002). There are many Jewish religious writings prohibiting the destruction of trees, including particularly fruit trees, even during times of war (Orr and Spanier, 1992). Similarly, I have been taken to an ancient tree in Estonia where Christians still tie on rags in the same way, and was told it was one of at least 300 left in the country; remnants of a far larger tradition that survived the banning of such practices under communism. In Islam, the Prophet Mohammed strengthened traditional *hima*, a form of protected area, including rangelands, forests, woods, watersheds and wildlife. Around both Mecca and Medina, the holiest Islamic sites, Mohammed declared a zone of protection where no tree shall be cut or animal killed and *hima* are now being revived in various countries of the region as protected areas (Bagader et al, 1994). Shari'ah law contains many specific strictures against deforestation and in favour of desert restoration (Llewellyn, 1992).

Attitudes within faiths also develop over time. Major religions manage to convey a feeling of timelessness and permanence while in reality changing perspectives and attitudes dramatically over the centuries, in a reflection of changes in the wider world. This is not a simplistic relationship and there are many examples of religious leaders clashing directly with the state, often with extreme courage and also often creating social and political havoc in the process. Most liberal innovations within religions promote a backlash and sects break away to return to what they interpret as the original or true doctrine. But religions are not insulated completely from what is happening around them and are constantly in transition: faiths also differ dramatically in their interpretation of doctrine between sects and in different parts of the world.

Our relationship with the rest of natural world is one of the areas where some faiths have changed position most dramatically. During the 20th and

21st centuries there has been a rapid increase in recognition of the duty of stewardship, with the result that senior figures in all the major faiths have now issued public statements acknowledging the moral obligation of humans not to destroy the rest of nature (Palmer and Findlay, 2003). This has included quite precise shifts in doctrinal thinking in some cases and also a general increase in awareness and recognition of the spiritual importance of the natural world and our obligations towards other species. Table 3.1 below summarizes how major religions view the natural world.

TABLE 3.1 Links between faiths and environmental thinking

Faith	Links to environmental thought
Bahá'í	Founded in the 19th century ACE by the Persian Bahá'u'lláh. Preaches that all religious leaders are manifestations of God and all scripture sacred. Nature and Scripture are the 'two books' of revelation. Shoghi Effendi, Bahá'u'lláh's great-grandson noted: 'Man is organic with the world. His inner life moulds the environment and is itself also deeply affected by it' (Landau, 2002).
Buddhism	Emerged in the 5th century BCE teaching respect for nature to help the interconnectedness of all that exists; plants and animals are included in schemes of salvation (Swearer, 1998). Buddha Gotama was born, attained enlightenment and died under trees. Sacred trees are sometimes decorated (Tucker and Williams, 1998). Buddhism creates practical protection measures, such as *ridam* in Bhutan, an annual prohibition on entering a designated mountain forest (Ura, 2004).
Christianity	Founded in the first century ACE. Teaches that all creation is a loving act of God and that humanity may not destroy God's creations without the risk of destroying itself. St Francis was an early proponent of Christian stewardship. There have been important statements by Christian leaders in response to the ecological crisis (Hessel, 1998). Pope John Paul II (1990) called for 'a more internationally coordinated approach to the management of the earth's goods'. Christian conservation groups exist.
Daoism	Traditionally believed to have been founded by Lao Tzu, author of the *Dao De Ching,* in the 6th century BCE. Stresses harmonious interaction with the environment, symbolized by a balance between two opposing forces of Yin and Yang (Girardot et al, 2001). Chuang Tzu, a Daoist scholar, teaches against the concept that all nature must be 'useful' and stresses its existence value (Merton, 1965). A modern interpretation lays particular stress on ecology.
Hinduism	Hinduism evolved around 3000 BCE. The earth is revered as *Bhumi*, 'mother earth'. There are many references to nature protection in texts; e.g., the *Arthashastra* prescribes fines for destroying trees (Narayanan, 2001). Damming India's most sacred rivers, the Ganges and Narmada, generated protests partly for faith reasons (Shiva, 2002). In the Chipko movement, women prevent forest loss by surrounding trees with their bodies (Weber, 1988).

(continued)

TABLE 3.1 *(Cont.)*

Faith	Links to environmental thought
Jainism	The sacred books of the Jain record teachings of Mahavira (599–527 BCE). Jains minimize harm to all life-forms, and teachings stress sympathy and compassion with all life (Chapple, 1998). Mahavira stated: 'One who neglects or disregards the existence of earth, air, fire, water and vegetation disregards his own existence which is entwined with them'. The Institute of Jainology produced the 1990 *Jain Declaration on Nature* (Singhvi, 1990).
Judaism	The Jewish faith was founded around 2000 BCE. In the past, reaction to pantheism downgraded the importance of nature, although this is changing (Vogel, 1999). The Tree of Life is one of Judaism's most powerful images. Planting trees has been a widely observed Jewish practice, particularly more recently and the Torah orders the creation of green belts around cities (*Numbers* 35:4). Trees remain a subject of worship in Israel today (Dafni, 2002).
Islam	Islam was formed in the 7th century ACE by Mohammed, who wrote down the teaching of Allah in the *Qu'ran*. This states that humans have stewardship over nature, but nature belongs to God (Foltz al, 2003). Rivers and lakes need a buffer zone, and tree planting and kindness to animals are encouraged. Islam developed the use of *Hima*, land protection for grazing, bee-keeping, forests or water (Bagader et al, 1994), still used in Saudi Arabia (Sulayem and Joubert, 1994).
Shinto	Shinto was the traditional faith of Japan before Buddhism. There are many deities but no formal hierarchy, no philosophical literature or doctrine, but strong links to nature. Ceremonies appeal to the *kami*, forces of nature in mountains, springs, trees etc. Sacred groves are important, including both cultivated and natural areas. Sacred forests are managed in part to provide timber for temple renovation.
Sikhism	Founded by Nanak, 1469–1539. Sikhs believe in one God and their sacred writings are in the *Guru Granth Sahib*. Nanak said 'Within the Universe, Earth was created to be a shrine'. All nature is sacred according to the Sikh faith. Sikhism follows a 300-year cycle, the most recent of which, 'The Cycle of the Sword' finished in 1999. The name of the current cycle, due to end in 2299, was chosen as the 'Cycle of Creation' putting an emphasis on environmental practices.
Zoroastrianism	Founded by Zoroaster (Zarathustra), in the 7th century BCE in what is now Azerbaijan. Later, many Zoroastrians fled from Muslim conquests to India, where they are known as Parsis. The practice of regarding the earth as sacred implies that life is also sacred. The decline of vultures in India due to chemical poisoning (Green et al, 2004), is a problem for Parsi communities because the birds are essential to the tradition of disposing of the dead in 'Towers of Silence'.

Sacred natural sites

The sacred and the natural come together most obviously in the concept of the *sacred natural site*, an area of natural habitat that has been recognized as sacred or perhaps more accurately as *especially* sacred by one or more faith groups. But the word 'natural' has many different interpretations within this concept. IUCN defines a sacred natural site as an: 'area of land or water having special spiritual significance to peoples and communities' (Wild and McLeod, 2008). Such places are typically distinguished either because of an historical association, for instance a place where a famous hermit lived or a spiritual teacher gained enlightenment, or because of some special living or geological feature, such as an ancient tree or an unusually shaped rock. The most common sacred natural sites are probably forest groves, but there are also a huge number of sacred lakes, rivers, springs, mountains, rocks and other distinguished habitats. Many faith groups decorate sites with flags, flowers and other offerings.

Sacred natural sites, often shortened to SNS, vary from tiny places of a few square metres to huge landscapes: from individual sacred trees to, for instance, much of the Yosemite National Park in California, which is considered sacred by several First Nations groups. Sacred sites criss-cross the landscape in an apparently endless pattern in Australia, made up of individual sites and the pathways between them, celebrated in stories that also cross vast areas and many language groups: these have been described most evocatively (although not always accurately) by the English writer Bruce Chatwin in *The Songlines* (1987). Many SNS are strictly protected; others are used for a variety of activities including sacred meetings or sacrifices and more mundane functions like the collection of medicinal herbs.

Some SNS are extremely ancient and many more are *assumed* to be ancient without any particular proof that this is the case; when Shonil Bhagwat (pers. comm.) took pollen cores from some supposedly ancient sacred groves in parts of India he found that the forests had only been in place for a couple of hundred years. In fact new sacred sites are still being created: in July 2005 we saw offerings left at the coast in Madagascar where archaeologists had recently discovered evidence of some of the first settlements on the island; this site had not had sacred values before but obviously gained note in local peoples' eyes because of the newly discovered historical links.

Many people assume SNS are confined to local faiths, animist traditions and perhaps to some of the more nature-orientated faiths, but when we carried out a survey of SNS within protected areas we found examples from all major faiths including the monotheistic faiths of Judaism, Christianity and Islam (Dudley et al, 2005). The early iconoclast, St Boniface is recorded as taking an axe to the sacred groves of the people he was attempting to convert in what is now Germany, and occasional stories leak out of Christian fundamentalists still doing the same today in countries where so-called minor faiths remain powerful. But for every fanatic with a chainsaw there are opposing

FIGURE 3.4 The small island of Nosey Vey in northern Madagascar is so sacred that no-one is allowed to land there

Christian traditions of sacredness in nature. This reverence often jumps between religions; in Africa many people who have converted to Christianity or Islam quietly keep their traditional sacred groves alive and a few of the oldest churchyards in Britain are known to be established on pre-Christian druidic sacred sites. The yew tree (*Taxus baccata*), a constant in many church-yards, was also sacred to the druids (Hartzell, 1991). Large sacred natural sites are often important to several different faith groups.

From our perspective here, some but by no means all SNS will be highly protected from interference and thus retain natural characteristics. In Madagascar I have seen a small conically shaped island in the far north that is so sacred no one is allowed to go there; local people want it to be declared an official protected area to ensure its safety. Many sacred mountains around the world are also off-limits, as described in the opening sequence of this chapter. The reason Bhutan does not allow climbing expeditions in the country is because of the sacred nature of the mountains, despite the tourist revenue that opening up the peaks would bring. When a local faith is flourishing, the levels of protection given to an SNS can be extremely high. Many SNS have been incorporated into national parks and other protected areas precisely because scientists have recognized the high biological values of the habitats that they contain (often without understanding *why* such habitats have survived).

Other SNS are far more open to visitation; more like the main part of a church building than the high altar, to use a Christian analogy. The *tembawang* of Borneo, described earlier, are used as places to collect fruit as well as sacred burial sites and this mixture of secular and sacred values is common: in the *kaya* forests of coastal Kenya for instance (Negussie, 1997) and in many sacred groves and medicinal plant gardens of India. The River Ganges is sacred, and many years ago I watched people floating paper boats with candles downstream in Rishikesh, where the river still ran fast and pure, but these sacred elements go hand in hand with a massive fishing industry and transport infrastructure based around the river. Another offshore island in Madagascar, on the southern tip, contains three sacrifice sites that are of high spiritual importance to the local fishing community, but access to the rest of the island is open. It is also the site of an important ground-nesting colony of red-billed tropic birds (*Phaethon aethereus*) that the local community protects due to their presence within a holy place. Local fishermen wanted the island to be included in the national protected area system to ensure protection of both the sacredness and the birds (Borrini-Feyerabend and Dudley, 2005). So secure do the birds feel that we were able to walk within a metre of females sitting on the nest without them appearing to be alarmed. Which is itself a common feature of SNS: because of the strong social traditions for sympathetic management they are often mini-hotspots of biodiversity.

In an initial and fairly quick survey, confined to papers that had appeared in peer-reviewed journals or published conference proceedings, a group of us collected over a hundred research projects that had measured the value of SNS in Asia and Africa, the large majority of which found a markedly high level of species diversity. Many contain rich biodiversity, sometimes exceeding nearby protected areas and forest reserves (Dudley et al, 2010a). In some places, SNS are the only remaining examples of a particular habitat, such as ancient lowland forests in Japan, which are now virtually confined to the environs of temples where they are strictly protected to supply timber of the right age for the occasional renewal of temple buildings. I have been told that the oldest written forest management records in the world are from these ancient forests, which are now also extremely important for the unique biodiversity that they contain.

Faith influences attitudes to nature although the extent to which this plays out in practice could be questioned; societies dominated by nature-orientated faiths, for example in many Asian countries, have not been notably better at preventing environmental degradation than those in countries where belief systems have in the past suggested that nature is provided for us to exploit; the massive deforestation in Asia has affected countries that are dominantly Moslem, Christian, Hindu, Buddhist and Shinto apparently indiscriminately. Similarly, Jewish traditions may revere trees but Jewish settlers have deliberately destroyed Palestinian olive groves. Most of the *hima* in the Arabian Peninsula have been degraded, and so on. But although a belief system has yet to be invented that can stop someone determined ('hell-bent' in fact) on exploiting natural resources, these underlying philosophies nonetheless help to shape our reactions to these issues and our approaches to conservation and management of land and water (Bhagwat and Palmer, 2009; Bhagwat et al, 2011).

Wilderness in the arts

In the last couple of centuries, the attitudes of many people to the natural world have been influenced more by writers, artists and latterly especially by film-makers than they have by religious or philosophical leaders. People in the creative arts, like the rest of us, emerge from particular traditions, which influence them in ways that they may or may not recognize. Many of the best known naturalists on film or in print during the latter part of the 20th century for instance looked upon the natural world from a secular perspective. Their opinions may come from very different philosophical roots to those of religious leaders, but there is often remarkably common ground in terms of practical attitudes to nature. The following section is mainly written from the perspective of Western art; over the course of the last century Western ideas about science and conservation have spread deep into cultures of Africa and Asia as well so the concepts that came out of the European Medieval period, the Renaissance and beyond have a wider application. But it should be remembered that many Asian cultures, for example the Chinese (Elvin, 2010) and Japanese, have a far longer and deeper engagement with nature through art than those of us in the West.

Landscapes and images

Kenneth Clark wrote that 'landscape painting marks the stages in our conception of nature' (Clark, 1949, p17) and, looked at in the right way, paintings, tapestries, bas-reliefs and even pictures on ceramics can tell us a lot about how people viewed the natural world, from cave paintings, through early representations of nature by cultures as diverse as the Incas and Sumerians through to the precise mosaics of the Romans and beyond. In Medieval Europe, when most art was intimately linked with and controlled by organized religion, paintings were imbued by both symbolism and a strong distrust of nature. Rare innovators risked the wrath of the establishment by depicting nature in the Christian church and a parallel process took place in the Moslem world as described compellingly in Orhan Pamuk's 1998 novel *My Name is Red*. Within Christendom we can trace a gradual emergence of appreciation for the natural world, initially through pictures and carvings of individual elements such as flowers or trees, which were slowly appreciated as prototypes of the divine. Carvings on Rheims cathedral are early 13th century examples that were not widely repeated for some time afterwards (Clark, 1949). Later, the garden came to be recognized as a symbol of natural beauty, albeit one controlled by humans. The word *paradise* comes from the Old Persian word for a walled enclosure and many of the earliest pictures of the Garden of Eden illustrate it as a walled garden, with 'paradise gardens' emerging in paintings from Sienna and references to natural beauty in the poetry of Dante. The change emerged most quickly in the various Italian city states that were supporting the newly emerging techniques and subjects of what we now call Renaissance painting. These positive views of nature only spread slowly; a hundred years later, the Flemish painter Hieronymus Bosch was still portraying a very ambiguous view – his triptych known as the *Garden of Earthly Delights* includes some startling accurate portrayals of birds (the goldfinch for instance), fruit and other elements of the natural world, but only as symbols of lust and temptation.

The painters of paradise gardens were drawing on real examples and it has been argued that the gardens of Italy provided a model against which to compare the less thoroughly tamed lands of the Americas and parts of Africa, thus helping to create the modern interpretation of 'wilderness' (Mitchell, 2001). They were also looking back to older ideas about *Arcadia*, a vision of pastoralism and harmony with nature, 'the perfect mid-point between wilderness and civilisation' (Eisenberg, 1998, p146). Literally a region of Greece, the wider vision of pastoral life embodied in the concept of Arcadia had been captured most powerfully hundreds of years previously by the poet Virgil in the *Eclogues*.

Similar developments were taking place in other parts of the world and garden building became a favourite pastime of the Mughal emperors in the Indian subcontinent. When I cycled out of Srinigar to explore the famous Mughal gardens of the Kashmir Valley in the 1980s I found them rather dried out and disappointingly poorly kept, but what was striking was the distinction between the formal garden and the harsh mountains slopes all around; again the garden was created as a very controlled sort of nature in contrast with its surroundings.

Although painters were starting to grapple with nature in a real sense, rather than just as a series of symbols, there were still limitations. The writer J. G. Ballard points out in one of his novels that the most interesting part of many Renaissance paintings is in the background. Peer around the standardized figures of the Madonna and child and a startling, rather surreal landscape can be seen as the artist was able to give full rein to an imagination otherwise kept in check by the orthodoxy of religious clients. These background landscapes developed as artists learned more about perspective and light and gradually the natural world started to be portrayed more accurately; first small elements like leaves and flowers and then gradually the wider landscape. The poet and philosopher Petrarch is the first person recorded as climbing a mountain just to see the view in the 1300s, but he remained an isolated innovator and illustrations of mountains generally remained symbolic in form long after the depiction of flowers, trees and animals had become more accurate.

The potential of art to convey real rather than symbolic landscapes changed forever in 1444, when Conrad Witz painted *The Miraculous Draught of Fishes* and chose to include a detailed picture of part of what is now the French shore of Lac Leman (Clark, 1949). Witz's picture shows barren hills where today there is a dense forest, which many people assume is natural and permanent. The hills are clearly visible from offices in the United Nations building in Geneva and Kit Prins, former head of the timber division there, used to keep a reproduction on his wall to make the point that Europe's forests are currently expanding again after an historical low. It was another 50 years before the realistic approach taken by Witz was generally followed but from then on a flood of recognizable landscapes and seascapes started to emerge and, among other things, these have created a rich body of evidence for those wanting to trace back ecological histories, as outlined in Box 3.1 below. Virtually any art gallery in Europe has, if you're prepared to dig around among the permanent collection, paintings that illustrate dramatic changes in natural vegetation. For

---

BOX 3.1 What paintings tell us about the environment

Paintings can tell us a great deal about changes in ecology, ecosystems and human relationship with nature if looked at with an ecologist's rather than an art historian's eye. Paintings can:

- **provide direct information about changes in vegetation cover**. Since early realistic artists like Conrad Witz first started painting real rather than imaginary landscapes, ecologists have been able to compare paintings with modern photographs of the same area to get a snapshot of changes over time. Pictures can also tell us about past climatic events and, through the colour of sunsets, even tell us something about volcanic eruptions.
- **tell us about developing awareness of naturalness**. Many early pictures showed stylized or idealized landscapes as a backdrop to the main interest, usually a portrait. Even when artists started painting more accurate representations they tended to choose places that fitted contemporary perceptions of beautiful landscapes or made subtle alterations to match the priorities of patrons or audiences (see later discussion on the mountain Cadair Idris). Paintings tell us what people *perceived* as being attractive or compelling ecosystems at a particular period in history.
- **literally give us a picture of how humans reacted to the natural world in the past**, such as pictures of animals killed for food (a far wider range of species than would now be considered in most parts of the world), hunting apparatus, management of trees and even the early presence of invasive plant and animal species in particular environments. For example, paintings show us that in the past people in the West ate a far wider range of wild species than they do today.
- **show the limitations of knowledge**. Painters tell us as much by their mistakes as their accurate representations: take the many weird drawings of whales, elephants, giraffes and other creatures that most painters would only have seen briefly or partially. Coreggio's famous painting of Leda and the Swan shows a highly accurate portrait of the swan on the ground, which could have been copied from a dead specimen, but a portrait of the bird in flight that seems inaccurate and clumsy to a generation brought up on photographs and slow motion films of birds in flight.

instance in Ljubljana National Gallery, in Slovenia, painters like Marko Pernhart and others from the mid-19th century illustrate a generally treeless landscape around what is now Triglav National Park, which is today densely covered with what most visitors and even inhabitants assume is natural forest.

For a long time, increasing accuracy in portrayal of the natural world focused almost entirely on *cultural* landscapes and seascapes, on places that humans had influenced and fashioned. J. M. W. Turner, England's great maverick artist of landscapes and seascapes, summed up the concepts from the perspective of one immersed in cultural landscapes: 'The Landscape is not seen for itself, but as a commentary upon the human condition, as a speculation upon the tension between order and disorder'.

With the coming of the Romantic period and the fresh interest in 'nature' that was emerging in the countries colonized by European states, artists started to focus for the first time on natural landscapes as the main purpose of a composition rather than as an incidental feature. Piero di Cosimo's picture of a forest fire was one of the first deliberately to remove humans as the main focus of a composition. The idea that a landscape portrayed without people would be regarded as radical is hard to imagine today, but the change was as dramatic at the time as the revolutions that shook the art world in the 20th century. Once accepted, the idea quickly spread and painting changed forever as artists consciously tried to understand the natural world around them. In 1891, the Ministry of Environment in Prague commissioned the landscape artist Julius Mařák (1832–1899) to paint a picture of Šumava Virgin Forest, now part of the Šumava National Park. The aim was to provide a record of ancient forest; this is the earliest example I have found of an explicit attempt to paint what we now know as old-growth forest, although the concept that artists might paint natural landscape was quickly adopted, particularly in the newly colonized countries, and art galleries in places like Washington, Canberra and Auckland contain important records of the ecosystems as they were at or soon after European settlement. These paintings tell us two things if we look carefully enough: first they give an idea about vegetation cover at a particular time, but just as significantly they also tell us about how people *viewed* landscape. With the coming of the Romantic movement, for the first time wild land was seen as something desirable and attractive; the small distortions that Romantic artists deliberately or subconsciously introduced into their work tells us a lot about what their patrons expected in a compelling scene. Dark, lowering skies, storms, jagged cliffs and ruined buildings all started to be used to portray a vision of wilderness as *sublime* that, for the first time, began to be considered attractive rather than repellent (see box on Cadair Idris for discussion of the changes in ways of looking at a single mountain).

The advent of photography made images of wild landscapes available to everyone who could get hold of illustrated magazines, and landscape photographers like Ansel Adams helped create a whole new way of understanding natural beauty, although their use of printing techniques, perspectives and

BOX 3.2 Cadair Idris

Cadair Idris is the nearest rocky mountain to my house in Wales; a volcanic massif that stretches down to the shore of the Irish Sea and from where, on exceptionally clear days, the Irish Wicklow Mountains can be seen rising up on the horizon. I've climbed it literally dozens of times, walking up every path and many of the faces where there are no paths. I have also slept on the top, although local legends say that anyone who spends the night on the summit ends up mad, dead or a poet. The slopes have rich birdlife and plants, there are ice gullies in cold winters and *brocken-spectres* – huge shadows thrown onto clouds opposite the sun – when the weather is suitable.

The thousands of people who climb the mountain each year are testament to its attraction. To the early settlers it must have seemed an extraordinarily forbidding and magical place; there are ritual standing stones on the lower slopes and some of the mysterious burial cairns that our ancestors left on mountaintops. The name means literally 'seat of Idris' and refers to the shape created by Llyn-y-Cae, a glacial lake tucked into one of the corries like a massive chair. Idris is a legendary character: perhaps a Welsh king killed in a battle with the Saxons near the River Severn around 630, but he is also said to be a giant and astronomer and has been persistently linked to Enoch, the great-grandfather of Noah who built the ark described in the Bible: a *Book of Enoch* was one of the lost texts discovered in the Dead Sea Scrolls. Only fragments remain, mainly lists of fallen angels, some astronomical musing and a haunting passage '[And beyond] those [mountains], roughly northwards, on their eastern side I was shown other mountains' (Vermes, 1962, p547). The Qu'aran refers to Enoch as Idris and some scholars argue that Cadair Idris is actually named after Enoch, but if this link is real we know nothing about how an obscure Middle Eastern prophet became associated with a similarly obscure Welsh mountain. We can assume that Cadair Idris was long considered sacred. Farmers eventually settled around the edges and gradually began to run sheep and at one time cattle on the slopes, building dry stone walls to mark out holdings.

When wars in mainland Europe curtailed the traditional 'grand tour' popular with wealthy young Englishmen, some of them started to explore the wilder parts of Britain. Initially travel was hard and there were no maps or anything but miserable accommodation, but despite the hardships climbers and botanists were soon regularly making their way up to the summit of Cadair Idris, which had early assumed a romance out of step with reality. Camden's *Britannia* described 'Kader Idris' in 1695 thrillingly but inaccurately as 'probably one of the highest mountains in Britain' (Rees, 1992, p50) and it became a huge draw to early tourists. The botanist John Ray was exploring there in 1658 for instance (Condry, 1981) and the German Johan Jacob Dillenlus in 1726 (Jones, 1996); followed in the 19th century by a stream of tourist celebrities including the writers Thomas Love Peacock (1811), John Ruskin (1826), Alfred Tennyson (1856 in heavy rain) and Francis Kilvert (1871) (Condry, 1966; Rees, 1992). Guiding became an important cottage industry in the local town of Dolgellau, a stone hut was built on the top to provide refreshments for visitors in 1830 and paths became better built (Condry, 1966). Many of the early visitors would have ridden much of the way on ponies. Even Charles Darwin, who often holidayed on the estuary below, wrote that 'Old Cader is a grand fellow' (Condry, 1970, p123).

By the time my father Brian cycled to Wales from the south of England in the 1930s, there was an old man who served cups of tea on the top during the season and sold enamel badges of the mountain; tourist innovations that have fortunately long since disappeared.

The mountain became a major attraction for artists as well and it is through their eyes that we can trace out changing attitudes to natural landscape, through the changing shape of the mountain as it was depicted in drawings and paintings. Before the 17th century Cadair Idris was almost certainly still regarded as bad-land – wilderness in the old fashioned sense of the world and a frightening place to be caught out in bad weather. There was widespread belief that the Creator had favoured some areas of the world more than others and an assumption that bare, rock-strewn mountains were among the areas that he had looked on with displeasure.

When the Romantic Movement swept through Britain, with its emphasis on grandeur and the awesome – in days before that word itself became debased into a catchphrase – this negative view was turned on its head. Early landscape paintings of Cadair Idris emphasize the grandeur of the scene, making the slopes perceptively steeper and more rugged than in reality: a painting of 1774 by the Welsh artist Richard Wilson is a typical example and J. M. W. Turner also painted several impressionistic views of the region that helped to establish a particular 'feel' for the mountains (Hourahane et al, 2008). In 2001 the Royal Welsh Academy held an exhibition exclusively of over 60 landscape paintings and photographs of the mountain (Anon, 2001), stretching from 1797 to the millennium: many of the earlier pictures are consciously or unconsciously exaggerated in terms of the steepness, size and harshness of the landscape.

Richard Wilson is a critical figure in this trajectory. Two hundred and fifty or so years ago, when people suddenly stopped looking at mountains as ugly and useless and started to perceive them as beautiful and sublime, his portraits helped to define the new aesthetic. Not without a struggle; the critic John Ruskin complained that his pictures focused too much on dark, rocky places and 'opposed to the natural tone of the English mind' (Jones 2001). But Wilson was Welsh not English and his view eventually carried the day. It is impossible to find the exact spot where Wilson sketched out the view for his painting of Cadair Idris in 1774 because the picture is partly imagined; the peak is too sharp and some of the foreground is transposed from lower down the mountain, but it tells us a lot about what Wilson thought his clients might want to see. It also shows the slopes below the lake as completely bare, whereas today they are covered with 'ancient' forest.

choice of light conditions also provided a particular interpretation of the view. Today artists work consciously in natural landscapes, either directly on the land as in the rock designs of Richard Long and the sculptures of Andy Goldsworthy or more traditionally through photographs and paintings. Many of these artists are consciously working within a conservation tradition and to support a conservation ethic. For example the Yellowstone to Yukon bi-national conservation corridor initiative has commissioned landscape artist Dwayne Harty to paint a series of pictures throughout the length of the biological corridor to raise awareness of its aesthetic values and I had the pleasure of watching him paint several studies for this huge work in northern Canada while putting together this book.

FIGURE 3.5 'Cadair Idris' literally means 'seat of Idris', referring to the glacial follow and lake carved out of the side of the mountain; a feature beloved of early British romantic painters and poets

Writing wilderness

The modern conservation ethic to a large extent began in North America and particularly in the United States, as settlers started to appreciate the aesthetic, biological and spiritual values of 'their' new land. Early writers were able both to experience and to chart the decline of 'wilderness' as it was gradually replaced by agriculture, although it should be noted that in many cases the empty landscapes that they wrote about had only appeared quite recently after settler wars and imported diseases had annihilated huge swathes of the original population. For the New World as a whole, the century or two following Columbus saw a decline of the original population of up to 95 per cent, mostly caused by imported diseases (Diamond, 1998).

John Muir and Henry David Thoreau are two hugely important figures in the development of modern conservation and both drew inspiration from the American landscape; I'll use them here as examples of a much wider field. Thoreau was the better writer, Muir the better explorer and activist; the latter's books were almost incidental to his life and he did not publish his first, *The Mountains of California* (1884), until he was 56. Muir was also predominantly a conservationist while Thoreau, during his short life, addressed many different social, environmental and philosophical issues directly in his life and writing.

The Scottish-born Muir spent the first two decades of his adult life travelling and exploring in parts of western United States that were virtually unknown to white people at the time, he then went on to write a series of hugely influential articles and books, particularly on the Sierra Nevada Mountains in California. He was an expert geologist and botanist and his writings still provide valuable data for ecologists today. Muir was also what would now be called an activist and among many other things he set up the Sierra Club, which remains one of the strongest US environmental organizations; he also lobbied successfully for the National Parks Act of 1899 and the establishment of Yosemite National Park. He has been criticized for some of his early dismissive writings about Native Americans, and for the model of exclusionary national parks which he helped to champion, but it is worth noting that he changed his mind later and was overtly sympathetic to the plight and mistreatment of First Nations people at a time when such views were unpopular. Muir remains an iconic hero to many North American conservationists; his books inspirational texts that are still all in print almost a century after his death.

Early settlers in New England in the 1600s believed they were transforming a 'wilderness' into an ordered garden and following Divine will in the process (whereas in fact they were transforming an ecosystem modified by the original inhabitants into one modified in different ways by colonists). Although the imagery was modified a little, by the 1800s the transformation was still seen as wholly positive (Cronon, 1983) and it is only with writers like Thoreau that questions about the implications of our impacts on natural ecology were raised. And Thoreau, unlike Muir, was writing from a land that had already been undergoing 'Europeanization' for a couple of hundred years.

Thoreau's most famous book *Walden* (1854), an account of living for two years alone in a small wooden hut in woods beside Walden Pond, marked the complete opposite to Muir's grand landscapes and daring journeys. It was set in the east of the United States instead of the west, in much gentler and non-threatening countryside and Thoreau's canvas was deliberately much smaller. He made no pretensions of living in wilderness, but instead was interested in the concept of wildness within a settled landscape (Haila, 1997). He lived on land owned by his mentor and fellow writer Ralph Waldo Emerson, two miles from the village of Concord where he walked every day to hear the news. His book, which has had a huge impact ever since publication, details what it is like to live simply, with time to think deeply. He describes what he does during the day, the books he reads, sounds that he hears in the woods, his attempts to cultivate a bean field and so on. Like desert hermits living outside cities, he was not alone but received plenty of visitors, including a runaway slave who Thoreau helped on his way to Canada. Thoreau and his friend Emerson were both transcendentalists, a group that emerged in New England in opposition to the narrowness of the Unitarian church and drew on philosophies and religions from several countries, including particularly Vedic thought, and he quotes from the *Bhagavad-Gita*; he was in some respects deliberately imitating the sages who withdrew from the world for a period of meditation. While Muir's books are the bibles for many conservationists, Walden became the inspiration for self sufficiency and back-to-the-land movements that periodically sweep North America (e.g. Houriet, 1971). Thoreau was also a compassionate naturalist; he 'preferred to hold a living bird in his affections than a dead bird in his hand' (Condry, 1954, p89). Like Muir, Thoreau was an activist although on different issues; he was imprisoned briefly for refusing to pay taxes to a government that supported slavery and wrote a famous tract *On the Duty of Civil Disobedience* (1849), which has created the philosophical underpinning of many an act of non-violent direct action, from anti-war protestors to Greenpeace action teams.

For all their differences in lifestyle and approach, Thoreau and Muir both played a critical role in alerting Americans, and gradually people in other countries as well, to the rapid loss of what they considered to be natural landscapes. Perhaps more significantly in the long term, they also argued for the irreplaceable *value* of such landscapes in human lives. Both writers consciously addressed the spiritual benefits derived from travelling and spending time deep into the natural world. Edward Hoagland writes that Muir 'believed that wilderness, like man, was an expression of one God' and quotes him as writing that 'I will touch naked God' when ice climbing (Hoagland, 1985, pvii). The concept of deliberate immersion in wild places being in large part a spiritual quest is a constant theme through generations of North American nature writing ranging from Annie Dillard's meditations around her home in *Pilgrim at Tinker Creek* (1974) to Peter Matthiessen's journeys into the high Himalayas in *The Snow Leopard* (1978). Jon Krakauer's 1996 book *Into the Wild*, on the surface a story of the tragic death of the young adventurer Chris McCandless in Alaska, is also a sustained meditation on the need that some people have to experience nature in its most untouched form.

Today, there is increasing understanding of the extent to which pre-European cultures had already shaped the ecosystem on the continent: something that many colonisers remained oblivious about. Karl Butzer identifies 'a pre-European cultural landscape, one that represented the trial and error as well as the achievement of countless hundred generations. It is upon this imprint that the more familiar Euro-American landscape was grafted, rather than created anew' (Butzer, 1990, p27). Rather than a static society, pre-European cultures went through many changes, in responses to altering climate (particularly long droughts), new technical approaches and changing cultures and politics, with different tribes living on game hunting, foraging for fruit and berries and various forms of agriculture including complex irrigation systems (Diamond, 2005). Different groups lived both as nomads and settled communities. Complex trade networks were in place long before the Europeans arrived. But the *idea* of an empty land still has a powerful resonance.

There is a long, albeit sporadic, history of writing as a meditation on nature in other parts of the world although in many places where people

FIGURE 3.6 Walking towards Lesotho

have leisure to write philosophical essays or novels the land has already been changed by human intervention over centuries if not millennia. Compare Richard Mabey's *The Common Ground* (1980) which laid out a kind of manifesto for maintaining wildlife within Britain's rapidly vanishing (and already deeply altered) countryside with Barry Lopez' *Arctic Dreams* (1986), which details his travels and encounters with nature in the far polar north. Most European nature writing consciously integrates humans into the narrative and focuses on human-populated and managed landscapes. *Tarka the Otter* by Henry Williamson (1927), one of the most famous animal stories, focuses for much of its plot on a long and ultimately unsuccessful battle that the otter has with the hunters setting out to destroy him. Indeed, the concept of writing a novel not centred on human characters is almost as radical as painting a landscape without people was a few hundred years ago and still something that fiction writers have not attempted in any major way.

The emerging books on the natural world were divided between those from explorers and travellers, who described an exotic 'other', and the dispatches from the gentler, tamed lands where most of the reading public spent their lives. Gilbert White's *The Natural History and Antiquities of Selborne* (1789, with more than 300 editions since), is made up of over a hundred letters that the clergyman White wrote to two friends detailing the natural history around his village. It occupies a similar place to Muir in the affections of English naturalists, although White's canvas is smaller and his landscapes much more heavily managed. These different perceptions of the natural world, from the pastoral tamed lands of Europe to the wilderness ethic of North America and similar colonized countries, are by now virtually hard-wired into national consciousnesses. They have an enormous impact on the way in which we address conservation management, as we will see.

Incidentally, if the description of the natural world in literature is limited, it is still far more complete than any attempt by writers of novels, poems and plays to address environmental issues and the ways in which these affect human society. Apocalyptic novels, like Cormac McCarthy's magnificent *The Road* (2006) generally use a vaguely defined disaster to create a canvas on which to tell a particular story, rather than attempting an accurate description about what might happen in the event of a plausible disaster. Literally a handful of people have attempted more: John Steinbeck in *The Grapes of Wrath* (1939), which looked at the impacts of soil erosion and the dust bowl on poor families in the United States; August Strindberg in *By the Open Sea* (translated version, 1987) included issues related to fisheries decline; Gao Xingjian's wonderful *Soul Mountain* (Gao, 1989) includes a detailed description of the plight of pandas and conservation efforts in Sichuan; and Edward Abbey's *The Monkey Wrench Gang* (1975) is a fictionalized account of a group of radical environmental activists. There are a few more, but the field remains very small. Having once helped form an environmental ethic, literature is now being left behind.

Today, instead, most peoples' exposure to nature comes from television and hugely successful wildlife series like *Life on Earth* and *Planet Earth*, along with many other less lavish productions on dedicated channels such as Animal Planet and the National Geographic Channel. About a quarter of all natural history films seen on television emerge from the BBC Natural History Unit in Bristol, and as discussed in the introduction, they predominantly focus on images of beautiful natural places and wildlife, without any people in sight. In fact many television programmes promote a Manichean view, alternating nature in the wild with the threats of losing this as a result of human activity. Television has for many people brought (often simplistic or downright false) images of wild landscapes and seascapes into their homes in a way that most written accounts do not. While it has played a critical role in promoting a conservation ethic, it has also helped to sustain a false picture of wild nature.

Where does all this leave concepts like naturalness and wilderness?

The kinds of changes described above are often presented as a series of distinct steps but I hope that the discussion so far has shown this to be an over-simplification. There was not a set period 10,000 years or so ago when everyone switched from being hunters to farmers and the same is true for all the other practical and philosophical changes described. Change comes in fits and starts, spreads around the world erratically and does not always move in the same direction. So the progressions described above should be seen more as additional layers of ideas and activities adding to the complexity of human society rather than as abrupt and permanent changes in direction. There are still many people living in the same ways and having approximately the same belief patterns as our pre-agrarian ancestors and sometimes doing so in deliberate rejection of alternatives: many of the surviving groups of indigenous peoples have made a conscious decision to maintain their traditional lifestyles. New faith systems may appear to bring dramatic changes but as we have seen many adherents do not wholly abandon older sacred beliefs. Older faiths, or modern variants thereof, emerge again and 'rediscovered' religions such as paganism consciously bring nature into the centre of human life rather than pushing it to one side.

This means that today there are a plethora of attitudes towards natural ecosystems, cultural ecosystems and, particularly, concepts of wilderness. For proponents of the wilderness ethic – followers of Muir and similar writers – wilderness remains a precious commodity with a wide range of practical and psychological values which, once 'degraded' will be almost impossible to regain. To many indigenous people, on the other hand, use of the word *wilderness* is viewed as an insult implying, they say, that land so designated has never been subject to management, whereas in fact it has often been lived in for hundreds or thousands of years. Deborah Bird Rose, an Aboriginal academic in Canberra, writes:

> *A definition of wilderness which excludes the active presence of humanity may suit contemporary people's longing for places of peace, natural beauty, and spiritual presence, uncontaminated by their own culture. But definitions which claim that these landscapes are 'natural' miss the whole point of Aboriginal people's country. Here on this continent, there is no place where the feet of Aboriginal humanity have not preceded those of the settler. Nor is there any place where the country was not once fashioned and kept productive by Aboriginal people's land management practices. There is no place without a history; there is no place that has not been imaginatively grasped through song, dance and design, no place where traditional owners cannot see the imprint of sacred creation.* (Rose, 2008, p28)

Deborah Rose's piece, a contribution to a debate about protected areas within IUCN, drew an angry response from some but not all wilderness conservationists. Some of her criticisms are spot on; others have already done a thorough job of analysing the number of pages written about wilderness in North America without mentioning the people who once lived there and I don't intend to repeat this process. But a quick reading through the history of environmentalism in the continent (see for instance the texts collected by Nash, 1989) shows that many wilderness advocates effectively viewed all unsettled land as permanently empty land. Callicott writes: 'The reserved wilderness idea has been and remains a tool of androcentrism, racism, colonialisation, and genocide ... The wilderness idea is associated with outmoded equilibrium ecology and ignores the ecological impact of at least eleven thousand years of human habitation of the Americas and Australia' (Callicott, 2000, p24).

To some extent, the ideas that Callicott summarizes could themselves now seem to be outmoded: organizations like the Wild Foundation deliberately define wilderness partly in terms of the cultures that helped to shape particular ecosystems and see such cultures as a benefit rather than a threat (e.g. Martin, 1982). There are an increasing number of cases where traditional, rural peoples and contemporary urban conservationists are finding common ground in arguing that large parts of the world should be set aside predominantly for nature and lobbying together against, for instance, mining or oil extraction. 'Wilderness protection can help maintain opportunities to continue traditional relationships with nature' (Watson et al, 2003). Exactly what 'setting aside' means we will need to come back to later.

In European countries on the other hand, the concept of wilderness is viewed negatively by many people, most often in the farming community but also generally in rural communities. It is common to see fears about the future of upland farming in the UK presented in terms of a return of 'wilderness' to the uplands, by which most people mean fields of thistles and other weeds (although in reality these would quickly be replaced by young forests in many areas). But on the other hand Paul Shepheard notes that today many people distinguish between 'wilderness' as being what was there before humans came and 'wasteland' – once regarded as the same thing – now being regarded as cultivation gone feral (Shepheard, 1997).

The very words used have resonance. IUCN sparked a huge debate when we suggested (Dudley and Phillips, 2008) that the names associated with various IUCN protected area categories be abandoned. The wilderness lobby in particular fought hard to retain the name 'wilderness area' within classification systems such as the World Database on Protected Areas. Yet in Europe feelings against 'wilderness' run so high that advocates use different phrases like 're-wilding'. It is hardly surprising that human attitudes to concepts like wilderness differ so much. A hundred and fifty years ago, John Stuart Mill (1850-58) wrote of 'nature' and 'natural' that: '... have thus become entangled in so many foreign associations, mostly of a very powerful and tenacious character, that they have come to excite, and to be the symbols of, feelings which their original meaning will by no means justify; and which have made them one of the most copious sources of false taste, false philosophy, false morality, and even bad law.' But this confusion is damaging and as far as possible views need to be reconciled.

Although I have described a series of philosophical steps in our relationship with naturalness, each of these has been an *addition* rather than a *replacement*; today we have a bewildering confusion of worldviews all struggling for attention on a crowded planet. How we reconcile these and try to make sense of our ever changing relationship with other species is the focus of the next chapter.

CHAPTER 4

Naturalness and Ethics

Key messages

- *There is a moral confusion about conservation, in particular its relationship with human rights.*
- *'Existence rights' for species are also often confused with 'animal rights' for individuals.*
- *A key facet of existence value is right of the global ecosystem to experience rates of species extinction no greater than the norm expected through natural evolutionary processes.*
- *In order to achieve effective conservation, we need to understand where we stand in relation to the rest of nature; who we are practising conservation for and what we are aiming to achieve.*

We're on a beach in southern Guatemala, in a poor village in a poor country. People are wearing what look like third or fourth-hand tee shirts and ragged trousers, many are barefoot. And some of the villagers are explaining their marine turtle conservation project. Turtle eggs have long been an important source of income for coastal communities throughout the tropics, but over-collection is contributing to a massive global decline. In this community people still dig up turtle eggs to sell, but now they voluntarily put aside a proportion of each clutch, which are then hatched and bred in special tanks and, when the young turtles are a little older, released back into the water. Giving them a secure environment for the first few weeks of their life, it is hoped, will mean that more of the young turtles survive, helping to balance out the losses from eggs sold in the local markets. I'm not sure about the science; whether getting into the water a few weeks older and stronger really boosts turtle survival enough to make up for the off-take. Nor do I know if the project survived; it's at least a decade since I was there. But that's not the point here. What struck me then, and on many other occasions over the years, was that the local people were really *committed*: the kids were excited about the baby turtles and the adults were knowledgeable and caring. No one wanted the turtles to disappear. And this was not just because they would lose a source of income; people were interested and concerned in the animals *as* animals, as sentient beings with a life to live.

Below, I start by discussing some of the moral confusion and criticisms associated with biodiversity conservation. A distinction is then drawn between animal rights and 'existence rights': that is, between the rights of individuals and species. Some core beliefs of conservationists are summarized and the chapter ends by suggesting answers to three critical questions:

1 Where do we stand in relation to the rest of nature?
2 Who are we practising conservation for?
3 What are we aiming to achieve?

A moral confusion

Concern about biodiversity and natural ecosystems is often written off as an indulgence confined to the wealthy and privileged, particularly by those with a vested interest in undermining conservation. I see no evidence for this generalization and there are myriad examples of people at all socio-economic levels living in harmony with the wider ecosystem. The phenomenon now referred to as 'community conserved areas', high biodiversity ecosystems voluntarily conserved by indigenous peoples and local communities, is a case in point (see for instance Pathak, 2009). On the other hand there is little reason to be over-optimistic either; human cruelty to animals and indifference to the natural world also has a long history. Some cultures appear to have an instinctive 'feel' and sympathy for other species, often related to long-held spiritual beliefs, while others do not, or at least not to the same extent. It is hard to find a constant moral baseline. The way that individuals react to the rest of nature is not wholly or even mainly determined by religious faith, race, background, economic class or gender. Most people have a set of ethical standards towards other animals and to some extent towards plants and ecosystems, which are often rather confused, confusing and ill thought out, but nonetheless real and important to them.

Chapter 3 looked at range of different ways in which people view naturalness, with one extreme being those who argue that concepts such as 'natural', 'wilderness', even 'nature' have no independent existence outside human discourse. But by stripping these concepts of anything distinct from our own opinions and emotions we create confusion and also risk a dangerous devaluation. There is only a small step from saying that the concept of nature is a human construct to assuming that it is something with no independent value or existence beyond our own human values, which brings us full circle back to the old views that 'nature' has been put there by an indulgent deity for us to use and abuse as we will.

And the results of this ambiguity are starting to become obvious to anyone involved in conservation on a day-to-day basis. To some extent, the whole philosophy of conserving wild nature is being questioned, but not just in thoughtful or constructive ways; there is a much deeper gut reaction at work. 'Biodiversity' and 'nature conservation' have almost become dirty words in some circles – not only in the boardrooms of corporations intent on stripping out natural resources as quickly as possible, but more insidiously in areas of social science, human rights and even now creeping into attitudes on display within conservation organizations. I've heard terms like 'fascist' used casually and publicly to describe individuals who argue for wilderness protection, by other people involved in the conservation field. And I have heard people working within mainstream conservation organizations say that the primary – or even the *only* – reason to conserve biodiversity is for the benefits it confers on human society.

This is sloppy and dangerous thinking. Although it stems in part from a growing confusion about the reality of what conservationists are trying to defend, it is also influenced by critiques of conservation from a human rights perspective. As a result it is mixing up two very different issues. First, that some conservationists have promoted an idealized and simplistic view of nature distinct and isolated from humans which has, among other things, encouraged approaches to conservation that disadvantage politically weak and vulnerable human communities. And second, that biodiversity conservation itself is somehow an ethical red herring. The first is certainly true but it does not lead to the second. This may seem like a digression, but it has distinct relevance to our discussions on naturalness.

Why conservation is being criticized by human rights activists

There is no doubt that some conservation projects have been carried out at the expense of people and usually of those people the least able to stand up for their rights. In particular, creating large protected areas by expelling the people already living there (often called 'The Yellowstone Model') has created a lot of unnecessary hardship. I'm going to follow the disreputable practice of quoting myself, not because I have anything original to say but to make the point that these are not new opinions. The following comes from a book three of us wrote about threats to protected areas a decade ago:

> *News of the creation of a new protected area is usually greeted with delight, and often relief, by conservation organisations … However, for the people living in or around a new protected area, the news is often greeted with far less enthusiasm and sometimes also vigorous opposition to the creation of a reserve. For them, protection may mean loss of access to things that have previously been available for little or no monetary cost – such as game, fish, non-timber forest products and agricultural land – or impose restrictions on their activities. In many cases, people have been physically expelled from new protected areas, or forcibly*

relocated to areas far away from their traditional lands. Most conser-
vationists would argue that conservation of biodiversity and ecology
are worth some sacrifices by people ... Such choices become much more
morally suspect when certain groups of people shoulder the majority of
the costs ... (Carey et al, 2000, p25)

These words still hold true today, although I would argue less so than they did when they were originally written.

The distinction made above is important; we were arguing that it is not the setting aside of areas for other species that is wrong but rather that the fault lies in choosing approaches and decision-making mechanisms that mean the poorest and least powerful carry most of the costs. All too often local people impacted by protected areas have not been asked their opinion, nor have they been adequately compensated. Some but by no means all the reasons why this happened was because of a view of wild nature as being necessarily and naturally empty of humans.

Generally speaking, we can expect conservation to disadvantage local communities in places with underlying problems of social inequity, corruption and poverty; conservation does not create these conditions but it often reflects them. In places where people are dispossessed of land in the name of nature conservation, they are generally also dispossessed by mining, farming and urban redevelopment, or just because someone rich and powerful wants to build a summerhouse or a golf course. Sometimes 'protected areas' are set up ostensibly in the name of biodiversity conservation when the land is actually being set aside for mining, or timber; it is far from uncommon for logging or mining to increase in an area after a park has been established. In fact where local communities support protected-area creation it is often precisely to avoid other land use changes that would make things even more difficult for them.

When we studied the ability of protected-area managers to use the resources of protected areas for delivering economic benefits and poverty reduction to local communities we found that success was intimately linked with overall quality of governance (Dudley at al, 2008). So there was an apparently perverse result that protected areas in places like Austria and Germany do pretty well in delivering economic benefits to relatively poor communities but protected areas in much of Africa usually do badly, even though the surrounding communities are far poorer and some African protected areas generate more tourist revenue money than most national parks in Europe. Efforts to address inequalities through integrated conservation and development projects often fail because, however well designed the individual project, it is undermined by wider corruption, crime and institutional weakness. A multi-year project to set up community ecotourism at the edge of a protected area in Senegal I visited a few years ago failed because a local businessman simply bought off the police and had the whole operation undermined. There are unfortunately many such examples and they give aid and development projects a bad name.

This is not to say that inability to run a perfect project should be equivalent to accepting the status quo. Conservation organizations have too often been complicit in inequitable conservation, either unaware or guiltily ignoring the human impacts of protection strategies. There has been a necessary backlash, with organizations like the World Rainforest Movement and the Forest Peoples' Programme drawing international attention to human rights abuses (Colchester and Erni, 1999; Nelson and Hossack, 2003); indigenous peoples' organizations using international processes to publicize their problems; and a great deal of soul searching. The 2003 World Parks Congress created a watershed in thinking about more participatory and socially just community approaches to conservation, and the Convention on Biological Diversity has provided a powerful framework for a more equitable approach in its *Programme of Work on Protected Areas* and its *Akwe Kon* guidelines for working with communities (SCBD, 2004). Environmental justice has emerged as an important concept (Campese et al, 2009). Things are changing though it would be over-optimistic to say that the changes are complete or have gone far enough.

But the original environmental justice critique of conservation, which I generally support, has developed into something else, which I do not. The argument goes something like this, usually inferred rather than stated in so many words. If nature is simply a human construct, and wilderness protection a game for rich kids and the super-privileged, shouldn't the whole approach be rethought? Do we need to set aside land particularly for nature? Aren't protected areas irrelevant and shouldn't we instead be 'mainstreaming biodiversity' into the wider landscape (whatever that means)? If bushmeat hunting is providing valuable protein and income for poor communities what right have we to try to stop it? Shouldn't human needs always come first? Over the last decade there has been a steady backlash against some key conservation strategies, not among the public who remain broadly supportive but paradoxically within many conservation organizations. People with a protected areas or biodiversity brief in some of the world's largest conservation NGOs have told me repeatedly of feeling isolated, regarded as old fashioned and being undermined. I have sat in a meeting in a government conservation organization and heard people grumbling that there was 'too much talk about biodiversity'. There is, at best, a certain amount of confusion around.

I rather like a lot of what I'll call for shorthand the post-modernist critique of conservation (e.g. Gare, 1995). It has made us think, knocked a few cherished preconceptions around and provided some important fresh ideas. It has encouraged conservationists to look at other values: like sacred values and cultural values for instance, and at the opinions of social scientists and historians. Human rights campaigners have made us listen more to what local communities want rather than just telling them what they ought to want. But it has also helped create an underlying confusion and lack of ethical focus that has left many of us uncertain about what we should be doing and how we should be doing it. So as an introduction to looking at what naturalness means today, it is important to draw some distinctions between different approaches within conservation and propose some parameters for looking at what a concern for naturalness implies, starting with the differences between animal rights and existence rights.

Animals rights, biodiversity rights and ecosystem rights

Until quite recently the concept that non-humans – animals, plants or ecosystems – had rights was almost wholly rejected within Occidental philosophy, sometimes very explicitly. Rene Descartes famously made an abrupt distinction between humans and the rest of nature; or more accurately 'man and nature' because many thinkers regarded women as 'near the animal state' (Roberts, 1983, p43). In *Man and the Natural World*, his magisterial study of changing relations with the natural world in England between 1500 and 1800, Keith Roberts traces the way in which attitudes gradually developed towards a greater sympathy for the non-human, but this must be contrasted with a continuing high level of cruelty or at least indifference among a large proportion of the population. And as he points out, this Manichean distinction between 'man' and 'nature' was not confined to Christian countries. The rejection – apparent hatred – of wildlife also survived and even increased among colonists who spread from Europe into the newly conquered territories in the Americas, Africa and Asia. The devastation of wild bison populations in North America is well known. But at least these made the hunters some money: many settlers killed wildlife and simply left the corpses to rot. 'Binge killing' of animals like birds, deer and alligators persisted well into the 20th century. The famous bird artist John James Audubon, revered today as a pioneer conservationist, is recorded as joining in the killing of hundreds of seabirds in a single afternoon on the coast of Florida including four hundred nesting cormorants and 'I thought by some unaccountable means or other we had killed the whole colony' (Kirby, 2006, p13).

During the last century, the concept that animals have rights has gained ground rapidly, boosted by a rich philosophical literature (e.g. Singer, 1975; Midgley, 1983). But the large majority of this writing focuses on the rights of individual animals; there is some discussion among philosophers about existence rights (see for instance Feinberg, 1974 and about what we might call ecosystem rights (e.g. Rolston, 1989), but this has been limited compared with the huge global effort aimed at putting the philosophy into practice.

Outside a narrow philosophical discourse, most people confuse concern for biodiversity or ecosystems (I'll lump these ideas together as *existence rights*) with concern for *animal rights*. But the two worldviews are very different; while it is certainly possible for one person to adhere to aspects of both it is not essential and at their extremes of interpretation they can and do come into conflict.

Animals rights focuses on individuals while existence rights focuses on species and ecosystems, with less concern for individuals. From the perspective of animal rights, the rights of an individual dog, horse, elephant or beetle are viewed in the same way as the rights of an individual human: hence donkey sanctuaries, organizations concerned with preventing animal cruelty, hunt saboteurs and so on. In practice, at least in Western culture, people interested in animal rights direct their attention mainly towards those animals most closely related to humans, mammals in particular and also birds, although this is not the position taken by philosophers such as Peter Singer, nor by faith groups such as the Jains. Many, possibly most, people who take animal rights seriously will be vegetarian, because they regard the killing and eating of an animal as unnecessarily cruel and something that humans should have developed beyond in a civilized society. Others who eat meat will have standards relating to the way in which such animals are kept and killed.

Existence rights address both plants and animals and embrace all species, regardless of their size, intelligence or the extent to which they remind us of ourselves. Proponents are less interested in the fate of individuals and more in the survival of species and complex ecological interactions. Although there are probably a higher proportion of vegetarians working for conservation organizations than in the population at large, they will likely be in a minority and conversely many conservation NGOs include hunters among their staff and supporters. This group would regard the killing of an *individual* for food as morally justifiable, particularly from the wild, fulfilling a natural part of the ecological cycle and acceptable as long as it was carried out with respect, with the minimum of unnecessary suffering and if the *species* was not put at risk of extinction as a result. It could be argued that this stance – of killing in a sustainable and respectful manner – is closely aligned to the views of many indigenous peoples and ethnic minorities.

It would be wrong to assume that supporters of animal and existence rights can be divided quite as neatly as the paragraph above suggests; in practice the cut off between what is and is not acceptable differs with every individual. Many meat-eating supporters of existence rights would never consider eating whales or the higher apes because of their intelligence and complex social structures, and avoid products from factory farms. Similarly, many animal rights supporters who avoid eating meat from mammals and birds are prepared to eat fish (although arguably a fish slowly suffocating on the deck of a trawler faces a harder death than a rabbit killed by a single shot).

Conflicts between animal rights and existence rights come when the rights of individual animals clash with the rights of ecosystems and species. Sagoff points out that organizations 'which promote a love and respect for the functioning of natural ecosystems, differ ideologically from organizations that make the suffering of animals their primary concern' (Sagoff, 1984, p40). These conflicts are not hard to find. In 2008, national park managers in Canberra, Australia told me of their frustration that a cull of 500 grey kangaroos had

FIGURE 4.1 The gradual replacement of the native red squirrel by the alien grey in Europe has been helped by a combination of factors, including protests from animal rights groups about the culling of the North American grey

been blocked by international outcry from animal rights groups. The cull was considered necessary to maintain a balanced ecosystem because, in the absence of predators, kangaroo numbers had increased to a level where vegetation was degrading and other animal species were losing habitat. Similar protests are preventing a cull of feral horses, which are proliferating rapidly and destroying vegetation throughout the Australian Alps in New South Wales (Worboys et al, 2010). In Scotland, introduction of hedgehogs (*Erinaceus europaeus*) onto the island of Coll devastated populations of ground-nesting birds, because hedgehogs eat the eggs. But proposals for eradication brought death-threats to staff at Scottish National Heritage (and an expensive security system at their headquarters in Inverness); culling was replaced with expensive capture and translocation. In Italy, animal rights organizations used legal means to delay plans to eradicate alien invasive grey squirrels for so long that they spread too far to make the cull practical, threatening loss of native red squirrels over a wide area (Bertolino and Genovesi, 2003). In all these cases the rights of individuals (and in fact individuals of mammal species that humans tend to hold in high regard) was placed above rights of ecosystems and implicitly of other species.

More subtly, because animal rights are concerned with the well-being and the consciousness of the *individual*, there is less concern about whether or not the *species* concerned is endangered. In California, the US National Park Service killed hundreds of rabbits on Santa Barbara Island to protect a few plants of *Dudleya traskiae* (no relation), endemic to the island and once thought to be extinct (Rolston, 1995). From the perspective of existence rights this makes perfect sense, because rabbits are an abundant, invasive alien species, which on this particular island were destroying the only known population of another species. But from an animal rights perspective the action is perverse; hundreds of sentient beings with complex social structures and the ability to feel fear, loss and pain are being destroyed to protect a non-sentient, relic plant species of little intrinsic value. The resulting tensions are real but generally suppressed: insiders in conservation organizations sometimes grumble about the 'bunny huggers' among their membership and some animal rights groups criticize organizations like WWF because of their tolerance of hunting and culling, but the ethical questions are seldom brought into the open.

The implications of existence rights

The issue of existence rights deserves to be much more carefully examined than it has been up to now, by philosophers who can provide a rigorous framework against which to measure actions and decisions. For a start, and based on discussions with many conservation biologists over the years, I'd like to suggest that proponents in what I have been calling existence rights generally believe in the following:

- The right of the global ecosystem to experience rates of species extinction no greater than the norm expected through natural evolutionary processes;
- *thus* the right of survival for virtually all species of plants and animals, in functioning ecosystems on a scale large enough to favour long-term survival;
- *thus* the maintenance of evolutionary potential.

Note that this is not just a utilitarian issue. Chapter 5 looks in more detail at what functioning ecosystems supply us in terms of goods and services but this is much more than that: a strong ethical case that humans have no right to drive species and ecosystems into extinction. There is a parallel need to approach the task of conservation in a socially equitable way and there are also situations where trade-offs will need to be made between human and non-human rights but neither of these caveats change the underlying messages. I suspect that most people who are deeply concerned with biodiversity conservation would state these three rights as an ethical position that also has strong overtones of an explicit or implicit spiritual nature. For conservationists with a religious faith then this is likely rooted in that particular set of teaching or belief system but even the most secular scientists often refer to our responsibility to nature in terms that come close to the sacred.

Three critical questions for those concerned with natural ecosystems

The foregoing is by way of background to the central issue: What are the ethical dimensions (if any) of conserving natural ecosystems? In order to understand this we need to understand first more about our own place in nature and our own motives. Below I attempt a very brief answer to three critical questions for conservationists:

1   Where do we stand in relation to the rest of nature?
2   Who are we practising conservation for?
3   What are we aiming to achieve?

Where do we stand in relation to the rest of nature?

In Chapter 3 we saw how old ideas of humans' innate superiority to the rest of nature are gradually being abandoned. I don't believe that we are innately *inferior* either, although some guilt-ridden conservationists seem to assume that we are. But nor are we just the same as everything else; we are distinguished by the sophistication of our reasoning ability, our ability to speculate about the future and our colossal and disproportionate ability to influence the ecosystems around us. While many species can create some havoc if a series of chance events give them a competitive advantage for a period, no other species has done so on the same scale. Many biologists and philosophers have struggled to 'place' humans in relation to other creatures; apart from the fact that the distinctions keep getting eroded a little every time someone discovers new reasoning ability in the more intelligent species and individuals among the primates, cetaceans and birds, not so much has changed since Darwin. But what that means in terms of our obligations has still been by no means fully explored.

Who are we practising conservation for?

Again we run into philosophical problems as soon as we step away from the easy answer that we practise conservation to please ourselves. There is certainly a lot of truth here: much conservation is, consciously or unconsciously, conserving a particular make-up of the natural world that some sections of society deem to be useful, aesthetically pleasing or spiritually significant at a particular time. Even in the short history of modern conservation, aims and priorities have shifted and will doubtless continue to change in the future. Many conservationists probably do not rationalize their actions too carefully and if they do their answers will lie somewhere on a spectrum that includes ethics, morals, social justice, ecosystem services, human rights and obligations to the rest of the living world. Informed self-interest is not a particularly bad starting point for the practise of conservation.

Can we also say that we are responding to the needs and desires of other species? We can't ask them, so we have to try to guess what their answer would be, if they had the reasoning power and if we shared a common language. I can imagine a few purists shuddering at the temerity. But given the efforts that plants and animals put into personal survival and into reproducing and maintaining the species I think it is fair to assume that they are not seeking oblivion. That being the case, it is also fair to argue that we should be addressing the survival needs of biodiversity as a whole, rather than simply the particular species or ecosystems of immediate benefit or interest to ourselves: indeed the term 'biodiversity' was to some extent coined explicitly to encourage this wider kind of thinking (Wilson, 1988).

The presumption that biodiversity has intrinsic value is also one of the core ideas underpinning conservation biology (Soulé, 1985), which has received additional support from studies of the role of diversity in promoting resilience, for instance against climate change (Thompson et al, 2009).

What are we aiming to achieve?

In Britain, Brooke Bond Tea used to give away illustrated cards that children could collect and paste into special albums. For years Brooke Bond Tea Cards were based around nature subjects and attracted a range of artists and writers quite well known in their day: *British Butterflies*, *Wildlife in Africa* and so on. Collecting their *Wildlife in Danger* set was probably the first time I realized wildlife might actually be in danger of *disappearing*: 50 carefully selected iconic and beautiful species from around the world with descriptions of the threats that they faced. I still have them, stuck carefully in their album.

Conservation organizations have proved surprisingly conservative and reluctant to move away from the Brooke Bond Tea philosophy of saving the spectacular and the pretty. It sounds bizarre now, but a proposal for Greenpeace to run a campaign on behalf of endangered great whales almost split the organization in half, objections coming both from anti-nuclear campaigners who saw it as a diversion and from activists who thought the public would never warm to something as large and alien-looking as a whale (Hunter, 1979). Similarly, in the UK staff at both Friends of the Earth and WWF were reluctant to expand their tropical species campaigns to an ecosystem-based message, centred on rainforests, because again they believed the public would never fall behind something as abstruse (and hot and hazardous) as a jungle. Both suppositions proved to be spectacularly wrong.

Gradually, the aspirations of environmental and conservation organizations moved away from just the charismatic (although these still dominate the media and raise the most money from supporters) to encompass all plants and animals, then gradually with the concept of biodiversity to embrace as well intra-specific variation and ecosystem interactions: to a concern for every living thing in fact. But what exactly does 'everything' mean? Is it enough to protect species? There are probably more captive tigers than wild tigers today, and tigers breed well in captivity, but most people would agree that tigers in zoos are not enough. Major contemporary campaigns by the Wildlife Conservation Society and WWF emphasize the importance of tigers in the wild (Walston et al, 2010). But is it enough to have just one population, or maybe one example of every sub-species? Are bacteria as important as blue whales? It is often difficult to even decide where a particular 'species' begins and ends. Ultimately species do not work as a good vehicle for explaining what conservationists are trying to achieve, not least of all because most have still not been described by science.

In theory, ecosystems should work better as a descriptor, because even if we do not know all their components and all their interactions, they form coherent enough units that they can be described. They are not isolated units: they have very fuzzy boundaries and there is considerable movement between ecosystems with only the global biosphere being really consistent as a concept; but for all these caveats ecosystems have proven to be quite useful ways of planning management. The concept of 'ecologically-representative', in terms of targets for conservation, is based on the assumption that ecosystems provide valid units for conservation effort. But ecosystems also face the same types of questions that we outlined above; in fact the problem is even greater because no one ecosystem is ever exactly like another. In addition, as we discussed earlier with respect to the Serengeti, ecosystems are not static; even without humans they change over time. The concept of 'saving' a particular ecosystem, in terms of freezing it at a particular moment, may be both practically impossible and inherently unnatural. Throw climate change into the picture and things become even more confused; if predictions and observations are correct, ecosystems are going to change dramatically over the coming decades so that conservationists and others will be placed in the position of trying to 'keep things going' in an increasingly fluid and evolving set of new ecosystems. The question of whether species or ecosystems are suitable units for planning and measuring conservation has created a heated and vibrant debate over the last few years (e.g. Brookes et al, 2004; Cowling et al, 2004). We return to these issues in more detail in Chapter 8.

Clarity of ethical position is important because it provides the fundamental drivers, often subconscious, that help to determine how we react in any particular situation. But in practice, whether we like it or not, ethics are seldom the sole reason decisions are made about natural ecosystems; self-interest plays an overwhelming role in many cases, which is one of the reasons the natural world is in such a mess. Changing perceptions, to recognize that we lose more than we gain if we undermine the planet's ecology, can help shift the balance of policy decisions and accompanying laws to give greater weight to conservation concerns. The next chapter therefore provides a rapid overview of our current state of knowledge about natural ecosystems.

CHAPTER 5

The Things We Get from Natural Ecosystems

Key message

- *In addition to their existence value, natural ecosystems have a huge range of livelihood, security, economic, cultural and spiritual values to human societies.*

Two of us are sitting in the back of an open truck in the rainforest, and it's raining. In fact it is pouring; a relentless deluge that drenches us so thoroughly that it is almost funny, as the truck slithers painfully along a dirt track for what seems like hours, down to a tiny hydropower station. By the time we get there the rain finally stops and the owner of the power station is there to greet us, looking considerably less bedraggled than we are. Our little expedition is to see one of Costa Rica's 'Payment for Ecosystem Services' (PES) schemes, where users of ecosystem services pay the owners of the ecosystems that provide them; clean water is a classic example of a product suitable for PES. Here the power company is paying local farmers to keep the watershed forested, to ensure that there will always be enough water to run the turbine. Tropical cloud forests in mountain areas are believed to increase water supply significantly, by scavenging droplets of water from clouds. But as is often the case in hydrology there is disagreement among the experts, with lots of strongly held and divergent opinions. We are in cloud forest now so paying to maintain forest is probably a good investment, but if the theories are wrong the owner may be wasting his money. I ask him whether he has been following the debate. He shrugs; yes he knows about it but he is committed to the scheme anyway. The money he pays isn't so much, a few thousand dollars a year, and he looks upon it as insurance. If the water supply slows significantly his investment of several million dollars is wasted and in those circumstances he is more than happy to make sure the forest stays healthy and wet. He's content and will keep the system in place whatever the experts eventually decide.

The last chapter set out some ethical reasons for conserving natural ecosystems. But the issue goes beyond a matter of conscience or philosophy; there is an array of very practical incentives for maintaining natural ecosystems so as well. Authentic ecosystems – healthy, diverse self regulating ecosystems – are not simply receptacles for biodiversity or playthings for the rich and privileged of the planet, but provide many ecosystem services, genetic resources and cultural and spiritual values that humanity wants and needs. Some of these are easy to present in economic terms, while others are mainly non-monetary: a brief overview of the benefits that natural ecosystems can provide is given below.

Over the last decade Sue Stolton and I have worked on a series of reports called 'Arguments for Protection', with much-needed support from WWF, The World Bank and other partners. Earthscan published the overview volume *Arguments for Protected Areas* in 2010 (Stolton and Dudley, 2010a) and there are to date seven other detailed reports on particular topics along with a host of shorter papers. Scraped together with limited resources, the series grew out of a simple idea to publicize a few of the wider benefits of the world's protected area network. But as we worked our way through the topics it developed into something more complex, an attempt to understand the enormous mixture of social, economic, cultural, ethical and spiritual values that protected areas provide – along with some of the costs that they can extract on individuals and society. And although we narrowed our scope to look just at protected areas – national parks, nature reserves and so on – many of the values we were investigating are found in any natural ecosystem. The following draws on this work and on that of the many other people who have attempted to collate and quantify ecosystem benefits. It should be regarded as a work in progress; there is still a lot to be learned. If I was writing five years ago, potential benefits in combating climate change would probably have been only a very small part of the whole (the issue hardly featured in the 2003 World Parks Congress for instance) but since then it has grown to be the single most important issue for many commentators. The next few years may well bring a few other surprises.

Natural ecosystems are probably best known in this regard for providing a set of benefits known collectively as *ecosystem services*: clean air and water, stable soil, wild foods and medicines and buffering against the extremes of climate. Most people also understand that they provide a still under-explored potential in terms of *genetic resources* for crop breeding, medicines and other products. As will already be clear to anyone reading this book sequentially, they also have enormous *cultural, social and spiritual values* to different groups. Finally, there is growing recognition of the importance of functioning ecosystems in supplying a more broad-based *resilience*; all of these issues are examined in turn below.

Ecosystem services

Natural ecosystems often remain the cheapest and most cost effective means of supplying many life support systems, including water for domestic use and irrigation, many foodstuffs, a host of other materials and protection against natural disasters and climate change.

Water

Demand for water increased twice as fast as population growth over the course of the last century (World Water Council, 2000), resulting in shortfalls and over a billion people living without access to clean water and sanitation. The UN Human Settlement Programme (UNHSP) attributes over two million deaths a year to diseases caught from contaminated water (UNHSP, 2003). This situation is likely to get worse under climate change (Bates et al, 2008). Providing enough clean water is already a priority for many countries and municipalities.

Well managed natural forests almost always provide higher quality water, with less sediment and fewer pollutants, than water from other catchments (Hamilton et al, 2008). Forests do not intercept every contaminant – they will not guard against parasites such as *Giardia* for instance, but in most situations they reduce or even eliminate the need for further purification of drinking water. Similar benefits can be gained from many wetlands. Some water plants can concentrate toxic materials in their tissues and thus purify water (Jeng and Hong, 2005) and municipalities recognize that natural wetlands can be an important filtering system for domestic water supplies. When we surveyed the world's largest cities we found a third (33 out of 105) of them draw a substantial amount of their drinking water from forest protected areas and at least five other cities obtain water from sources that originate in distant watersheds that also include protected areas. Others had integrated land management strategies in place to help protect the purity of water supplies (Dudley and Stolton, 2003). While some of these benefits occur almost by accident, local government officials in cities like Melbourne, Bogotá and Jakarta are well aware of the values of these natural areas and have set protection policies to maintain water quality. Other municipalities bemoan degradation of forests because of the impacts on water quality, currently the situation in Mount Kenya National Park outside Nairobi. Companies like Coca Cola, Pepsi Cola and Perrier situate some of their bottling plants to take advantage of this natural capital.

The situation is not quite as clear cut in terms of water flow. Some natural vegetation types, including many forest ecosystems, reduce net water flow, because trees have higher evapotranspiration rates than vegetation like grassland and crops. However, other natural forests (particularly tropical montane cloud forests) increase total water flow; water from the clouds condenses on leaves and increases net flow into the watershed (Hamilton et al, 1994). Cloud forests cover 381,166km^2 of the planet's surface (2004 figures); 60 per cent in Asia, 25 per cent in the Americas and 15 per cent in Africa. The theoretical range is considerably larger; large areas have already been cleared (Bubb et al, 2004). Many of the remaining cloud forests are already supplying water to cities like Quito in Ecuador and Tegucigalpa in Honduras. Older eucalyptus

FIGURE 5.1 Paramos vegetation in the watershed helps to provide clean and plentiful drinking water to the city of Bogotá, Colombia

forests are also believed to increase flow and in Melbourne and several other Australian cities old-growth eucalyptus are conserved partly to maintain water supplies. Other natural ecosystems, such as the *paramos* found in Colombia, Ecuador and surrounding countries, also increase net water flow.

Food

Most of us rely on wild food for at least some of our nutrition; often more than we realize. Many of the world's poorest people catch wild animals or collect animal products to supply a major part of their diet (Scoones et al, 1992), including bushmeat, fish and shellfish, bird and turtle eggs, invertebrates, honey and flavouring products (Ntiamoa-Baidu, 1997). Bushmeat makes up more than a fifth of animal protein in rural diets in over 60 countries (Bennett and Robinson, 2000) rising to 80 per cent in areas such as rural Kenya (Barnett, 2000). Although overconsumption of wild meat is a major conservation problem, as described in Chapter 1, if managed correctly it can provide a critically important 'free good' for people with no other nutritional options. It also provides a rare source of cash income in many rural areas; a UK government study put annual global value at around US$7 billion (Elliott et al, 2002), although much of this is currently from unsustainable sources. While bushmeat consumption is highest in the tropics it is not confined to poor countries and for example consumption of moose is a major protein source in the Arctic regions of Scandinavia (Helle, 1995). Moose management gives an idea of what might be possible elsewhere. Hunting is carefully controlled to retain a sustainable population and families are allocated a quota; moose makes up an important part of the diet of many low-income families without endangering a wild population. If current overkill in many tropical countries could be controlled and managed, sustainable sources of meat would be available from many wild populations.

Wild plants are also major food sources for poor people. The UN Food and Agriculture Organization (FAO) estimates that 18,000–25,000 wild plant species are used as food in the tropics (Heywood, 1999). Precise statistics for global dependency on wild food are hard to find although there have been some important national studies; in India 50 million people are directly dependent on wild foods (Shaankar et al, 2004). In many cases wild plants are used as supplements to agricultural crops or as an emergency supply when crops fail. Typically, hunter–gatherer societies collect a wide range of food plants and rely on long-standing traditional ecological knowledge to identify edible species; they know which are likely to be in season at particular times and understand the mixture needed for a balanced diet. In forest regions of Thailand, for instance, around a hundred plant species are eaten (Ogle, 1996).

Much of the world's livestock still grazes predominantly on natural vegetation. There are 100–200 million pastoralists around the world (Hatfield and Davis, 2006); the massive range of the estimates gives an indication of how hidden many of these users of natural and semi-natural ecosystems are from governments and policy-makers. Many other farmers use natural and semi-natural pastures for grazing livestock and gathering wild fodder, which is itself one of the most important non-timber forest products according to the FAO, particularly in Asia (FAO, 2006).

Although primarily a nutritional source for the poorest in society, collection of wild food may also be a more economically efficient way of living than agriculture for some communities (Delang, 2006). As with animals, wild plant collection can be a sustainable and rational use of natural ecosystems if managed correctly. Many models of sustainable natural resource management exist, both operating bottom–up at a community scale (Borrini-Feyerabend et al, 2004) and developed in a more top–down way through government agencies. An increasing number of protected areas, for example, are now opening up their natural resources for use by local communities in a managed way as a supplement to farming (e.g. in Uganda as described by Wild and Mutebi, 1997).

Wild plants provide a major addition to food even in some of the richer countries. In Finland, yields of the 36 wild plants with edible berries reach 900 million kg/year (Raatikainen, 1988) and of these 16 species are regularly collected, with over 50kg/person/year being harvested in some regions (Salo, 1995). Yet the strategies used in non-timber forest product (NTFP) production differ markedly from place to place (Belcher et al, 2005); some systems have been practised on a sustainable basis for hundreds or even thousands of years while others rapidly deplete resources through overcollection or bad management.

Most of our marine and freshwater fish still also come from the wild, scooped up from the natural ecosystem in much the same way as they have been for thousands of years, albeit at a different scale and often with more efficient and ruthless technology. Roughly two thirds of fish, crustaceans and aquatic molluscs come from capture fisheries and just over three quarters of aquatic production is from the sea: in 2004 this meant wild catch was around 100 million tonnes (Brander, 2007). An estimated 250 million people in developing countries are directly dependent on small-scale fisheries for food and income (World Bank, 2004) and many more throughout the world also benefit from wild caught fish. While mismanagement and overexploitation of fisheries has caused what could without over-statement be described as a global crisis in fisheries, there is also growing recognition that with better management (including set-aside areas for breeding, reduction of waste and by-catch etc.) the total available could actually be increased and remain sustainable. The Economics of Ecosystems and Biodiversity (TEEB) programme estimated that with restoration and good management total value of a sustainable catch could increase by US$50 billion a year (TEEB, 2009).

In most of these cases, the availability of wild food relies on healthy ecosystems and managers are increasingly recognizing this interrelationship. For instance, setting aside areas of water to act as nurseries for fish is the fastest, often the only, way of restoring overfished ecosystems (Halpern, 2003); such approaches have been understood in the Pacific Islands and some other tropical areas for hundreds of years, and are codified in traditional laws, but are being trumpeted as a new innovation (or still being resisted) in other coastal fishing communities. On land, overuse of insecticides destroys not only pest insects but also beneficial species, such as those needed for pollination, leading to some radical rethinking of pest control strategies on farms. A study by Taylor Ricketts and colleagues (2004) for instance revealed a strong economic relationship between forests, coffee plantations and bee populations in Costa Rica.

Materials

Plant and animal-based products continue to provide raw materials for industry: collection of materials such as rubber, latex, rattan, plant oils, bamboo, textiles, cosmetics and other NTFPs remains important for subsistence and trade (Lewington, 2003). NTFPs are usually regarded (indeed described) as 'minor forest products', but in fact they can exceed the value of timber in some cases; for instance this has been measured in Botswana (Taylor et al, 1996). Global trade in NTFPs is estimated at US$15 billion a year (Roe et al, 2002), although this involves food products as well. A study that compared 54 cases of income generation among people living near or in forests found that forests provided resources that contributed an average of 22 per cent

FIGURE 5.2 Tropical rainforest has been referred to as the 'primary source' of genetic material, due to the huge variety of biodiversity that these ecosystems support

of families' total income – the equivalent of US$678 per household per year (adjusted for purchasing power parity) (Vedeld et al, 2004).

Physical and mental health

Natural ecosystems play a key role in maintaining health through purifying water, as described above and in some cases by hampering the movement of disease vectors (Colfer et al, 2006; Stolton and Dudley, 2010b); several studies have shown that malaria and other insect-transmitted diseases are markedly less prevalent in forested areas than in nearby places that have been deforested (e.g. on the island of Flores in Indonesia: Pattanayak et al, 2003). A study in the Peruvian Amazon found that primary malaria vector, *Anopheles darlingi*, had a biting rate 278 times higher in deforested than in forested areas (Vittor et al, 2009); avoiding deforestation or restoring natural vegetation can thus reduce risk of malaria (Oglethorpe et al, 2008). Conversely, natural wetlands can help to spread malaria and this has led to wetland drainage in some areas, with other side effects in terms of water availability and fish production.

Natural ecosystems also provide us with places to exercise: as obesity overtakes malnutrition as a global health problem, managers of nature reserves and national parks are increasingly promoting their sites as safe and attractive places to keep fit (Stolton and Dudley, 2010b).

These values are increasingly recognized but only because they are in danger of being lost, as generations grow up and pass their lives alienated from natural environment. Aston Park is the remnants of an old deer park on the edge of Birmingham in the English West Midlands, bordered by an expressway and Aston Villa football ground. There are some nice open spaces and a hall in the middle but it is not, in my memory, really very exciting and certainly not anything that could remotely be described as wild. When I was living there around 1980 a schoolteacher acquaintance took a bunch of inner city kids out there for a run around. As soon as they got off the bus two of the boys were so terrified by all the space around them that they filled their pants on the spot. Things have almost certainly got worse in the 30 years since.

The idea that people are being alienated from nature, and that children are becoming *particularly* alienated is already well known and Richard Louv's 2005 book *Last Child in the Woods* makes an impassioned plea for bringing children back into contact with the natural world. Television, computer games, urbanization, lack of public transport and a perception of increasing risk for children left alone is creating a degree of separation from nature that would have been hard to imagine a generation ago. The children living in the small town near me in Wales literally have to walk a few hundred yards at most to be in rough pasture and woods but I can't remember the last time I met any kids away from the streets or the manicured lawns of the local parks. And although this alienation is often talked about as a side effect of late industrial society it is likely to be even more acute in many developing countries where people do not have the time or money to even venture beyond the city boundaries. A friend in Nairobi told me of his assistant's amazement when she first took a flight to Mombassa and saw open countryside below her; his description was hilarious over a beer in a downtown café but deeply depressing in its wider implications. Accessible quasi-natural places, such as urban nature reserves, can play a critical linking role by giving people access to some aspects of nature without scaring them off.

The immediate health benefits from natural ecosystems add up to more than just a place to work out. The importance of natural environments to mental health is also being increasingly recognized (Pretty, 2004; Maller et al, 2006), stemming from concepts such as 'therapeutic landscapes' (Gesler, 1992) and 'Nature Deficit Disorder', which defines a range of health problems associated with a lack of connection and direct experience of nature by children (Louv, 2005). In Australia, this has led to a pioneering link-up between Parks Victoria and the state mental health authorities, to provide access to national parks for mental health patients in the *Healthy Parks, Healthy People* programme (Senior, 2010). Similar exercises have been undertaken with people suffering from drug addiction in Glasgow, Scotland. The soothing effects of an attractive natural landscape, instinctively recognized by most people, have also been shown to have positive therapeutic effects for troubled adolescents at relatively low costs (Russell, 2000).

Natural ecosystems give us medicines as well. Wild plants are used in traditional herbal remedies, which remain the primary medicines for 80 per cent
of the world's people (WHO, 2002). Overall, researchers estimate that around
50,000 higher plant species are used worldwide for medicines (Hawkins,
2008), a vast natural pharmacy. Researchers in Nepal have discovered 1624
plant species having medicinal and aromatic values, Sri Lanka has about 1400,
India some 2500 and China around 5000 (Kunwar at al, 2006). At least 60 per
cent of medicinal plants are gathered from the wild and countries like India
and China reportedly harvest 90 per cent and 80 per cent respectively of their
medicinal plants from wild sources (Muriuki, 2006; Alves and Rosa, 2007).

About 3000 medicinal and aromatic plant species are traded internationally
and most of these are collected from the wild (Medicinal Plant Specialist Group,
2007). In Europe, 1200–1300 species are used and in the 1990s at least 90 per cent
were still wild-collected. Almost 100 per cent of medicinal plants were then being
wild-collected in countries like Turkey and Albania, but even in heavily industrialized Germany, 50–70 per cent still came from the wild (TRAFFIC, 1998).

Energy

As the world gradually wakes up to the limits and costs associated with fossil
fuels, there is a slow but increasing shift towards use of renewable resources.
Virtually all these come with associated environmental and social costs of
their own, and the conservation movement is currently splintered on this
issue, with environmental groups actively opposing every possible energy
source, thus effectively neutralizing their voice (Dudley, 2008a). But whatever
the path chosen, some of these renewable energy systems rely on functioning
natural ecosystems: for instance hydro-electricity schemes only work so long
as reservoirs do not silt up, which remains a danger in areas of rapid deforestation (Douglas et al, 2007).

More significantly, in developing countries some 2.4 billion people – more
than a third of the world's population – still rely on wood or other biomass
fuels for cooking and heating (International Energy Agency, 2002). At one
time, fuel use was identified as a major source of deforestation (Eckholm,
1975) and photographs of women carrying bundles of sticks on their heads
was an iconic 1970s image from the emerging environmental movement.
Since then, a number of research projects have concluded that environmental
impacts of fuelwood collection have sometimes been exaggerated (e.g. Leach
and Mearns, 1988), although poor management can create localized impacts
(Utting, 1991) particularly in dry forests (Arnold et al, 2003). Collection of
wood for fuel is increasingly seen as an income source: in Kenya, the charcoal
economy is estimated at over US$350 million a year, which one estimate put
on a par with tourism (Kantai, 2002).

FIGURE 5.3 Wood and charcoal still supply heat energy for 2.6 billion people around the world; collection in countries such as Morocco can lead to forest degradation and loss, but with good management can provide renewable resources from natural forests

Ecosystem stability

More subtly, but no less importantly, natural ecosystems provide an effective buffer against both regular and irregular stresses: vegetation binds soil and prevents erosion and desert formation; forests and wetlands ameliorate flooding; vegetation on steep slopes helps to block landslides and avalanches; while coral reefs, coastal marshes and mangroves can dissipate much of the energy from ocean surges and coastal storms (Stolton et al, 2008). Some of benefits are given in Table 5.1 below.

An extreme climatic event or earthquake is transformed into a 'natural disaster' when people, crops and infrastructure get caught up, damaged and destroyed. Governments have recognized for hundreds or even thousands of years that some forms of ecosystem degradation – such as deforestation on steep slopes, can increase the risks of a natural disaster occurring in the event of something like a huge storm. The Millennium Ecosystem Assessment notes that: '*Changes to ecosystems have contributed to a significant rise in the number of floods and major wild fires on all continents since the 1940s*' (Millennium Ecosystem Assessment, 2005). The potential for conservation and restoration of natural ecosystems to help mitigate the huge human and financial costs of natural disasters is also increasingly being recognized by institutions like The World Bank and the UN's International Strategy for Disaster Reduction (ISDR). The ISDR has noted that: '*the management of ecosystem services should*

TABLE 5.1 Protective functions from natural ecosystems

Impact	Role of natural ecosystem	Examples
Floods	Natural vegetation such as forests can help to ameliorate any but the most severe floods. Marshes and floodplains can absorb excess water.	Flooding in **Malaga, Spain** has been dramatically reduced by forest restoration and protection in the watershed (Dudley and Aldrich, 2007).
Tidal surge and coastal storms	Coral reefs, coastal marshes and mangroves can all help to absorb the force of water from both coastal storms and abrupt surges as with a tsunami.	Areas of **Sri Lanka** with healthy mangrove ecosystems suffered less from the 2004 Indian Ocean tsunami than places where all natural vegetation had been cleared (Caldecott and Wickremasinghe, 2005).
Avalanche and landslide	Vegetation cover, particularly mature forests, provides a physical barrier against slippage of earth, rocks and snow: loss of such cover is implicated in increases in landslides in many tropical countries.	Some 17 per cent of forests in **Switzerland** are managed to protect against avalanches and floods; services which have been valued at US$2–3.5 billion per year (ISDR, 2004).
Typhoons and hurricanes	Forests can protect directly from wind damage and also from associated flooding. Mangroves and other natural coastal defences also give protection and wetlands provide space for floods to dissipate.	Differences between deforested **Haiti** and the more forested **Dominican Republic** were identified as a major reason why a 2004 hurricane caused > 3000 deaths in Haiti and only 7 in the DR (Aide and Grau, 2004).
Fire	Fire responses are complex. Many countries manage otherwise natural forests to reduce fuel load through prescribed burning, but in the wet tropics selective logging within forests can increase fire spread.	In Indonesia, selectively logged forests suffer more fire damage due the opening of the canopy, which creates a drier climate, with logging debris providing additional dry fuel for fires (MacKinnon et al, 1997).
Drought and desertification	Natural vegetation, control of grazing and trampling pressure and conservation of drought-resistant food plants are key steps in slowing or halting dryland degradation and desert formation.	Local responses to desertification include re-introduction of traditional management approaches, such as the *hima* reserves (Bagader et al, 1994) and protection to ensure continued plant cover (Omar, 1991).
Earthquakes	Although the occurrence of earthquakes is not influenced by ecology, much of the resulting damage comes from landslides and these will be influenced by health of ecosystems, particularly on slopes.	Analysis of thousands of landslides triggered by the 2005 earthquake in Kashmir found that forested slopes suffered less slippage than bare, agricultural and shrub-covered slopes (Kamp et al, 2010).

be recognized as an integral part of disaster risk management' (International Disaster Reduction Conference, 2006)

There are still plenty of questions about exactly when and by how much natural ecosystems can protect us. A few years ago the Center for International Forestry Research (CIFOR) and the UN's Food and Agriculture Organization published a report attacking the notion that forests can prevent major floods (CIFOR and FAO, 2005; soon after publication this was used by a Philippine timber company in a full page newspaper advertisement to justify its logging within a national park). Similarly, there has been a long debate about the usefulness of mangroves and coral reefs in protecting coastal communities after the 2004 Indian Ocean tsunami (Danielsen et al, 2005; Kathiresan and Rajendran, 2005; Dahdouh-Guebas and Koedam, 2006). The consensus seems to be coming around to the idea that natural ecosystems will never be able, on their own, to neutralize very exceptional events, like a once-a-century flood, but that they can play a critically important mitigating role in many, probably most, situations.

Take the city of Malaga for instance, in Andalusia, Spain. City officials explained to us that regular floods were recorded for around 500 years when heavy rains fell into the mountains surrounding the city and were regarded as an unavoidable problem. Many flood defences were built but they all failed in one way or another. Reforesting even quite a small part of the watershed, which was achieved by the municipality either coming to agreements with landowners or purchasing parcels of land, has eliminated the regular flood events. Not only that, the forests have become important tourist destinations, with rich bird life and plant species that could not survive on the dry slopes (Dudley and Aldrich, 2007).

Climate change

All of these services gain a sharp new focus when the added pressures expected under climate change are taken into account: the Intergovernmental Panel on Climate Change (IPCC) predicts additional water stress, food shortages, extreme weather events and the emergence, or at least further spread, of many crop pests and human diseases. In this context, natural ecosystems provide a further additional benefit that was scarcely even recognized until a few years ago (Dudley et al, 2010b). Many of them store and continue to sequester large amounts of carbon, thus slowing and potentially helping to mitigate the release of carbon dioxide (Trumper et al, 2009). These natural carbon stores are characterized by their extreme importance but also their instability: environmental degradation and feedback from existing climate changes threaten to flip many terrestrial and marine ecosystems from being carbon stores to sources of carbon in a few years unless urgent steps are taken to address management problems.

Forests contain the largest terrestrial stock of carbon, and forest loss and degradation is responsible for 17 per cent of global carbon emissions (Nabuurs et al, 2007). Tropical moist forests are the most significant forest type in terms of storage and continue to act as sinks even in their old-growth stage (Baker et al, 2004; Lewis et al, 2009), as do old-growth boreal forests (Luyssaert et al, 2008); however some of the boreal carbon gains are likely to be offset by the increased fire likely in these regions under climate change (Stocks et al, 1998; Bond-Lamberty et al, 2007). Meanwhile temperate forests are in many areas recovering from a long historical retreat and currently expanding, thus sequestering additional carbon (e.g. Janssens et al, 2003).

Other ecosystems are also important carbon stores. Inland wetlands tend to be sinks for carbon and nitrogen but sources for methane and sulphur (Ramsar Secretariat, 2002); peat in particular is an extremely important store. Although only covering about 3 per cent of the land surface, peat is believed to contain the planet's largest store of carbon (Parish et al, 2007): some of this peat-land is also covered with forests, which is why we can have two 'largest' carbon stores. However, ecological degradation, including widespread drying of peat and the impact of forest fires, is currently resulting in rapid loss of some of the carbon formerly stored in peat (Ramsar Scientific and Technical Review Panel and Biodiversity Convention Secretariat, 2007); most scenarios for runaway climate change are based on drying of peat and massive additional release of carbon in the polar and subpolar regions. Marine ecosystems contain huge amounts of carbon, particularly in coastal zones where capture is equivalent to 0.2Gt/year in salt marshes, mangroves and seagrass (Duarte, 2002). Natural grasslands store carbon mainly but not entirely within soils (Schuman et al, 2002). Indeed, some analysts say that soils hold more carbon than the atmosphere and vegetation combined (Lal, 2004), although estimates vary.

The United Nations Environment Programme has noted the critical role that natural ecosystems can play in capturing carbon (Trumper et al, 2009). Funding opportunities emerging from the UN Framework Convention on Climate Change and various voluntary schemes may provide the support to provide natural ecosystems with sufficient economic benefits to withstand demands for alternative uses, but the magnitude and limitations of these schemes is still being worked out as I write. There are high hopes for Reduced Impact from Deforestation and Degradation (REDD) schemes (Bond et al, 2009) with a REDD+ scheme being proposed that would include natural forests and perhaps in time other natural ecosystems, and might also be suitable for protected areas (Dudley, 2010). Ambitious plans have been proposed, for example using REDD to ensure protection of large areas of the Amazon (Ricketts et al, 2010).

Genetic resources

Natural ecosystems also, as we have seen, generally contain many more species than managed ecosystems or at least contain species that will not be found in cultural landscapes. Some ecosystems, particularly tropical moist forests within so-called 'biodiversity hotspots', can contain quite astonishingly high numbers of species and a rich (and in many cases scarcely explored) within-species variation. Medical researchers, crop breeders and other biologists draw on this rich natural cornucopia in developing a vast array of materials: most people have no idea the extent to which we are still drawing on natural genetic capital from what Norman Myers has called 'the primary source' (Myers, 1984). Two fields where wild genetic resources are still indispensable are medical and agricultural research.

Pharmaceuticals

Wild plant and animal products form the basis of many commercially available pharmaceuticals (ten Kate and Laird 1999): over half the synthetic medicines produced today originate from natural precursors; including some well-known drugs such as aspirin, digitalis and quinine (WHO, 2005). At least 89 plant-derived medicines used in the industrial world were originally discovered by studying indigenous medicine (Beattie, 2003), yet the professional medical industry still often looks down on such 'primitive' approaches. Today natural products play a dominant role in the development of drugs for the treatment of human diseases (Newman et al, 2003). Finding new genetic material with potential medicinal properties is now a large and frequently cut-throat business (Juma, 1989). As early as 2000 there were over two hundred corporations and government agencies in the United States studying rainforest plants for their medicinal capacities, with plant-based pharmaceuticals estimated to be earning over US$30 billion per year (Zakrzewski, 2002). Defence of national rights over genetic material was an early stimulus for signing of the Convention on Biological Diversity (CBD). Global sales of pharmaceuticals based on materials of natural origin are worth US$75 billion a year (Kaimowitz, 2005); collection of valuable medicinal plants can often supply a source of income to people without land title or other means of making a living.

Crop breeding

Much material used for crop breeding and improvement also comes from the wild precursors or near-relatives of crops; usually known as crop wild relatives or CWR. Careful screening of CWR can identify genes that help crops resist new climatic conditions, new diseases and other stresses. CWR have helped improve yields or addressed serious diseases in potatoes (potato blight); rice (grassy-stunt virus); maize (corn blight); tomato (increased yield); and wheat (addressing problems of drought, heat, salinity and water-logging). Estimates of the global value of plant genetic resources for food and agriculture vary from hundreds of millions to tens of billions of US dollars per year (Stolton et al, 2008).

In addition to CWR, crop scientists are increasingly recognizing the benefits of some traditional crop varieties – landraces – many of which were abandoned or pushed aside when the 'green revolution' promoted higher yielding varieties reliant on similarly high inputs of fertilizers. Yet the old varieties were often better adapted to local conditions. Losses of over 90 per cent of traditional varieties of some crops have been recorded (Fowler and Mooney, 1990); in a couple of decades the accumulated wisdom of centuries of crop breeding was thrown away on a gamble that modern varieties would be able to fulfill all our requirements. Today the remnant traditional landraces are being sought out and conserved, although many varieties remain at risk of disappearing.

Until recently, crop scientists relied on seed stores in major collections to protect genetic diversity – so-called ex-situ conservation – like the recently opened huge seed store in Svalbard in Norway. While these places are essential they are also limited; they can only contain a certain amount of the available genetic material and are then 'frozen' in time; that is, there is no opportunity for further evolution of the species. Another option is to conserve the varieties *in situ*. This usually conserves far more genetic variation *within* a CWR or variety and also preserves the opportunity for evolution: populations in living ecosystems will naturally evolve over time and this may include characteristics useful to crop breeders, particularly during a period of rapid environmental change. Most crop conservation experts advocate a mix of ex situ and in situ collection; yet many of the world's centres of crop diversity are poorly represented within the protected area network (Stolton et al, 2008).

Cultural, social and spiritual values

Our first two 'human-centred' value types have been strictly utilitarian; descriptions of what ecosystems provide us in terms of services and materials. But we are not, thank goodness, a strictly utilitarian species and things of the spirit matter too, whether or not these are expressed formally in religious and philosophical terms. These issues have already been touched upon in Chapter 3, with respect to the role that faiths have had in shaping our attitudes to naturalness, the dual role that sacred natural sites have in protecting both sacred values and biological values (many faith adherents would castigate me for distinguishing the two) and the importance of concepts like wilderness in shaping modern experiences.

Aesthetic

Ever since the Romantics opened our eyes to the significance of wild nature, there has been a movement explicitly calling for protection of the natural for values that are hard to define in economic terms. (There are plenty of attempts to define the economic value of a view, through contingent valuation studies, house pricing and so on but none are without major limitations.) Most of the earliest national parks were not set up to protect biodiversity. The word was not invented until the 1980s and the concept of protecting entire ecosystems is relatively recent. Instead the momentum behind the establishment of parks was primarily scenic and the reason most people continue to visit these places is aesthetic rather than particular interest in species or ecosystems. The World Heritage Convention has a criterion for listing within the World Heritage list: 'contain superlative natural phenomena or areas of exceptional natural beauty and aesthetic importance'. The large majority of the 180 natural World Heritage sites are considered beautiful or magnificent because of the natural ecosystems they contain, regardless of whatever additional geological, ecosystem or biodiversity values they may contain.

Such values are common in our society and there is convincing evidence that they are important for many physical and psychological reasons, but they are neither universally recognized nor always innate. People isolated from such values can find them frightening or disturbing as the earlier example from Birmingham suggested; conversely those who have grown up experiencing hardship in natural environments sometimes prefer to stay within a more comfortable urban milieu. Schools increasingly recognize that time is needed to learn to appreciate the natural and invest resources to bring children into outdoor environments to teach both life skills and appreciation of the natural world.

Sacredness

Similar naturalness values relate to countless sacred natural sites, straddling both mainstream and minor faiths. Many of the sacred mountains of Asia, for example, are maintained in pristine condition within national parks particularly because of their sacredness. The Tiger's Nest monastery in Bhutan, perhaps the most extraordinary religious building in the world, is built literally hanging on the edge of a cliff hundreds of feet tall and visitors need to creep round to it on a narrow path carved out of the rock. The sacred Mount Halasan, which dominates the island of Jeju south of the Korean peninsula, attracts tens of thousands of visitors every year, being of importance to both Buddhists and followers of the island's local animist traditions. But naturalness is valued in sacred sites even in less remote places. Within the city boundary of Seoul there is Mount Baekundae contained in Bukhansan National Park, which attracts an awe-inspiring ten million visitors a year, yet still manages to maintain natural vegetation; it is estimated that at least 10 per cent of visitors also stop off at various temples built on the route to the summit. Visiting these places is a strange experience for someone not used to the tradition of pilgrimage; a mixture of noise and confusion but also deep reverence in the main sites of worship. A similar juxtaposition of natural and sacred can be found in countless other sites. Even around my home in Wales there are sacred wells lost in the hills and I sometimes find Buddhist prayer flags tied to cairns at the top of mountains in the Snowdonia National Park.

Resilience

The values described above derive from natural ecosystems but they are not tied to naturalness as such; many can be replaced by human constructions like purification plants and avalanche fences or by semi-natural habitats. In some cases an artificial ecosystem will do as well as a natural ecosystem; a plantation of exotic conifers probably provides not dissimilar protection against landslides to a natural forest. It can be argued that natural ecosystems usually provide a wider range of products than the simplified managed systems that replace them, and often at a lesser cost, but the individual components are seldom unique.

However, a new ecosystem function more directly related to naturalness has recently come to prominence in the face of accumulating evidence of climate change: a growing number of conservation biologists identify strong links between biological diversity and biological productivity and claim that both are directly linked to ecosystem *resilience*.

Links between biological diversity and resilience have been noted by several researchers (e.g. Peterson et al, 1998; Carpenter et al, 2006) who also propose a connection between biodiversity and provision of ecosystem services: in other words more diverse ecosystems are more likely to maintain their functions (biological, chemical and physical) in the face of disturbance, including from climate change. The CBD commissioned a detailed review of resilience in forest ecosystems (Thompson et al, 2009) in recognition of this important new aspect of biodiversity. Resilience comes in a number of forms. Ecologists distinguish between *engineering resilience*, the ability of an ecosystem to return to its pre-disturbance state and *ecological resilience*, also known as *equilibrium dynamics*, the ability of an ecosystem to absorb impacts, change and adapt to maintain itself below a threshold where the system changes into a different state altogether (Walker et al, 2004). The first refers to the ability of an ecosystem to return to pretty much the same state as it was before disturbance, which as we have seen is unlikely in many cases today, while the second reflects a more rough and ready form of recovery, perhaps not exactly the same but pretty much functioning in the same way. It also recognizes that ecosystems may exist in more than one stable state (Schroder et al, 2005), suggesting that there is no simple 'right' and 'wrong' in terms of future development. From the perspective of authenticity, ecological resilience is more significant. The importance of both inter- and intra-species variation has been noted in these situations (Schaberg et al, 2008).

Connections have also been proposed between high biodiversity and high ecosystem productivity, with a suite of competing hypotheses to explain this: the *rivet hypothesis, keystone hypothesis, niche complementarity hypothesis* and *sampling effect hypothesis* for instance. This is still speculative but a meta-analysis of studies in forest ecosystems in 2009 found three quarters of research projects suggest increased productivity with higher biodiversity while the remainder are neutral (Thompson et al, 2009). In a further link in this complex interrelationship it is suggested that more productive ecosystems are also more resilient (Stone et al, 1996). There is also recognition that ecosystems with high carbon frequently have high biodiversity (Kapos et al, 2008). A climate-resilient ecosystem would be more likely to retain its functions and ecosystem services in the face of climate change.

To make things even more complicated, an increasing number of researchers are drawing links between human cultural diversity and biological diversity (Pretty et al, 2009). Loh and Harmon (2005) talk of biocultural diversity as total richness in natural and cultural systems and attempted a first global assessment, finding the highest levels of biocultural diversity in the Amazon, Central Africa and Indo-Malaysia-Melanesia. Cultural and biological diversity are also linked to linguistic diversity (Maffi, 2005) and a database of linguistic diversity shows a decline even steeper than that of biodiversity (Harmon and Loh, 2010). There is now a growing movement focusing on protection of biocultural diversity (Maffi and Woodley, 2010). Associations between natural and cultural diversity are not confined to the tropics and are sometimes apparently counter-intuitive. Bird species richness increases as human population increases in Britain, except at the highest human population densities (Evans et al, 2007). There are numerous examples of species diversity persisting (or even increasing) in managed landscapes: two examples among many are small mammals in Canadian spruce-fir forests (Sullivan et al, 1999) and endemic plants in Bolivian montane forests (Kessler, 2000).

There are two schools of thought on the subject of how to manage ecosystems adaptively to maintain ecosystem resilience. One proposes that greater species richness within ecosystems increases ecosystem resilience by increasing the interdependencies and robustness of the system (the so called stability–diversity hypothesis) and thus the emphasis should be on maintaining the full diversity. A second school argues that it is not species richness as such but functional diversity that plays the pivotal role: this argues in effect that managers should manage ecosystems for their functions. Species that maintain key biological functions (such as seed dispersers, pollinators, top predators etc.) should be the primary target of management interventions, with less attention placed on 'passenger species' whose presence or absence do not make a significant difference to the way that the ecosystem functions. As George Orwell (almost) wrote in a different context: 'All species are equal but some are more equal than others.'

While the emphasis on function makes sense, and incidentally fits well with our definition of authenticity, it may be difficult to put into practice in part because judging which species are or are not important will become increasingly difficult as conditions change. Some species with a narrow ecological niche, which we might expect to be particularly vulnerable to climate change, may be far more resilient than expected and grow in importance within the ecosystem if conditions change in their favour (Thompson et al, 2009). Making judgements about management approaches will depend on conditions and opportunities on a case-by-case basis. However, the emerging discipline of studies on ecological resilience looks likely to make some major changes to aspects of ecosystem management in the future.

Calculating the value of an ecosystem

We may know that natural ecosystems provide us with valuable goods and services but many politicians and policy-makers will only take the issue seriously if we express these values in terms of number of dollars. Unfortunately, calculating the value of a forest or a watershed remains challenging even if a single good is under consideration, while attempts to work out the total benefits from something like a tropical forest ecosystem are extremely complex. Once calculated, they also need to be offset against the potential benefits from replacement uses, such as conversion to cattle ranching or oil palm production. It is difficult to make generalizations; when the World Bank carried out an overview of water and NTFP benefits from tropical forests they found a lot of variation from place to place (Chomitz and Kumari, 1998) so that a compelling study from one forest will not necessarily transfer to another. Lastly, values need to be linked to particular people: a value that accrues entirely outside an ecosystem (like watershed values) may provide little incentive to the people who have control over that ecosystem unless some way of paying them can be agreed.

Total economic valuations are the most useful; these are costly and open to challenge but those that have been completed provide valuable ammunition for people arguing for ecosystem protection. Studies in Cambodia, for example, suggest that the coastal Ream National Park provides subsistence and income worth US$1.2 billion a year (Emerton, 2005). Cambodia's freshwater capture fisheries equal 400,000 tonnes a year and contribute an estimated 16 per cent of national GDP; over 1.2 million people rely on fish from Tonle Sap Lake alone (van Zalinge, 2003). In Laos, 81 village communities depend on the Nam Et National Biodiversity Conservation Area for NTFPs with a value estimated at US$1.88 million/year. Of this amount about 30 per cent is cash income and the remainder is for subsistence. In 2003, the sale of NTFPs accounted for 41–76 per cent of average family income in the Nakai district (ICEM, 2003). In Cape Province, South Africa, estimates of costs and benefits for marine protected areas found benefits outweighing costs (Turpie et al, 2006).

Even if accurate data on economic value are available, there is also the critical question of who gains. It may be reasonably easy to show that the total values of a standing tropical rainforest exceed those of the timber gained by felling trees (e.g. Ruitenbeek, 1990) but most of these values will be diffuse – that is they will accrue to many different people near and far, the majority of whom will not even necessarily recognize the benefits as coming from the forest. This may be little compensation to the owner of the forest, who would get more money from selling the timber. Working out how to ensure that those responsible for maintaining ecosystem services receive adequate compensation is proving to be a major stumbling block. Although economics is not our primary business here, the following brief digression looks at how economists have gone about working out such values.

Valuation studies

There are two views about valuation studies: one that understanding the economic benefits from biodiversity and ecosystem services is an important step in ensuring their conservation and the other that it is irrelevant or even dangerous, in that whatever the opinions of fiscal conservatives, decisions are seldom taken exclusively for economic reasons. Some opponents go further and argue that it is immoral to attempt to put a price on something like the survival of a species or an ecosystem. Whatever the ethical case, in reality questions are asked about economic value as soon as ecosystem services (ESS) are integrated into the planning of national or local governments, or when industry is asked to pay for particular ESS.

The TEEB process was set up both to promote understanding of these values and also to provide information on likely economic benefits and how these might be realized to a range of stakeholders (e.g. TEEB, 2009). I was involved in a couple of the TEEB reports and had the chance to look at how they were developed (Kettunen et al, 2011, Berghöfer and Dudley, 2011, see Box 5.1 below). Other processes, such as IUCN's long-term involvement in assessment of economic values of ecosystems, add valuable data and case studies. But there are still a plethora of different valuation options available; some of these are outlined in Table 5.2. Many suffer from the problem that they are theoretical: it is fine to work out the value of an ecosystem like a piece of wetland or a coral reef using damage cost limitation, net factor income or contingent valuation but the figure that emerges from the calculations doesn't mean much unless someone is prepared to stump up the money.

Our ability to make these calculations is likely to change, in part driven by the zeitgeist created around the TEEB process. The IUCN World Commission on Protected Areas has a task force looking specifically at valuation methods for protected areas. There are a plethora of methodologies being tried and

TABLE 5.2 Options available for valuing ecosystem services

Valuation method	Example	Limitation
Market price	Timber and non-timber forest products, fish, water	Can be distorted, e.g. by subsidies and tax breaks. Not all ecosystem services are traded on markets
Replacement cost	Coastal protection by mangroves, water filtration by forests and wetlands	Overestimates value if society is not prepared to pay for human-made replacement; conversely under-estimates value if human-made replacement does not provide all the benefits (e.g. biodiversity benefits)
Damage cost avoided	Landslide/avalanche protec-tion, carbon storage in peat	Difficult to relate damage levels to ecosystem services
Net factor income – revenue from sales of ESS minus cost of other inputs	Filtration of water by wetlands, commercial fish-eries supported by protected nursery areas	Tends to overestimate ecosystem values
Production func-tion – value of ESS as input in production of marketed goods	Commercial fisheries supported by protected nursery areas, materials collected from the wild and used in handicraft making	Technically difficult to calculate
Hedonic pricing – influence of environ-mental characteristics on price of goods	Air quality, scenic beauty, cultural benefits	Technically difficult for some ESS unless part of a recognized certifi-cation scheme
Travel cost	Any site used for recrea-tional purposes, e.g. national park	Hard to use when trips are to multiple destinations
Contingent valuation – asking people what they would pay for a particular service	Protection of endangered species, protected areas, clean water, pure air	Expensive to implement and diffi-cult to ensure accuracy – people do not do what they say
Choice modelling – ranking willingness to pay for various ESS	Protection of endangered species, protected areas, clean water, pure air	Expensive to implement, techni-cally difficult but probably more accurate than contingent valuation
Value transfer – using values estimated at other locations	Any ESS that has compar-ison studies	Can be inaccurate as characteristics can vary even when the contexts appear to be similar

Source: Adapted from Pabon-Zamora et al, 2008

tested for carbon values created by the spurt of interest in carbon storage. A new Alliance for Water Stewardship looks set to bring water values into sharper focus. There are likely to be more and more robust tools available for valuation over the coming decade.

BOX 5.1 TEEB

TEEB (The Economics of Ecosystems and Biodiversity) is a multi-institution research project set up to raise awareness of the economic value of ecosystems and biodiversity. TEEB is has produced several reports and books aimed at:

- scientists (Report D0, book published as TEEB, 2010);
- national/international policy makers (Report D1, book published as TEEB, 2011a);
- local government (Report D2, book TEEB, 2011b);
- business (Report D3, book TEEB, 2011c);
- citizens (Report D4);
- climate change issues (supplementary).

Key messages

TEEB has an impressive number of messages in these reports and books, plus numerous papers and presentations. Nonetheless, some clear themes emerge.

- **Undervaluing of natural capital is leading to its loss.** Values of 'natural capital' – ecosystems, biodiversity and natural resources – are seldom fully taken into account in markets or in day-to-day decisions by governments, business or citizens. The economic invisibility of nature's flows into the economy is an important reason why ecosystems are degrading and biodiversity is being lost.
- **Good biodiversity and ecosystem management is good business.** There are sound economic reasons to integrate biodiversity and ecosystem services into different sectors. The TEEB reports make recommendations to policy makers, business and local government.
- **Some critical steps are needed to avoid loss of natural capital.** TEEB highlighted four key conservation priorities needed immediately:

  1 Halt deforestation and forest degradation
  2 Protect tropical coral reefs
  3 Save and restore global fisheries
  4 Recognize links between ecosystem degradation and rural poverty.

TEEB also produced a special supplement outlining critical threats and opportunities relating to climate change.

- **A mixture of market, policy and regulatory responses are needed.** TEEB identified five responses in particular:

  1 Increase use of market mechanisms, like Payments for Ecosystem Services (PES), REDD and other carbon market schemes, and certification
  2 Remove perverse subsidies that encourage unsustainable use of natural capital
  3 Strengthen regulation and pricing policies to encourage sustainable use
  4 Invest in ecological infrastructure, particularly restoration (mangroves, forests on steep slopes etc.)
  5 Expand protected areas as critical tools for ecosystem and biodiversity management.

- **Valuation tools are needed:** Despite interest in natural capital, we are still lacking many of the basic tools needed to measure the values of biodiversity and ecosystem services. Filling these gaps is an urgent priority.

Fortunately, as in the example given in the introduction to this chapter, economists and businesspeople are starting to investigate the options for producing economic benefits from natural ecosystems such as Payment for Ecosystem Services schemes (Pagiola et al, 2002) and much useful work has already been done, particularly in Latin America.

Many sectors of society are waking up to the values of natural ecosystems. It remains to be seen whether or not these people have enough power and influence to maintain such ecosystems against the pressures for unsustainable exploitation.

CHAPTER 6

Global Attempts to Assess Naturalness

Key messages

- *There have been a handful of attempts to assess global naturalness, with estimates that range from 17 to 52 per cent of land surface in a 'natural' state.*
- *The differences illustrate among other things a lack of clarity in understanding what we mean by naturalness.*
- *A number of biome and regional studies help build a picture of the state of the world's ecosystems, but there are still large gaps in our understanding of the amount of near-natural ecosystems remaining.*

Many years ago I took the night flight from Helsinki to Tokyo, the flight path taking us along northern Russia, with clear skies, a full moon and deep snow on the ground. I didn't shut my eyes: over the course of a long night I saw a couple of ice-bound ports; some unidentifiable groups of buildings with a few lights twinkling and hour after hour of nothing but forest and tundra. I've since taken a few more long flights over Russia and Canada and it is easy to start thinking that the world is a very empty place. But the boreal forests of the polar regions are almost unique among ecosystems that contain more than ice or rock in the extent to which they have so far been left alone, protected by bitter cold in winter and millions of biting flies in summer. Even these tough places have long-settled indigenous peoples groups and nowadays also mineral exploitation and logging creeping over hitherto untouched areas. The lines cut for seismic surveys in northern Canada create a series of scars running across a landscape that is otherwise virtually empty of humans.

Three decades of conservation work have given me the privilege of travelling to many of the world's wild places: I have for instance been to two thirds of the major 'wilderness areas' identified by Conservation International (CI) (see below). And in most I have been pretty deep too: working in protected areas that are chosen because of their naturalness. But I seldom see places

FIGURE 6.1 Lines cut for seismic testing are the only indication of human interference over huge areas of northern Canada

that are truly uninfluenced by humans, at least where there is enough water and vegetation to stay alive. I mentioned northern Canada and other boreal countries, particularly anywhere high. Mountain tops are often untouched for practical reasons or because they are considered sacred and there are empty areas high in all the continents. I've talked to people who have been deep into Congo basin forests where even the pygmy people do not go, but the only forests I have walked in there show strong evidence of human presence and this is now probably the majority. Human traces appear in the oddest places. I was once days from anywhere in the Swedish Arctic on my own (I thought) and saw a new footprint in a patch of snow in front of me; presumably a Sámi was sitting nearby chuckling away at my inability to see them.

But although fully natural ecosystems no longer exist, many *near-natural* ecosystems are still very much with us and continue to have a high importance for a wide variety of cultural, economic, spiritual and ethical reasons. How much near natural ecosystem do we have left? There have been surprisingly few attempts to find out: four global studies, mainly by non-governmental organizations (NGOs), plus a few local or biome specific projects also predominantly driven by NGOs or independent research bodies. Academics and international organizations such as United Nations Environment Programme (UNEP) have generally not yet tried to develop global statistics about naturalness.

FIGURE 6.2 Large areas of boreal and sub-boreal Russian taiga have such a low human population and lack of industrial activity that they are among the areas that might most closely be described as 'untouched' by humans

Global assessments

The four global assessments completed to date come up with figures ranging from 17 to 52 per cent of land cover natural or undisturbed; I have been unable to find any attempt to look at extent of natural ecosystems in the ocean in anything but the broadest terms (e.g. Halpern et al, 2008). All four studies used different methods, different criteria and different thresholds, making comparisons difficult. The natural areas they identified did not by any means entirely overlap. Although they show increased sophistication of approach over time, the results do not demonstrate any particular trend and it would be fair to say that we still do not have a detailed understanding of naturalness at a global scale.

The first is over 20 years old. McCloskey and Spalding (1989), working for the Sierra Club and reporting at the fourth World Wilderness Congress, used jet navigation charts to identify areas of 400,000km² or more of 'undeveloped land still primarily shaped by the forces of nature'. They concluded that about a third of the world qualified in this very broad classification of naturalness. However, 41 per cent of this was in the Arctic or Antarctic. According to their criteria, most settled continents have between a quarter and a third of their land surface as wilderness; Europe is an exception with most of the land surface settled and transformed.

Lee Hannah and colleagues at CI (1994) next created a geographic informa-tion system (GIS) analysis based on human disturbance, dividing the world's terrestrial area into three main classes: (1) *human dominated*, (2) *partly disturbed* and (3) *undisturbed*; the latter defined as having a human population of less than ten people per km^2. Advances over the previous study included improved mapping resolution, expanded categorization systems and an ecologically based definition of habitat. They found 52 per cent of the land 'undisturbed', of which roughly half was rock, ice and desert. Three quarters of the habitable land area had been disturbed. This analysis suffered from the weakness that some land areas with low population levels have nonetheless been extensively modified, such as many large livestock grazing and transhumance areas, but it marked a major step forward by setting up measurable classes of likely disturbance.

Over at the International Programmes Section of the Wildlife Conservation Society, then operating out of a series of portable cabins in the grounds of the Bronx Zoo, New York, Eric Sanderson and colleagues also started looking at the amount of natural habitat left on the world's land surface through development of a *human influence index* drawing on information relating to population density, degree of land transformation, human access points and electricity power infrastructure. The human footprint expresses as a percentage the relative human influence in every biome on the land's surface. This more sophisticated analysis dropped the amount of land classed as 'wild' to just 17 per cent, or 27 per cent if Antarctica were included. The authors concluded that 'the global extent of the human footprint suggests that humans are stewards of nature, whether we like it or not' (Sanderson et al, 2002, p902).

Finally, once again at CI, Russ Mittermeier and an associated research team (2003) created a *wilderness index* based on three factors: human popula-tion density of less than five people per km^2; an area threshold of a million hectares; and a habitat intactness threshold of 70 per cent. Using these, CI measured remaining wilderness as 46 per cent including the Sahara and Antarctica. If the population threshold was reduced to less than one person per km^2, the total wilderness dropped to 38 per cent. The analysis drew on the broad philosophy of the earlier CI study by using population density as a critical indicator but added additional parameters.

CI has probably done more than any other institution to look critically at naturalness as an indicator around the world. Using the analysis summarized above, CI identified 24 major wilderness sites. Nineteen of these had popula-tion densities of less than one person per km^2. Table 6.1 below outlines CI's wilderness areas. (Other analyses from CI have subdivided some of the wilder-ness areas, increasing the number but not affecting the overall areas involved.)

All these studies, while useful in providing an indication of low popula-tion areas likely to be natural, should be treated with caution as a measure of the broader classifications above; the fact that there are not many people present, and not much modern infrastructure, does not guarantee that areas are untouched. In the CI list above, for instance, the Australian desert has

TABLE 6.1 Conservation International wilderness areas

Biome and wilderness	Area in km²	Intact %
Tropical humid forest		
• Amazonia	6,638,926	80
• Congo Basin	1,725,221	70
• New Guinea	828,818	70
Tropical dry forests and grasslands		
• Chaco	996,600	70
• Miombo-Mopane	1,176,000	90
• Australian savannahs	585,239	100
Mixed mountain temperate rainforest and needle-leaf forest		
• Rocky Mountains	570,500	70
• Pacific Northwest	315,000	80
• Magellanic forests	147,200	100
• Tasmanian World Heritage Wilderness Area	13,836	90
• Boreal forests	16,179,500	80
Wetlands		
• Llanos	451,474	80
• Pantanal	210,000	80
• Banados del Este	38,500	80
• Sundarbans	10,000	80
Warm and cold-winter deserts		
• North American deserts	1,416,134	80
• Patagonia	550,400	70
• Sahara	7,780,544	90
• Kalahari-Namib	714,700	80
• Arabian deserts	3,250,000	90
• Central Asian deserts	5,943,000	80
• Australian deserts	3,572,209	90
Tundra		
• Arctic tundra	8,850,000	90
• Antarctica	13,900,000	100
Total	**75,863,801**	**83**

Source: Mittermeier et al, 2003

been extensively influenced by introduced species such as the camel and in eastern and southern Africa the miombo woodlands includes major areas of cultural management. The Chihuahuan desert, one of the North American deserts, has undergone major transformations according to a biological assessment – 'virtually the entire ecoregion has been heavily grazed' – while rivers have been altered by groundwater extraction and keystone species like the Mexican wolf and grizzly bear have been extirpated (Dinerstein et al, 2000). Similar changes have taken place in many other 'wilderness areas'. The immense biological richness remaining in such areas should not be underestimated but naturalness is already severely impacted in many cases.

Conversely, by focusing only on large areas the four studies necessarily omitted many smaller natural habitat fragments, some of which are highly significant from an ecological perspective. But what the combination of these research projects does tell us is that up to half the world's land surface is still *relatively* untouched; that depending on how high we set the bar in terms of intactness will make a big difference to the precise total; and that not all of this is just rock and ice, with large forest and wetland areas still surviving in a more-or-less natural state into the 21st century.

Another global assessment should be mentioned, although it started from a slightly different perspective. Jon Hoekstra and colleagues at The Nature Conservancy and WWF (2005) looked at habitat loss and degree of protection for 13 terrestrial biomes and again for their 810 constituent ecoregions (for technical reasons Antarctica and mangroves were excluded). They found habitat losses ranging from 48.5 per cent for tropical/subtropical dry broadleaf forests to 0.4 per cent for tundra. This necessarily looks at broad habitat occurrence rather than quality, but provides a snapshot of how much of various habitats remained for us even to worry about their level of naturalness at the turn of the century. Habitat conversion for the 13 biomes is summarized in Table 6.2 below.

TABLE 6.2 Percentage of habitat converted in major biomes

Biome	Percentage converted
Temperate grasslands, savannahs and shrublands	45.8
Mediterranean forests, woodlands and scrub	41.4
Tropical/subtropical dry broadleaf forests	48.5
Temperate broadleaf and mixed forests	46.6
Tropical/subtropical coniferous forests	27.3
Tropical/subtropical moist broadleaf forests	32.2
Tropical/subtropical grasslands, savannahs and shrublands	23.6
Flooded grasslands and savannahs	26.6
Deserts and xeric grasslands	6.8
Montane grasslands and shrublands	12.7
Temperate conifer forest	12.6
Boreal forests and taiga	2.4
Tundra	0.4

Source: Hoekstra et al, 2005

We need more detailed studies. The World Resources Institute (WRI) published an important series of biome assessments in 2000 (see Box 6.1) but these only provide very partial information. Scattered facts and statistics are available in some ecoregional plans or protected area gap analyses and anyone prepared to work through the several hundred regional studies available might at least be able to tell where the biggest gaps in information remain. These will be considerable. Even in well-studied areas such as North America many data are lacking; for instance the 2004 ecoregional assessment of the Northern Great Plains was unable even to identify the proportion of prairie that remained under native species (Forrest et al, 2004). Research has understandably tended to focus on presence of key species like birds and mammals, where information is more likely to be available, but this doesn't necessarily tell us much about overall naturalness of the ecosystem.

BOX 6.1 The PAGE analysis

To coincide with the Occidental Millennium, the Washington-based World Resources Institute, an independent research institution, carried out a Pilot Analysis of Global Ecosystems (PAGE), which looked at the global status of five key ecosystems, focusing on freshwaters, coastal areas, grasslands, forests and agro-ecosystems. Although the studies did not primarily consider naturalness, analysis of the PAGE assessments findings throws up some interesting statistics, albeit necessarily at a very general level:

- **Coastal:** status of land within 100km of the coast was considered for 19 global coastal ecosystems; of these only five had more than 50 per cent of their coastal areas dominated by crops, crop and natural habitat mosaic and cities: these were the NE Atlantic, Black Sea, Mediterranean, South Asia and SW Atlantic (Burke et al, 2000).
- **Freshwater:** some 60 per cent of the 227 largest rivers are strongly or moderately fragmented by dams, diversions and canals, but these include most of the largest rivers, with 90 per cent of the total water from the 227 rivers flowing through altered river systems (Revenga et al, 2000).
- **Grasslands:** grassland area shrunk dramatically during the 20th century and 40 per cent of remaining grasslands are lightly to moderately degraded, while 5 per cent are heavily degraded (White et al, 2000); this statistic refers mainly to erosion and risks of desertification, with much less reported on ecological status of the grasslands.
- **Forests:** less than half of the remaining forest exists in its natural state, due particularly to clearance and regrowth in the United States, active management in Europe and shifting cultivation in tropical and subtropical forests. Frontier forests, defined as highly natural forests, cover 40 per cent mainly in the far north in Canada, Alaska and Russia and in Latin America from the Amazon to the Guyana Shield (Matthews et al, 2000).
- **Agro-ecosystems:** although the study looked briefly at natural ecosystems in agricultural areas, no statistics were produced (Wood et al, 2000).

Biome specific assessments

The practical challenges of trying to measure naturalness across the entire planet have doubtless deterred many potential researchers. There is a richer, albeit patchy, collection of research projects focusing on naturalness of specific biomes. As in the case of definitions of naturalness, discussed in Chapter 4, forests have received the lion's share of attention in terms of both regional and global surveys, spurred on by fears of rapid deforestation and latterly also concern about decline in forest quality. There has been some consideration of grasslands and freshwater wetlands and very little for ocean ecosystems.

Naturalness in forests

The concept of forest quality has bothered me for years; my attempts to get my head around what defines a natural forest is a major stimulus for writing this book (Dudley et al, 2006). But I haven't been alone in worrying about these things: over the previous two decades there has been a concentrated effort to understand exactly how much and what kinds of forests are left around the world, an ambitious and continuing series of projects involving governments, intergovernmental agencies, academic institutions and NGOs. Two UN agencies, the Food and Agriculture Organisation (FAO) and the Economic Commission for Europe (UNECE) have played a critical role by assembling periodic Forest Resource Assessments, which have gradually extended their focus to values beyond timber supply. But regional initiatives have also been important, particularly the Ministerial Conference for the Protection of Forests in Europe and the Montréal Process, as has Global Forest Watch, an initiative of the World Resources Institute, which has both defined and mapped natural forest areas in many parts of the world (see Box 6.2). Some individual governments have also taken the initiative to consider issues of forest quality and area of natural forest, such as Austria (Grabherr et al, 1998).

Much of this work has taken place in the rich countries of Europe and North America. While the focus of concern in the tropics remains deforestation, in the temperate regions forests are recovering from a historical low (Dudley, 1992) and the concern has switched more towards what type of forests are left; there are also greater resources available to make the investments needed to provide such overviews.

In the year of the millennium, the UNECE published a landmark volume in its periodic Temperate and Boreal Forest Resource Assessment (TBFRA) (UNECE, 2000). These reports, which mirror the ones that FAO publishes on tropical forests, focus on Europe, North America, the Commonwealth of Independent States, Japan, Australia and New Zealand. They remain the best global picture we have of the bulk of the temperate and boreal forest estate. Traditionally the UNECE study focused on trade issues but gradually widened its remit and in 2000, for the first time, national correspondents were asked for information on the area of 'forests unmodified by man', which the UN defined fairly precisely:

> *Forest/other wooded land that shows natural forest dynamics, such as natural tree composition, occurrence of dead wood, natural age structure and natural regeneration processes, the area of which is large enough to maintain its natural characteristics and where there has been no known significant human intervention or where the last significant human intervention was long enough ago to have allowed the natural species composition and processes to have become re-established.* (UNECE, 2000)

According to the responses received, 55 per cent of temperate and boreal forests in the countries examined fell into the 'natural' class: much higher than expected. However, this global average is enormously distorted by the presence of huge, unmanaged forest estates in Canada and the Russian Federation; these made up the bulk of the natural forest with another 7 per cent of the total divided between the United States and Australia. In Europe, by contrast, virtually all forests are secondary and are either currently or recently managed. In the whole of Europe, almost nine million hectares fell into the natural category, with the large majority of this falling in Scandinavia and European Russia. Sweden, defined 16 per cent of its forests as natural in the year 2000, Finland almost 6 per cent and Norway 2 per cent. In central and western Europe, most countries either reported zero natural forests or a total that was less than 1 per cent of the forest estate as a whole. A few countries in the far east of the continent reported high percentages of natural forests, such as Armenia, but these small nations made little difference to the global average.

All these data must be treated with caution. While some countries have carried out careful studies of forest naturalness, these are in the minority and we can assume that some correspondents had to make judgements using poor information, or put down zero simply because no one had bothered to look. A few countries, particularly in the far east of Europe, put down surprisingly high figures and this may reflect lack of understanding about what was being asked. In other cases results have been disputed. For example the correspondent for France estimated that there were 30,000 hectares falling into the natural category, less than 0.2 per cent of the total forest estate, which is itself a fraction of original forest cover. Independent analysis has challenged even this tiny fraction and proposed 30,000 hectares as a maximum with 10,000 hectares as a more probable figure; in addition less than 20 per cent of these ancient forests were found to be in protected areas (Vallauri and Poncet, 2002).

The global total is inaccurate. Russia and Canada, which together dominate the statistics, both admitted that their figures were highly approximate; since the TBFRA study the WRI carried out 'frontier forest' studies for both countries (Aksenov et al, 2002; latest version of Canadian study Lee et al,

TABLE 6.3 Statistics for natural forests in temperate countries from the 2000 TBFRA

Country	Percentage of forests	Country	Percentage of forests
Europe		Slovenia	4.5
Albania	8.2	Spain	0.0
Austria	0.9	Sweden	16.1
Belgium	0.0	Switzerland	0.6
Bosnia and Herzegovina	0.0	The FYR of Macedonia	0.0
Bulgaria	7.1	Turkey	1.9
Croatia	0.1	United Kingdom	0.0
Cyprus	0.0	Yugoslavia	0.1
Czech Republic	0.0		
Denmark	0.1	**Commonwealth of Independent States**	
Estonia	0.1	Armenia	85.0
Finland	5.8	Azerbaijan	42.8
France	0.2	Belarus	0.6
Germany	0.0	Georgia	18.4
Greece	N/a	Kazakhstan	0.0
Hungary	0.0	Kyrgyzstan	13.7
Iceland	0.0	Republic of Moldova	0.0
Ireland	0.2	Russian Federation	91.8
Israel	0.0	Tajikistan	5.3
Italy	0.1	Turkmenistan	0.0
Latvia	0.1	Ukraine	0.6
Liechtenstein	21.7	Uzbekistan	10.5
Lithuania	0.6		
Luxembourg	0.0	**North America**	
Malta	0.0	Canada	50.7
Netherlands	0.0	United States of America	8.8
Norway	2.9		
Poland	1.6	**Other TBFRA countries**	
Portugal	1.6	Australia	12
Romania	3.7	Japan	12.7
Slovakia	1.0	New Zealand	20.1

2006), which recalculated the figures, increasing the percentage of untouched forests in Canada but slashing estimates for natural forest in Russia. If these figures are used instead, total global coverage for TBFRA countries is closer to 40 per cent natural forests remaining (Dudley and Stolton, 2003a). Since the UNECE study, the Ministerial Conference for the Protection of Forests in Europe (now known as Forest Europe) carried out its own analysis and concluded that some 26 per cent of the forest in the continent is essentially uninfluenced by humans, mainly in the north and east; if Russia is excluded only 5 per cent is uninfluenced (as compared with 8 per cent plantations) (MCPFE, 2007).

The figures for southern and western Europe are sobering in terms of the survival of whole ecosystems. If we are to consider naturalness to include large-scale and long-term dynamics the statistics are even starker. In practice, the presence of large protected areas in the Republic of Komi in European Russia provides our only real source of information on naturally functioning forest ecosystems in the continent.

Data for other temperate countries are even patchier. Temperate forest in Uruguay, never extensive, has been reduced to a few fragments (Carrere, 2001). In South Korea, 0.4 per cent of vegetation is believed to be in a natural state (Choi, 2007), and so on. In the tropics, the only comprehensive data comes from occasional country-level studies and from the efforts of Global Forest Watch (see Box 6.2).

BOX 6.2 Global Forest Watch

In the late 1990s, the WRI set up a unique project – Global Forest Watch or GFW – to monitor the status of the world's forests. GFW was based, at least initially, around the idea of *frontier forests* (see Chapter 4), which for our purposes are effectively natural forests. The first report, published in 1997 (Bryant et al) found that 40 per cent of forest qualified as frontier forest. Almost half the Earth's original forest cover had gone, much of it destroyed within the previous three decades, leaving a fifth of the original forest cover as large, relatively undisturbed tracts. Almost 70 per cent of this was in three countries: Canada, Russia and Brazil; conversely WRI found 76 countries that had lost all their frontier forests. Half of the remaining frontier forest was boreal and most of the rest tropical: only 3 per cent was entirely temperate. More than a third of the remaining forest was threatened by logging, agricultural clearing and other human activity.

Over the following eight years, a string of reports, maps and atlases provided far more detailed data on the extent and location of natural forests than had been available hitherto. While not attempting to cover the whole world, GFW provided a picture of some of the richest and most threatened forests in the world. (Note that given the difficulty in collecting data, and to some extent due to different end-uses of various reports, not all the statistics below use the same criteria: that is, they are not directly comparable.)

In **North America**, less than half (42 per cent) of the region's forests are in low access tracts greater than 200km², with over 90 per cent of this being in Canada and Alaska. Only 6 per cent of forests in the lower 48 states of the United States are large, low access forests (Noguerón et al, 2002). **Alaska** had 67 million ha of intact forest in 2006, with 59 million ha in the boreal region and 7.5 million ha in coastal temperate rainforest, along with about 28,000 undisturbed islands (Strittholt et al, 2006). Over half **Canada's** forest area (and a third of the whole country) exists in intact landscapes; of this forest land roughly a third is naturally treeless. Intact landscapes are commonest in the north and at higher elevations in the west (Lee et al, 2006).

Approximately 289 million hectares (26 per cent of the forest zone) remained at the millennium as large, intact forest landscapes in **Russia**, mostly in Eastern Siberia, the Russian Far East and Western Siberia (Aksenov et al, 2002). Undisturbed forest landscapes with an area of at least 50,000ha made up around 14 per cent (31.7 million hectares) of the total forest in **European Russia** at that time, including the Ural Mountains, with the vast majority of this confined to the most remote areas of the north (Yaroshenko et al, 2001). A study in **Primorsky Kray** in the Russian Far East found 2.94 million hectares of High Conservation Value Forest, some 17.8 per cent of the region's forest cover (Aksenov et al, 2006).

Although GFW has never assessed the whole of the Amazon region, a 2002 study in **Brazil** found 47 per cent of the Brazilian Amazon was under some form of pressure, although this included both current pressure from logging or agriculture and potential pressure from existence of mining exploration leases (Barreto et al, 2006). Further north in **Venezuela**, around half the country remains forested although data were admitted to be out of date (Bevilacqua et al, 2002). In **Chile** less than 45 per cent of forest remains as mature, native forest. About 34 per cent qualifies as frontier forests – tracts of at least 5000 hectares: many of these remain on steep slopes or at high altitudes. Smaller fragments of native forest are often last habitats for particular species (Neira et al, 2002).

Research in **Central Africa** was inconclusive: in 2002 two thirds of forests were still in tracts of at least $10,000km^2$ with no public roads, but the analysis did not include logging roads; around half that area was in unaccessed $10,000km^2$ tracts and only around a third of the remaining forest has yet to be allocated to logging (Minnemeyer et al, 2002): the extent of unaccessed forest has likely decreased since. Data for **Cameroon** were out of date but by 2000 over 80 per cent of forest outside protected areas had been allocated to logging (Bikié et al, 2000). Over half **Gabon's** forests had been allocated for logging by that date (Collomb et al, 2000) in a rapidly accelerating process that has continued.

GFW has been less active in Asia; a report on **Indonesia** focused mainly on forest extent and found in 2002 (Matthews, 2002) some 98 million hectares remaining, although undergoing rapid loss; roughly half that area had been fragmented by roads etc. Continued clearance will have since reduced these figures.

More recently a number of institutions including university departments, WRI and Greenpeace joined forces to identify and map remaining 'intact forest landscapes', which were identified in 66 out of 149 forested countries. Total area considered intact was 13.1 million km^2 or 23.5 per cent of remaining forest, the large majority being in tropical and subtropical forest (45.3 per cent) and boreal forest (43.8 per cent); very little temperate forest remains intact (Potapov et al, 2008).

Naturalness in inland waters

There is generally far less recognition of naturalness issues in freshwater systems, although the 'wild rivers' movement in some parts of the world is

FIGURE 6.3 Many remaining tropical forests, while modified in subtle ways by the indigenous peoples that live there, have retained more-or-less natural ecosystems, as this one in Ecuador

starting to grapple with these issues. In many cases no serious attempts have been made to define naturalness for particular wetland habitats. Global data sets do not exist. The WRI did a groundbreaking analysis of 154 major watersheds around the world (Revenga et al, 1998) but this only touched briefly on integrity. Similarly, some global studies are starting to look at impacts of chemicals on freshwaters at a broad scale, such as a modelling exercise that compared current nitrogen loading with pre-industrial levels in river systems (Green et al, 2004). While useful, such broad assessments tell us little about a particular ecosystem, let alone individual sites. The concept of 'wild rivers' has gained increasing currency, to describe rivers that are undammed or otherwise have their flow impeded, and the term has gained legal standing in countries like the United States, with specific rivers being designated as 'wild'; however the term itself refers mainly to flow and many 'wild' rivers have been compromised ecologically through introduced species, past overfishing, chemical pollution and the like.

Naturalness in grasslands

Most analyses are confined to whether or not grasslands still exist, rather than nuances of species compositions or natural functioning. Bill Henwood

TABLE 6.4 Status of temperate grasslands

Grassland region	Remaining area (km²)	% remaining in native cover
Eurasia		
Eastern Europe	43,120	3–5
Black Sea-Kazakh steppe	64,600	76
Russian steppe	49,500	15
East Asia		
Mongolia	Undetermined	90
China	Undetermined	53
Russia's Amur Basin	5000	5–20
Australia, New Zealand and South Africa		
Southeast Australia	4800	0.5–2
New Zealand	Undetermined	44
South Africa	28,900	65
North America		
Tallgrass	57,000	1–3
Mixed grass	62,000	36–40
Shortgrass	24,000	40–48
Intermontane shrub steppe	2200	46–70
Chihiahuan	43,000	15
South America		
Northern paramo	Undetermined	60
Central paramo and puna	Undetermined	Unknown
Pampas	49,100	30
Campos	20,500	65–80
Patagonian steppe	40,000	95

(2010) collected information on the status and trends in the world's temperate grasslands, and found massive differences in areas remaining between regions, from less than 1 per cent to 90 per cent. Some of the figures he collected, from multiple sources, are summarized in Table 6.4 below; there is clearly variation in data quality.

No similar compilation has been found for tropical grasses. Nor, despite some efforts, has there been any systematic attempt to even define the criteria of wholly natural grassland; this issue is returned to in Chapter 7.

Ocean ecosystems

The concept of naturalness in oceans has still been only very sketchily addressed: mainly in terms of whether or not the wilderness concept fits marine ecosystems (e.g. Foster and LeMay, 1988; Sloan, 2002). A global-level study found that no marine areas were uninfluenced by humans; over 40 per cent of the ocean has been impacted by multiple drivers, yet large areas, particularly close to the poles, are still relatively unaffected (Halpern et al, 2008).

Conclusions

When I was planning this book the preceding chapter was provisional, depending on whether I found enough to put inside. And there was, but only just. Despite four or five studies, we have only a very approximate idea of how much of the world's land surface could be considered natural: something between a quarter and a half depending on how the parameters are set. We haven't even really tried to think about naturalness in ocean systems, except for very limited studies of the health of certain biomes like coral reefs or mangroves, presence of invasive species and the health of particular fish populations. Questions of naturalness of substrate, chemical composition, connectivity and ecosystem functioning remain largely ignored.

But we also know some things as well. We know that despite the massive changes that have taken place, many of them over millennia, there are still huge areas of the planet's surface that retain largely natural ecosystems. We have learnt quite a lot about some of these ecosystems, particularly forests. And we also now know enough to start thinking about how information can be improved in the future, particularly through use of satellite data, which are becoming increasingly sophisticated in their ability to distinguish between different levels of change in vegetation.

Information is also becoming more public. When I go to a new part of the world now I look it up on GoogleEarth – often a sobering way of judging the isolation of a particular habitat: as the World Database on Protected Areas refines its links with Google it is becoming easier to see directly whether particular protected areas are ecologically connected or isolated for instance. It is becoming more difficult for governments and others to fudge; several countries have had to radically revise their forest cover data (usually downwards) as better satellite imagery has become available. But these welcome advances cannot cover up the fact that there is still an awful lot to be learned.

CHAPTER 7

Defining Naturalness and Authenticity

Key messages

- There have been a number of very useful attempts to define naturalness, integrity and wilderness, but most of these are based around ecosystems that are relatively unchanged.
- A new definition of authenticity is suggested to embrace elements of naturalness in both fairly pristine and substantially altered ecosystems.
- New approaches to naturalness will be particularly important as ecosystems respond to climate change and old baselines disappear.
- An authentic ecosystem is described as: **a resilient ecosystem with the level of biodiversity and range of ecological interactions that would be predicted as a result of the combination of historic, geographic and climatic conditions in a particular location.**
- A tool for assessing elements of authenticity is proposed and applied to some case study sites.

Savolinna National Park in Finland is based around a huge, sprawling lake with hundreds of islands, large and small, mostly covered with spruce and fir and, when we were there, carpeted with wood anemones, wood sorrel and lilies. It is famous for having the world's biggest population of Saima seals (*Pusa hispida saimensis*), one of the few freshwater seals, already reduced to a remnant population and under intensive conservation management. Metsähallitus, the Finnish Forest and Parks Service runs a comprehensive conservation and restoration programme, which includes restoration of the beaver (*Castor fiber*), which had at one time been hunted to extinction. Beavers play a key role in freshwater ecology through their practice of damming streams and clearing trees from beside rivers. They're extremely good engineers; I was shown a tree half chewed through in Latvia once, which the forest owner told me had been like that for a couple of weeks; the beaver was waiting for the wind to be in the right direction before dropping the trunk exactly where it wanted. Beavers are circumpolar, existing in a band through North America, Russia and much of Europe, so when the Finns were looking for beavers to replace their lost population, they brought some over from Canada where they are abundant. But then, some bright taxonomist decided that the North American beaver (*C. canadensis*) was a distinct species from the one found in Europe, in much the same way as we have both an American and European mink. Should the Finns laboriously kill or capture all the beavers, which are now doing rather nicely in their protected environment, and bring some over from the Baltic States instead? As we have seen, invasive species can be ecologically disastrous (and beavers can be a disastrous invasive species as experienced in southern Argentina, where they have disrupted natural forests). But does it really matter that the species being reintroduced into Finland (where beavers traditionally live) is a near identical one from Canada rather than an identical species from somewhere else in Europe? How do we make decisions about something like this? Are the tools we have available robust enough?

To recap: Chapters 1 and 2 described two common beliefs about natural ecosystems: that they still exist in a pure form and that they are irrelevant. Ecosystems distinct from human influence no longer exist, but this does not make the *concept* of naturalness obsolete or irrelevant, in fact it is becoming more relevant than ever in the face of increasing rates of environmental

FIGURE 7.1 Reintroduction of beavers into their original habitats is a controversial issue in many countries, including exactly where the beavers should come from. The picture shows damage from beavers in Tierra del Fuego, Argentina, a place where they never originally occurred

change. And as described in Chapter 3, one reason why this issue has become so confusing is that as a species we have changed our attitudes to natural ecosystems dramatically on at least two occasions, moving from being an unthinking part of nature, to deliberately distancing ourselves from the natural world, to the situation today where we are taking tentative steps to re-engage. Philosophically things are still rather a mess. While there have been some clear thinkers wrestling with these issues, too much of what passes for debate tends to be the repetition of slogans rather than carefully considered positions.

One of the problems relates to terminology. A term like *wilderness* has radically different interpretations depending on who is speaking: a powerful rallying cry for parts of the environmental movement, but a slap in the face for many indigenous peoples and ethnic minorities, and often seen as a descent into primitivism by rural communities in Europe. The word *natural* creates similar problems, particularly when the concept is translated into other languages. Although ecology and conservation are disciplines that already suffer from a surfeit of terms, acronyms and titles, I suggest we need to think seriously about a new definition more suited to conditions at the beginning of the 21st century. This chapter looks at ways in which scientists and others have defined naturalness to date and discusses their strengths and weaknesses. Then to give some wider context we will look outside the ecological field at how cultural experts have addressed these questions in the context of the built environment and archaeological remains. Then finally a definition of *authenticity* is proposed for natural ecosystems as a way of looking at the values we have been describing in the context of rapid environmental and climatic change. Finally some of the practical implications are discussed.

Defining naturalness

The concept of what does and does not make up a natural ecosystem has fascinated ecologists for decades. Efforts have been directed towards finding overarching definitions that would work anywhere; definitions that can be applied to particular management situations; criteria and indicators for defining naturalness; and baselines or targets as an aim for management. A proper overview could fill a book by itself; here some of the most important trends and conclusions are outlined.

In terms of ecological definitions, three concepts stand out: *naturalness*, *biological integrity* and *ecological integrity*, these are all distinct from each other although they address similar concerns. *Wilderness* is slightly different but is such an important idea that it will be discussed here as well. Definitions of wilderness move away from strictly ecological issues to embrace cultural and social values, paving the way for the discussion of authenticity that follows.

The most commonly quoted approach to **naturalness** was defined by Anderson 20 years ago (1991). He identified three main components: (1)

the degree to which the system would change if humans were removed; (2) the amount of cultural energy required to maintain the functioning of the ecosystem as it currently exists; and (3) the complement of native species currently in an area as compared with the suite of species in the area prior to human settlement. Anderson's paper drew immediate attention and has been quoted regularly ever since. Götmark (1992) replied quickly criticizing the whole concept of naturalness as a useful management tool, which he argued was largely a political concept: a Swedish perspective countering one from North America and many others have contributed to this debate ever since. The Anderson model differentiates humans from nature and assumes a human-free baseline: it would be difficult to apply, for instance, in places where ecosystems have developed in the presence of humans. Others have used different parameters to define naturalness. Aplet et al (2000) distinguished between *naturalness*, defined as wholeness relative to historic norms, and *freedom*, by which they meant the extent that the ecosystem was outside human control. In the last 20 years our ideas about the significance of settlement, and particularly white coloniser settlement in the colonial period, have also undergone some major changes. For instance Oliver et al (2002) have criticized standards such as 'before white settlement', as has often been used in Australia, as overly simplistic. Naturalness remains as an important concept, but one that has a number of different interpretations within conservation; almost all of these to one extent or other assume that an 'original' ecosystem exists against which to make comparisons.

Next **biological integrity** gained attention, due in no small part to a stream of papers by J. R. Karr and associates, who over time developed a relatively wordy but thorough definition: 'the capacity to support and maintain a balanced, integrative, adaptive biological system having the full range of elements (genes, species and assemblages) and processes (mutations, demography, biotic interactions, nutrient and energy dynamics, and meta-population processes) expected in the natural habitat of the region' (Karr, 1996, p101). From a conservation perspective, biological integrity was proposed as being more useful than biodiversity (Angermeier and Karr, 1994), the latter being difficult to use as a measure because of the problems in setting a baseline. More species may not necessarily be better (for example an invasion of weed species into freshly cleared forest will boost the total number of species but will reduce the biological integrity). Angermeier (1994) points out that the term 'biodiversity' is often assumed to include what he calls 'artificial diversity' such as invasive species, which diminish biological integrity. Importantly, concepts of biological integrity have been incorporated into US federal law, particularly with respect to inland waters.

Ecological integrity has emerged as what is now generally considered to be a more complete concept than biological integrity, although the two are closely connected and their various definitions sometimes seem to merge and overlap. Karr and Dudley (1981, no relation), looking at the issue from a freshwater perspective, proposed that ecological integrity was the sum of the physical, chemical and biological integrity. The concept has been developed much further by Stephen Woodley and colleagues at Parks Canada (Woodley et al, 1993), who have made ecological integrity the basis of a detailed management effectiveness monitoring system for Canadian protected areas. Ecological integrity is a legal mandate for Parks Canada. It is defined as: 'a condition that is determined to be characteristic of its natural region and likely to persist, including abiotic components and the composition and abundance of native species and biological communities, rates of change and supporting processes' (Woodley, 2010, p109).

Parks Canada developed a comprehensive framework to support its efforts to measure ecological integrity in national parks by identifying a set of indicators which: includes both structural and functional processes; measures the main stressors; accounts for a range of spatial scales; has the power to assess change; is sensitive to a range of ecological stressors; assesses both vital signs and known problems; and aims to be more than just a collection of indicator species. Core issues to be measured included *biodiversity* (species richness, population dynamics and tropic structure), *ecosystem functions* (succession or retrogression, vegetation age-class distributions, productivity, decomposition and nutrient retention) and *stressors* (human land-use patterns, habitat fragmentation, pollutants, climate and park specific issues).

Parks Canada uses this information to produce simple to understand score cards for press and politicians, which summarize the state of the parks in a few images and scores but draw on a mass of underlying monitoring data. This means that any visitor to a national park like Banf or Jasper can have immediate access to a data-rich picture of how the park is performing over time and the extent to which ecological values are being maintained. Systems of this type rely on availability of sufficient money, effective monitoring and political will and are likely to remain a dream for many countries for a long time.

Lastly, in this brief roll call of definitions, the term **wilderness** has also frequently been defined, including under law in a number of countries (Kormos, 2008), giving it some direct policy implications that tend to overshadow scientific debate.

The legal ways in which individual countries have defined a wilderness (Kormos, 2008) vary both in the framework used and in what might be called the units of measurement: many definitions remain vague and include condition, size and social criteria. Legal definitions may not match the understanding of the general public (Shultis, 1999, p59). Terms used for condition include *substantially undisturbed, capable of being restored, no artificial structures* while other countries define condition more ecologically, in terms of being able to sustain populations of species for instance. Size is defined by area, width or distance from modern infrastructure in measures that vary from quantitative to qualitative: *at least 25km², at least 15km from modern infrastructure, two days' foot travel* and so on. (Many of these terms seem extremely hard to define in any quantitative way.) Social issues include variously opportunities for solitude, recreational uses, hunting and fishing. Cyril Kormos (2008a), a lawyer working with the Wild Foundation, talks about wilderness as a three-dimensional concept embracing the *biological, social* (both separate from and integral to human culture, depending on the starting point of the person concerned) and *iconic*.

An important overarching definition of wilderness was developed by Kormos, Vance Martin, Harvey Locke and others in the IUCN World Commission on Protected Areas' Wilderness Task Force (Dudley, 2008, page 15): 'usually large unmodified or slightly modified areas, retaining their natural character and influence, without permanent or significant human habitation'. Among the distinguishing features identified by the task force, in this case explicitly related to a wilderness that is also a protected area (IUCN category Ib), are that the area should be characterized by a high degree of intactness: containing a large percentage of the original extent of the ecosystem, native fauna and flora, intact predator–prey systems, and of sufficient size to protect biodiversity, maintain ecological processes and ecosystem services. In other words basically the same characteristics as biological and ecological integrity. But the wilderness definition goes much further in specifying the relationship of humans to the landscape or seascape, specifying that the area should generally be free of modern infrastructure, development and industrial extractive activity; agriculture including intensive livestock grazing; commercial fishing; low-flying aircraft and so on; preferably also with highly restricted or no motorized access. While some of the above features would directly impact on ecological integrity and thus their absence is implicit in earlier definitions, constructions such as cellphone towers and pipelines can in theory be incorporated within ecosystems without causing huge ecological disruption; here the emphasis is more towards social and cultural values and what we expect to see (or rather not see) in a 'wilderness'.

These values become more explicit in the other distinguishing features. 'Wilderness areas offer outstanding opportunities for solitude, enjoyed once the area has been reached, by simple, quiet and non-intrusive means of travel and be free of inappropriate or excessive human use or presence, *which will decrease wilderness values and ultimately prevent an area from meeting the biological and cultural criteria listed above*' (my emphasis, Dudley, 2008, p16). IUCN is thus deliberately distancing itself from the idea that wilderness should always be empty of humans, recognizing that many areas that share the ecological and cultural features identified with wilderness are also the homes of indigenous peoples, ethnic minorities and other groups who choose to have a very light impact on the rest of nature. This sophisticated approach to wilderness concepts is still not universally accepted and some people still popularly equate wilderness with an empty, 'untouched' ecosystem.

Attempts to define naturalness within biomes

Alongside the global theorizing, there have also been a number of attempts to define naturalness for specific biomes, most notably forests, inland waters and grasslands, often at a national or regional level. In some other ecosystems, including particularly the marine ecosystem, such issues are only just beginning to be explored.

Regional efforts to define naturalness in forest

I'm sitting in a conference chamber in Montréal, back in September 1993. Representatives from temperate forest countries have been invited to a workshop to develop criteria and indicators for sustainable forest management, something that eventually became the so-called Montréal Process (Montréal Process, 2007). We have spent over a week in intense and somewhat tetchy discussions among a strange international mix of foresters, scientists and politicians. Looking back a lot of the ideas now seem very simplistic. Suddenly, after delegates had almost talked themselves into the ground one hitherto silent man put up his hand and demanded, in passionate terms, what the devil we had been talking about for the last week. The *only* criterion of a good quality forest, he averred, was the amount of biomass it produced; anything else was just nonsense.

The Montréal Process emerged at a time when the global consensus was shifting, at least within the forest products community, from a focus solely on production to recognition that control over large forest estates brought other social and environmental responsibilities as well. Many forestry companies literally had to learn to accommodate a whole new set of demands. Fears about deforestation and latterly also about decline in forest quality led in the 1990s to a flurry of attempts to define and measure the various values available from forests. Different institutions jostled for control of this process (Dudley et al, 2006). At a global scale, institutions such as the Convention on Biological Diversity (CBD, 1997) and International Tropical Timber Organisation (ITTO, 1993) identified indicators that started to consider naturalness. A series of regional efforts to develop criteria and indicators of good forestry also emerged, in Europe and other temperate countries, the Amazon, Central America, Dry-Zone Africa, North Africa and the Middle East and by the Africa Timber Organisation (most did not progress beyond an initial meeting); individual countries like France (Anon, 1994) and Finland (Eeronheimo et al, 1997) did the same thing for their own forests and increasingly independent certification organizations like the Forest Stewardship Council started to outline their vision of a high-quality forest estate. In particular, the process running in Europe, now known as Forest Europe (formerly the Ministerial Conference for the Protection of Forests in Europe (MCPFE) or even earlier the Helsinki Process) not only survived over time but also established a set of clear criteria and indicators about forests that member governments agree to report upon.

Many of these were extremely general – an identification of the need to conserve a proportion of forests in the natural state for instance, and provide little useful information for us here. Others are quite precise. Forests Europe defines 'forests undisturbed by man' as '*forests where processes, composition of species and structure remain natural or have been restored*' (MCPFE, 2003). Critics complain that the MCPFE definition is too vague but it is significant that it includes the concept of restoration; it has also been successfully applied to produce a set of results, which might prove a challenge for some of the more complicated definitions applied by theoreticians. Some of the many ways in which natural forests have been defined are given in Table 7.1 below.

BOX 7.1 Definitions of natural forest

More effort has been spent on trying to define naturalness in forests than in any other vegetation type, in part because of the intense debate about intensity of management and its social and ecological impacts. The following provides a brief overview of some definitions that appear in English.

TABLE 7.1 Ways of defining naturalness in forests

Definition	Explanation and sources where relevant
Definition by degree of disturbance	
Virgin forest	Forests never significantly altered by humans. 'It is original in its structure and has developed untouched by humans under natural conditions. Virgin forest is not limited only to the climax stage, although the majority of virgin forests are old-growth forests. The terms "primeval forest", "primary forest" or "pristine forest" are often used interchangeably with the term "virgin forest"' (Parviainen, 2005, page 11).
Natural forest	Forests that regenerate with natural succession but can show evidence of past human influence (Parviainen, 2005); in other words less strict than virgin forest.
Frontier forest	Forests large enough to support a full range of indigenous species with structure and function shaped by natural events, used by the World Resources Institute. 'Relatively undisturbed and big enough to maintain all their biodiversity, including viable populations of the wide-ranging species associated with each forest type'. Criteria include: primarily forested; natural structure, composition and heterogeneity; dominated by indigenous tree species (Bryant et al, 1997, page 121)
Intact forest landscape	Defined as 'an unbroken expanse of natural ecosystems within areas of current forest extent, without signs of significant human activity, and having an area of at least 500km^2' (Potapov et al, 2008).

TABLE 7.1 *(Cont.)*

Definition	Explanation and sources where relevant
Definition by degree of disturbance	
Undisturbed by man	Definition used by the UN Food and Agriculture Organisation and UN Economic Commission for Europe among others. Defined as 'forests where processes, composition of species and structure remain natural or have been restored' (MCPFE, 2003).
Wildwood	'Wholly natural woodland unaffected by Neolithic or later civilisation' (Rackham, 2006, page 14: a definition used in the UK).
Definition by age	
Primary woodland	Forest that has existed continuously since original forest first developed, various definitions, e.g.: 'Land that has been wooded continuously since the original-natural woodlands were fragmented. The character of the woodland varies according to how it has been treated' (Peterken, 2002, page 11).
Old growth forests	Forests with mature structural and functional characteristics. There are various definitions, e.g.: 'stands in which the relic trees have died and which consists entirely of trees which grew from beneath' (Oliver and Larssen, 1990, page 262) and (for the Pacific Northwest of the USA): 'A forest stand usually at least 180–220 years old with moderate to high canopy cover; a multi-layered multi-species canopy dominated by large over-storey trees …' (Johnson et al, 1991, page 19).
Ancient forests	Forests that display characteristics associated with primary forests but where there is no proof that they have always been undisturbed: precise age limits to be considered ancient woodland varies but in the UK 400 years is commonly used (Kirby, 1992)
Definition by composition	
Native forests	Meaning is variable: often forests consisting of species originally found in the area – may be young or old, established or naturally occurring, although in Australia often used as if it were primary woodland (Clark, 1992).
Definition by multiple factors	
High conservation value forests	Definition used by the Forest Stewardship Council and others, which includes reference to naturalness along with other social and ecological factors (Jennings et al, 2003)

Source: Adapted and expanded from Dudley, 2003

Forests therefore labour under a plethora of definitions making comparisons sometimes rather difficult. The intense debate about forest definitions, which has now gone on for over 20 years, has also provided the time and space to think about naturalness in ways that have wider applicability.

Inland waters

Many freshwater systems have already undergone such profound changes – in terms of flow, chemicals and the introduction of alien species – that identification of a baseline is now virtually impossible. Most efforts at assessment have aimed at measuring overall ecosystem health, particularly presence or absence of pollution, through the Index of Biological Integrity (IBI) approach, originally developed by James Karr some 30 years ago (Karr, 1981). IBIs draw on sophisticated use of biological indicators and are often set for specific regions; they have gained widespread use in the United States through integration within Environmental Protection Agency standards. The idea of using indicator species to define integrity is popular in other counties as well. On a simpler scale, *The Sunday Times* in the UK ran a project with children using simple biological indicators to measure water and air quality, helping to create the public support for massive efforts to address pollution (Mabey, 1974).

Important though the IBIs have been, they tell us only a limited amount about naturalness on a broad scale, with their main focus being on water quality. We can list a wide range of likely changes to freshwater systems (see Box 7.2 below) but so far relatively few attempts have been made to look at how to define naturalness on a broader scale when it occurs.

BOX 7.2 Factors reducing integrity in inland waters

All inland waters:

- Excessive extraction of natural resources, e.g. overfishing
- Invasive species of plants and animals
- Pollution from nutrients, agrochemicals, waste products, etc.

Particularly rivers:

- Changes for navigation (canalization, straightening, etc.)
- Flood control measures
- Dams for drinking water reservoirs, irrigation and hydro-electric power
- Water withdrawal for agriculture, industry and domestic use
- Changes to sediments and nutrients (either dredging to reduce or extra added)

Particularly lakes, ponds and other wetlands:

- Drainage
- Changes to banks and edges

Others:

- Changes to groundwater resources through pollution or extraction

Source: Drawing on analysis in Revenga et al, 2000 but with additions

---

In contrast with forests, where definitions tend to focus on age and composition, in freshwater systems much of the emphasis within discussion of naturalness (although the word itself is seldom used here) is on flow regime (Poff et al, 1997) and composition of critical species assemblages. In the case of rivers, there is now widespread recognition of the value of remaining 'wild rivers' or 'free-flowing rivers', which are defined variously but are generally taken to mean rivers flowing without interruption (dams etc.) from their source to the sea (WWF, undated). The Nature Conservancy has developed a framework for assessing hydrological integrity, based around 32 parameters divided into five main groups: magnitude, magnitude of annual extremes, timing of annual extremes, frequency and duration of high and low pulses and rate of change in water conditions (Richter et al, 1996). It has been suggested that estimation of biological integrity in freshwater systems needs to draw on historical records, comparisons with other sites and modelling studies (Jackson and Davies, 1994). Alongside interruptions to flow, integrity of river banks is also important with many rivers now artificially canalized or otherwise altered.

The Ramsar Convention on Wetlands recognizes the need for ecological integrity within its sites but does not give specific guidance of identifying naturalness, although some convention signatory countries have done so in

FIGURE 7.2 The Dyfi Valley in Wales floods regularly, dissipating excess water harmlessly over grazing land and nature reserves rather than impacting on towns and villages further downstream

relation to management. For example, studies in New Zealand identified a range of possible characteristics of naturalness, including: aspects of the hydrology such as fluctuations in flow; geomorphic features such as sediment size; physico-chemical water quality parameters like water clarity, temperature or pH; presence of key fish or bird species; aspects of flora and fauna such as the presence of particular species of periphyton, submerged or emergent aquatic plants; characteristics of the surrounding riparian zone or wetland margin; absence of waste, pollution or litter; and opportunities for community activity and involvement (Ulrich and Ward, 1997). This definition, with its final point about recreation, again moves beyond the strictly ecological.

Grasslands

A generally neglected biome, grasslands have undergone huge modification throughout their range, in ways that people often do not even recognize, with grazing patterns altered, flora reduced in variety and changed through introduction of non-native species and, increasingly, wholesale replacement of dominant grass species with alien or bred varieties. Fundacion Vida Silvestre in Buenos Aires, Argentina, developed an indicator for High Value Grassland (Bilenca and Minarro, 2004) drawing mainly on expert judgement, and used this to map remaining high value grasslands in Argentina, Uruguay, Paraguay and southern Brazil. The Institute for European Environmental Policy has attempted to define the criteria for identifying natural grasslands in the context of guidelines for biofuel production and their text implicitly acknowledges the extent to which grasslands have already been altered:

> ... *non natural grasslands are assumed to be those created by extensive human interventions that have dramatically changed the natural system, for example via deforestation. Despite not being created by human intervention many natural grasslands may be maintained by human activity, for example domestic livestock populations or mowing which have replaced the maintenance role previously provided by wild herbivore populations. In the majority of cases natural grasslands will be 'used' by humans in some way.* (Bowyer et al, 2010, p10)

New efforts by the IUCN Grasslands Task Force to develop a global strategy for grassland conservation use a necessarily crude approach using three categories: (1) Highly Modified and Fragmented Landscapes; (2) Moderately Modified and Fragmented Landscapes; and (3) Large, Relatively Intact Landscapes (Henwood, 2010). However, interest in grassland conservation and values is increasing rapidly and we might expect more detailed assessment systems to develop in the near future.

Marine systems

Other biomes are even less well covered; the debate about naturalness in marine systems is only just beginning for example. Studies in Californian kelp forest found such major impacts through loss of megafauna and changes in population and size of many other species that identifying a baseline was by now impossible (Dayton et al, 1998). The virtual lack of remaining natural marine coastal systems has been identified as a critical lack in attempts to understand marine ecosystems and an argument for strictly protected marine reserves (Dayton et al, 2000). Apart from gross damage to marine systems discussed earlier, a general trend to simplification is identified (Airoldi et al, 2008). However, much work remains to be done in presenting this in systematic form. The question of ecological values within marine systems is touched on in developing selection criteria for marine protected areas (e.g. Roberts et al, 2003); but in general these questions remain to be explored in more detail. Brad Barr of the US National Oceanographic and Atmospheric Institute has been exploring options for wilderness protection in oceans (e.g. Barr and Lindholm, 2000) and it is likely that this will become an increasing feature of marine conservation efforts.

Moving forwards

The definitions described above, in general terms and linked to specific biomes, are all useful in helping to understand ecosystems and particularly ecosystem change. Sue Stolton and I have used modifications to the Parks Canada approach in assessing ecological integrity in a number of protected areas and it provides a viable and practical framework. In Serengeti National Park for instance park staff selected key indicators of ecological integrity which together embrace key values of the ecosystem (Mwamgomo et al, 2005) including: the migration; the Mara River; riverine forest; *Acacia* forest; *Terminalia* forest; kopje habitat; black rhinoceros; and wild dog, the last named being a restoration target as they are currently not found in the protected area. This doesn't mean that managers ignore other issues, for instance if elephants start to decline or an invasive plant species sweeps across the savannah, but it provides a logical and repeatable framework for understanding how the ecosystem is holding together over time. So what follows is not a suggestion that we abandon these ideas, but rather that today we need something in addition.

Most of the existing definitions of naturalness or integrity make three assumptions that do not work in many parts of the world: they assume the possibility of finding places without people, the opportunity for ecosystems to continue to function more-or-less indefinitely in the same way and the possibility of finding a baseline against which to measure change.

There are still ecosystems without people; a few places where humans have never settled or wandered and others where by accident or design humans have been removed. Such areas have particular ecological, cultural and often also spiritual value: the mountain tops of Bhutan for example. Some 'human free' ecosystems have achingly sad histories. Central Tasmania is empty because of a campaign of genocide against the Aboriginal inhabitants, despite its vast beauty and scientific and social values today. But these areas are vanishingly small in global terms, at least outside icecaps, deserts and bare rock. They have been discussed in greater detail in Chapter 6. Attempts to define naturalness as the absence of humans in places where humans have been modifiers for millennia, or where ecosystems have developed alongside humans, make little sense. Chapter 1 showed that definitions like 'before white settlement' are based on an implicit, false assumption that anyone originating from outside Europe had little impact on ecology (and incidentally these assumptions cause considerable offence).

Even in 'normal' conditions ecosystems do not remain stable for as long as we sometimes assume, if by stable we mean with exactly the same composition and ecology, and in any case we are not living in normal conditions. Many, probably most, ecosystems are going to change radically under conditions of rapid climate change and we need to recognize and manage for this situation. The type of change expected will differ in ways that it is still hard to predict and is nothing like the natural variability concepts that ecologists have used until now (e.g. Landres et al, 1999a). A definition that regards any permanent change from the status quo as a *loss* is going to be of little practical use for land and water managers over the next few decades except as a yardstick for defeat. Helping ecosystems to adapt, move and reform into viable units as climate changes, without shedding most of the world's biodiversity in the process, is perhaps the single most critical challenge facing conservationists today. We need to have some measure against which to judge if the emerging suite of 'new' ecosystems is of high or low value in terms of resilience, richness and genetic value. At least, concepts like biological or ecological integrity need to be modified so that they can accommodate these kinds of changes.

Last, one of the main reasons for identifying a measure of naturalness is to provide a baseline against which to measure change. In much of the world, we are already working in a dramatically altered set of ecosystems that have in many cases been beaten around for centuries, where climate change is also shifting the goalposts and where conservation has to compete with many other legitimate interests. Developing a conservation model which is predicated on our absence doesn't work, or at least it only works in a few atypical places.

I suggest that we need another definition, which I call *authenticity*, to encapsulate the values of naturalness in an increasingly unnatural world. I don't really care whether this actually means loading scientific literature down with another new term or simply bringing some of the ideas that follow into one or more of the existing definitions: the point is that we need to be thinking innovatively about naturalness and its role in the 21st century.

But first a small digression: while ecologists have been struggling to define naturalness in ecological terms, cultural experts have been discussing much the same topics with respect to historical, archaeological and sacred sites. I think we can learn a lot from these debates and that many of the ideas are transferable; a brief outsiders' summary follows.

If ecosystems are so heavily influenced by cultures, what can we learn from management of cultural sites?

As we walked towards the gates of one of the main temple complexes in Angkor Wat, Cambodia, the road ran between twin rows of carved heads and torsos. Most were weatherworn, broken and battered and a good few had been stolen, but about a quarter were brand new, carefully carved to replace damaged or missing heads. The temple complexes of Angkor Wat, Angkor Thom and the surrounding ruins are the finest surviving examples of Khmer Hindu buildings in the world. Throughout, craftsmen were hunched shading under umbrellas, working diligently to restore the damage caused by time, the Khmer Rouge and losses from thieves operating in the chaos that followed the civil war. For western tourists the view is unsettling: isn't it little more than vandalism to be messing around with one of the most iconic historical and spiritual sites in southeast Asia? Answering that question can tell us a lot about

FIGURE 7.3 In Southeast Asia, the concept of repairing ancient buildings is accepted as good practice, as in the case of workmen repairing damaged parts of the Angkor Wat complex of temples in Cambodia, whereas in much of Europe such interference with an historical site would be considered virtual sacrilege

management of natural sites. Although the parallels are not exact, for reasons that we'll discuss, the debates about cultural heritage contain similar issues to those addressed in this book and some of the answers that have emerged are interesting for ecologists as well.

For the past decade I have been involved in a UNESCO project led by Marc Hockings of Queensland University, developing and applying assessment systems for natural World Heritage sites (Hockings et al, 2008) aimed to increase their management effectiveness. The details don't matter here, but the significant point is that this approach is now starting to be applied to cultural sites as well (Castellanos, 2008), including all the cultural World Heritage sites in Finland for example. The process of thinking through how something developed for monitoring ecosystem conservation can be applied to cultural sites, such as ancient buildings and historic cities, has meant grappling with what values cultural heritage experts are looking for, and why. And some of the debates are remarkably similar to those we have been engaged in within the nature conservation world, which as we've seen is heavily influenced in management terms by cultural issues. There is also an important difference of opinion about approaches to conservation of historical sites around the world that closely matches the debates about wilderness in conservation.

Britain and Japan mark opposite poles of the debate about the meaning of 'authentic' in a cultural context. In Britain, conservators of historical sites have for a hundred years or more attempted to a greater or lesser extent to 'freeze' them; historically important ruined monuments would be conserved to the extent that they do not deteriorate further ('consolidated' in the language of archaeology) but would not generally be restored in terms of replacing fallen walls or putting on a new roof. Since the Romantics highlighted the charms of atmospheric ruins, all but a handful of our prehistoric monuments, castles or the many abbeys destroyed during the Reformation have been kept as they are. While the attitude of restorers to buildings has changed and is changing, there is still an emphasis on retaining the original fabric wherever possible. This is largely because for the British the individual components of the buildings are imbued with an historical and cultural importance that cannot simply be replaced by a copy. The *originality* of the particular stone, wood or metal is part of its historical interest; to be more precise, the fact that the visitor is looking at something that a craftsperson worked on hundreds or thousands of years ago is one of the main reasons why it is significant.

In May 2007, vandals started a fire on the historical ship *Cutty Sark*, a famous tea clipper moored at Greenwich in London. The ship was in the middle of a restoration programme and many of the original timbers had been removed but some were burned. The reaction of Richard Doughty, Chief Executive of the Cutty Sark Trust, speaking to the BBC neatly summarizes the British philosophy: 'When you lose original fabric, *you lose the touch of the craftsman, you lose history itself* ... And what is special about Cutty Sark is the timbers, the iron frames, that went to the South China Seas' (BBC, 2007, my emphasis).

The Japanese see things differently. Their culturally important buildings are mainly constructed of wood and, particularly in the humid climate of summertime Japan, wood has a relatively limited lifespan. People in charge of managing these buildings expect to replace component parts gradually over time as the fabric crumbles away, because that is what has been happening since time immemorial. We discussed earlier that many temples conserve particular forests to supply new timber. For example Itsukushima Shinto shrine on an island offshore from Hiroshima is a World Heritage site famous for temple gates that sit in the shallow water of the bay; ancient forests cover much of the rest of the island, to supply timber for rebuilding and incidentally today providing an important wildlife haven. For the Japanese cultural heritage experts, the issue is less about whose hands touched a particular piece of the building as whether the overall structure, feel and composition of the whole building is maintained. There is an old joke about the man who boasted that he had kept the same hammer for 50 years, though he had replaced the handle four times and the head three times; Plutarch tells a similar story about the ship used by Theseus being kept by the Athenians and continually restored as timbers rotted: when did it stop being Theseus' ship? I hope I'm not misrepresenting or oversimplifying, but I think that for the Japanese, as long as the hammer or ship had the same shape, used the same materials, did the same job and was repaired by craftspeople trained in the same traditions, they would still be authentic. I am going to argue later that we need a little more Japanese cultural thinking in our attitudes to natural ecosystems.

The situation is further complicated in the case of World Heritage sites that are also cities, like Lübeck in Germany or Vilnius in Lithuania, where there is a debate about how much the city should be 'allowed' to develop in line with the needs and wants of communities. Does having a *McDonald's* right next to the Minster and the Roman baths in the city of Bath undermine its World Heritage status? Who decides? What are the rules?

And what happens when something is destroyed? The sloping bridge in Mostar, now in Bosnia-Herzegovina, was built in the 16th century by an Ottoman architect and was a symbol of this town where Christians and Muslins lived together in harmony for centuries. I was there a couple of months before the 1992 war started and old men were still selling carvings and engravings on the streets nearby as people must have been doing for centuries. During the chaos and blood-letting that attended the break-up of Yugoslavia, the bridge was blown up, but was rebuilt in 2003, using original stone where possible. Significantly, UNESCO continues to list the centre of Mostar as a World Heritage site, specifically noting the reconstruction as: 'a symbol of reconciliation, international co-operation and of the coexistence of diverse cultural, ethnic and religious communities' (UNESCO website). Here the authenticity is also closely related to intangible values, which may be more important than the tangible stones used to build the bridge. The destruction of the bridge was symbolic and so was its reconstruction some years later. We might compare this with the restoration of a degraded ecosystem or threatened species; something like the reintroduction of the white rhino that has taken place in protected areas throughout southern Africa: the rhino is probably not essential to maintain a balanced ecosystem but the symbolic importance of its recovery from a tiny, remnant population has been culturally enormous. Indeed, ecological restoration can also be a hugely significant step in political and social reconciliation in some cases.

The parallels with ecology are surprisingly precise in some cases. UNESCO defines both authenticity and integrity for both natural and cultural sites. Cultural integrity is defined in this context in terms of wholeness and intactness, and the absence of instructive development, while authenticity is much more vaguely spelled out as something like 'cultural values truthfully and credibly expressed through a variety of attributes'. As in nature, the steps needed to maintain these attributes are sometimes in conflict; management approaches such as preservation and conservation, are generally best for authenticity while restoration and reconstruction may be needed for integrity but threaten authenticity (Alberts and Hazen, 2010). Ecologists similarly identify a potential tension between managing ecosystems for naturalness and wilderness (Landres et al, 1999). And in the same way that British and Japanese cultural experts disagree about continuity of form or process as determinants in cultural sites, similar debates take place in ecology. In Sweden, for example, Ohlson and colleagues (1996) showed that, counter-intuitively, age was not a primary determinant of lichen and fungi diversity in old-growth swamp forests but that the main thing affecting diversity was the presence or absence of dead wood; the ecological processes present were more important than ecological continuity in this case.

In UNESCO, the debate about what was meant by 'authenticity' spilled out into a significant international meeting in Nara, Japan in 1994, when the differences between various cultural approaches were discussed (Lemaire and Stovel, 1994). This was about the same time that we were starting to define authenticity as an aspect of forest quality (Dudley et al, 1993), albeit with no idea that a parallel process was going on in the cultural world. It was generally agreed by UNESCO members that a European perspective had until then been too dominant in determining approaches to cultural heritage, particularly with respect to issues of permanence. Jokilehto points out that 'the claims related to "intangible cultural heritage" were justified on the basis that this was **constantly being recreated** and could therefore not be seen in the light of historical authenticity, which was understood as "static"' (Jokilehto, 2006, p7, my emphasis). It was agreed that interpretation of authenticity needed to be much more culturally defined, drawing on issues such as design, materials, workmanship, setting, traditions, techniques, language and other intangible heritage, spirit and feeling (UNESCO, 2005).

We must be careful not to overplay the links between culture and nature in this context, not least because cultural sites are by their definition predominantly about culture, a completely human concept, whereas as argued earlier we have to try to consider ecosystems from more than a purely human perspective, however difficult this may be. But the questions that emerge from the debate about authenticity and culture – about whether or not elements are replaceable, about integrity *versus* authenticity and about the influence of history – are repeated almost verbatim in debates about naturalness in ecosystem management. Some of the solutions that cultural experts have come up with may in turn help us think through responses in natural sites.

Authenticity as a new term to describe natural and near natural ecosystems

And so to one of the central elements in this book: a proposal that we need to think again about terminology and definitions with respect to naturalness.

What follows is by no means entirely new. The idea of authenticity being a concept that had wider environmental and social resonance came originally out of work on food quality (Woodward et al, 1990). I have already examined authenticity at some length with respect to definitions of forest quality; these have gone through various iterations (e.g. Dudley, 1996) and the most recent is outlined in Box 7.3 below. However, many of these ideas were put together in the early 1990s, when far less was known about the extent of impacts likely under climate change. The 'original' definition of authenticity was nested within wider group of criteria, also covering *environmental benefits* and *socio-economic benefits* (earlier versions included a fourth criterion, *forest health*, which was later subsumed within the others). The following text builds on what has been learned since and applies it more generally to all biomes.

BOX 7.3 Authenticity as a criterion of forest quality

Forest quality is defined as *the significance and value of all ecological, social and economic components of the forest landscape* (Dudley et al, 2006). The basic criterion of forest quality is further subdivided into three other criteria: **authenticity, environmental benefits** and **social and economic benefits**. A definition of an authentic forest might be a forest in which *all the expected ecosystem functions can continue to operate indefinitely*. The components of authenticity are listed and include **composition, pattern, function, process, resilience, area, fragmentation and management practices**:

1 Composition: Composition of species, ecosystems and genetic variation
2 Pattern: Spatial variation of trees with respect to age, size, etc.
3 Functioning: Continuity, proportion and type of dead timber, etc.
4 Process: Disturbance patterns, life cycles
5 Resilience: Tree health, ecosystem health, ability to tolerate environmental stress
6 Area: Size, edges, connectivity
7 Fragmentation: Degree of fragmentation
8 Management practices: Mimicking natural ecological processes, integration of forest into the landscape

---

A definition of authenticity

The definitions discussed above all have their foundations in the concept of a *baseline*; a certain 'original' status against which to compare changes and plan management interventions. Much of this book has been an accumulation of evidence showing that in many places ecosystems have been so profoundly altered that making our way back to the baseline may already be impossible. More fundamentally, the whole concept of a steady-state ecosystem has been all but abandoned by ecologists in favour of much more mobile, fluctuating ecosystems that are constantly changing and evolving (e.g. Christensen et al, 1996). And even if we *could* define some kind of arbitrary baseline, climate change is combining with a host of other pressures to ensure that this baseline is likely to unravel over the next few decades.

In the face of these factors, many ecologists and a few conservationists and land managers are abandoning concepts such as naturalness altogether. But naturalness has its own unique values and by cutting it out of the picture we are left planning and implementing ecosystem conservation in the absence of any yardstick against which to measure progress. If we want to avoid sliding inexorably towards ecosystems dominated by weeds, brown rats and feral pigeons, and if we want to continue drawing on ecosystem services from natural ecosystems, we need to have be able to understand concepts of naturalness in a rapidly changing world, which means that we also need a definition that fits conditions in the 21st century.

I agree with the people who say that the concept of naturalness is becoming increasingly problematic, which is why I'm suggesting that a new term might help, and having already experimented with the term *authenticity* for some time, this seems to offer some advantages. Although it happened by chance, the choice of authenticity to describe both an ecological state and, through the World Heritage Convention, a condition relating to the built environment, is actually quite useful, because the way I'm using it in ecology has a lot of cultural elements reflected as well.

So, a suggested definition of an authentic ecosystem is: *a resilient ecosystem with the level of biodiversity and range of ecological interactions that can be predicted as a result of the combination of historic, geographic and climatic conditions in a particular location.*

Each of the substantive words in the definition is discussed in more detail in the box below. To elaborate: the definition is designed for the present time, when the global biosphere is undergoing a period of unusual flux. It seeks to provide a usable framework both for places where ecosystems remain relatively unchanged (e.g. climate refugia) and those places that have been changed, or will soon change, to a dramatic extent. Chapter 4 has argued that biodiversity rights assume no human-induced species extinction. But where will species go as conditions change? Even supposing it was possible to manage the impacts of disturbance at this scale, conservation planners are going to be faced with a hugely complicated task. Authenticity embraces the change and proposes that the sum of the 'new' ecosystems, where they emerge, should maintain, as far as possible, all their constituent species. In other words, on a landscape scale (and here 'landscape' may be a very large unit) we should be aiming to minimize loss of species diversity and ecosystem functions, but at a site scale many ecosystems will be transformed. Authenticity therefore focuses on flexible, durable ecosystems composed of the variety of species that might be predicted from the past ecological history and the current climatic and geographic conditions. In relatively pristine conditions, the practical application of this concept will be similar to biological or ecological integrity. In changed, or changing, conditions, management aims will be focused more on maintaining (restoring, or even developing) an ecosystem that can keep functioning and maintain current biodiversity, without worrying too much about the extent to which it has already been changed.

BOX 7.4 An authentic ecosystem

An authentic ecosystem is: *a resilient ecosystem with a level of biodiversity and range of ecological interactions that can be predicted as a result of the combination of historic, geographic and climatic conditions in a particular location.* Each of the main elements in the definition is discussed below.

Resilience: refers here to overall ecosystem health and in particular ability to withstand stress. The numerous attempts to define ecological resilience include reference to disturbance without major change, return time to a stable state following perturbation and adaptive capacity (Gunderson, 2000). Resilience has taken on new significance as ecologists search for clues about what ecosystem characteristics are likely to confer the ability to withstand climate change (IPCC TAR, 2001). Here our focus is primarily on adaptive capacity.

Level of biodiversity: as species' habitats move as a result of environmental change, diversity will ebb and flow, some locations becoming less diverse while other places increase in diversity. In a time of rapid ecosystem transformation, authenticity of composition is less a precise and unchanging list of named species as a degree and completeness of diversity as predicted from the combination of historical, physical and climatic conditions: biodiversity represented at all trophic levels, in a wide range of microhabitats. Exactly where these species started out may be less important than the role they play in the current ecosystem.

Range of ecological interactions: ecosystems that have lost some of their ecological interactions have also lost some authenticity. A focus on the importance of critical interactions (food webs, mycorrhizal associations, phenolic pathways, pollination, hydrological cycles, nutrient cycles and so on) means in theory that *functional species*, that is those that play an important role in the overall ecosystem functioning (Chapin et al, 1996), are more important than species that do not play such a keystone role. In practice we often do not know which species are important; for example aspects of ecosystem resilience may be linked to apparently redundant species (Peterson et al, 1998).

Predicted: climate scientists and ecologists are already working together to develop models for where particular species may end up in the new ecosystems that are developing (e.g. Araújo et al, 2004); such predictions will inevitably be rather rough and ready in most cases – the definition might more accurately read as 'predicted, estimated or guessed at ...' in many situations.

Historic factors: levels and types of diversity are in part a function of ecological history (Willis and Birks, 2006): for instance some ecosystems have unusually high levels of diversity for reasons of chance or accident, through being isolated or undisturbed for exceptionally long periods (Jetz et al, 2004). Other ecosystems have already been hugely changed and in some cases impoverished or added to; it will not always be possible either to recover lost elements or to remove additions. What an ecosystem is likely to contain in the future needs to be based in current realities, which have in turn been affected by historical events.

Geographic and climatic factors: in addition, ecosystem richness and complexity is now known to be heavily influenced by factors including location and climate: hot and humid terrestrial ecosystems are generally richer than cold, dry ecosystems although influencing factors are complex. As climate change creates rapid changes in ecosystem characteristics and location, those responsible for managing change will need to work out expected level of authenticity based on current conditions as well as ecosystem history.

Management implications of focusing on authenticity rather than naturalness

What are the practical implications of such a change in emphasis? Principally that it elevates *ecological process* in importance above the minutiae of *ecological components*. In other words the fact that an ecosystem is functioning at the expected degree of diversity and complexity is more important than whether it contains all its 'original' components, or has picked up some additional components along the way. The presence of alien species, or introduced chemical compounds, only seriously reduces authenticity if they disrupt the functioning of the system to a significant degree; for instance if chemical pollutants exceed their 'critical load' and eliminate whole species or groups or if an invasive species eliminates a whole group of species. Determining what *significant* might be in this context will be a task for ecologists as environmental change progresses.

Authenticity is also affected to some extent by the size of the area, although exactly what this means is still unclear. Island biogeography tells us that isolated ecosystems quickly whither and lose species and functions, but we know much less about exactly how to ensure connectivity and avoid fragmentation; in other words about what really constitutes 'an island' in ecological terms. Whenever conservation biologists calculate the minimum areas to maintain viable population of species it is usually very depressing news for those of us trying to undertake practical conservation. For example Archer and Beale (2004) used historical analysis of species loss from New Zealand after it had broken away from the main Gondwanan land mass to suggest that at least 260,000km^2 is needed to retain mammal populations in the long term. Similarly Chiarello (2000) suggests that in Brazil, Atlantic rainforest protected areas need to be nine times the size of New Zealand to retain viable mammal populations, a statistic so way beyond the present reality as to render any conservation efforts irrelevant. There are many such calculations: most do not factor in potential manipulation by ourselves, which is increasingly relied on to retain populations of larger mammals.

Ideally, authentic ecosystems should also be self sustaining; they should not need constant and often expensive manipulation to maintain their values. There are many ecosystems that require and deserve such attention, such as nature reserves carefully managed to maintain particular species, but these should not be confused with authentic ecosystems. Self regulation is an ideal that becomes progressively more difficult to achieve as ecosystems are disrupted, but could be given much higher priority in management actions than is currently the case.

I would propose that whether or not 'self-regulation' can realistically include human management depends on time, place and social desires, although this caveat is likely to be contentious. In long-managed cultural landscapes it could be argued that human intervention is part of the natural regulating process, although this assumes that successive generations of people will be interested in or prepared to maintain the same kind of lifestyles and management interventions in perpetuity. This issue is discussed more in the box below. The practical implications of climate change mean that in many cases humans will have to play an increasing and a long-term role in active ecosystem management; that we will need once again to become 'part' of the ecosystem, but this time in a much more deliberate fashion than hitherto.

The view of authenticity from my cottage

So far, so theoretical: to give some practical examples of how authenticity might provide a slightly different perspective, I'll start with some things that I can see from my back door in Wales, on the edge of the Snowdonia National Park. The examples I am going to cite have all been presented in the past as conservation problems. I believe *from the perspective of authenticity* that many are not really problems at all. (They clearly have very important cultural implications for some people, but that's a different issue.) Grey squirrels (*Sciurus carolinensis*) live in the woods behind my house and steal down into my garden to grab nuts from the bird feeder. When I went camping in Wales as a boy it was still possible to see the original red squirrel (*Sciurus vulgaris*) and I remember thrilling to the sight of one crossing the River Ogwen in spate,

---

Box 7.5 Can humans play a role in an authentic landscape?

If humans are part of the ecosystem, shouldn't we be part of its management? This is the essence of the protected landscape approach and of indigenous and community conserved areas (ICCA); both assume we can help maintain diverse and functioning ecosystems. Many examples of rich, managed ecosystems exist and if humans and livestock have replaced functional species (which we may have caused to go extinct), removing human influence can cause abrupt ecosystem change. Some community management stretches back many hundred years. Supporters of landscape and community approaches argue that humans may well have changed the composition of the ecosystem, but there is no reason why this should pose any philosophical or ethical difficulties.

Are such ecosystems *authentic* in the way defined here? This is more than just an academic point; it relates directly to our expectations of management in many of the world's apparently natural or authentic areas.

Humans are not part of the ecosystem in the same way as other species: our reasoning power stops us being a stable ecological factor: we can choose to change. The protected landscapes approach relies on maintaining traditional interactions between people and ecosystems: 'safeguarding the integrity of this interaction' (Dudley, 2008). But traditions change. While I've lived in Snowdonia National Park 'traditional' farming has changed from *transhumance* with shepherds tending flocks on foot in rough pasture; through *intensification* with road proliferation in the uplands, a doubling (at least) of sheep, reseeding and a massive expansion of conifers; followed a decade later by *extensification* to reverse some of these changes. Both changes were paid for by the European Union. Shepherds used to be slim and fit and often wracked with arthritis from constant rain; their grandchildren are supple and plump and race around the hills on quad bikes. At least some 'traditional' management that is good for wildlife requires a cost in terms of money or discomfort that most people reject if they get the chance.

So if authenticity implies some measure of sustainability in ecosystem function then the role of humans becomes more questionable. Many community-based management systems are facing a challenge as traditional societies undergo rapid social change. Long-established management approaches may come under pressure because younger people are no longer interested in them or have lost the skills needed to maintain them. Many indigenous communities are currently struggling to keep their ICCA viable during rapid cultural shifts. Although interest is often rekindled later, possibly for other reasons, the values may have been lost in the interim. Managing the transition between an approach driven primarily by pragmatic reasons (food, environmental services etc.) to one more consciously aimed at ecosystem management is difficult, because it often involves different stakeholders and different motives. So although humans probably can play a part in an authentic landscape, any attempt to measure the degree of authenticity will depend on how stable this role is likely to be over time. Stabilizing responsible management, through rewards, customs, ethical frameworks, policies or laws, is one of the main challenges facing conservation managers.

---

leaping from rock to rock. But the grey, originally from North America, has staged a notorious and controversial takeover since its first appearance in 1876 (MacKinnon, 1978), forcing the red back into Scotland, the Lake District and a few offshore islands. The reasons for the red's decline are complex and still argued about but it seems likely that the grey has a competitive edge over the red (Gurnell et al, 2004), which may have been exacerbated by impacts of introduced disease on the red (Tompkins et al, 2002). The decline of 'our' red squirrel has caused huge emotional upset and the UK government has invested a lot in schemes to maintain remnant populations. There are whole societies set up to protect the red squirrel. But from an ecological point of view no one has provided persuasive evidence that the switch has made an appreciable difference except in the colour of the coat; the grey squirrel in North America occupies much the same niche as the red squirrel does in Europe. Does the ecosystem function any less effectively because the grey has replaced the red? There is much concern about the economic impacts of grey squirrels on forests through bark stripping, but the red also does the same thing; the principle difference seems to be that the red squirrel is at a lower density (Huxley, 2003).

A few hundred yards up the back road at the end of my village there is a beech wood (*Fagus sylvatica*): hundred-year-old trees spilling down the hillside providing shelter for a rich diversity of birds and, in the season, forest fungi. But the wood is planted and strictly speaking it shouldn't be there; beech is not native this far north in Wales. On the other hand the only reason it *isn't* 'native' is that it has not yet had time to spread this far naturally following the last ice age twelve thousand or more years ago. Under the proposed definition of authenticity, this hardly matters; the beech tree is close enough to its natural range to have brought along most of its associated flora and fauna and in any case would be arriving as a result of natural dispersal in a few hundred or thousand years' time.

More controversially, the existence of Norway spruce (*Picea abies*) and larch (*Larix decidua*) may be less of a problem in Wales than we usually assume. Although spruce and larch are not native to the UK they are found over much of the rest of Europe in similar habitats. In Snowdonia, the problem is not so much the species themselves as the way they are planted, in dense, straight rows so crowded that all understorey vegetation disappears; there is certainly little authentic about these plantations and they have for instance contributed to a steep decline in several bird species. However, the presence of a few spruce and larch trees self-seeding in nearby oak woods may be *culturally* unappealing but it is unlikely to upset the natural *functioning* of the ecosystem. And how about sitka spruce (*P. sitchensis*)? This comes from further away in Alaska, but does it have a radically different functional role in the forest from Norway spruce? They are not identical of course: for instance they differ in the way that litterfall varies with stress for instance (Pedersen and Bille-Larsen, 1999), but does that add up to differences that are likely to disrupt ecosystems? These questions need more careful consideration than is usually the case. Similar arguments could be made about the sycamore (*Acer pseudoplatanus*), another visitor from mainland Europe. Although I spent days felling them out of native oak woodland a few miles down the valley (actually almost certainly *planted* native oak woodland by the way) when I first started out in practical conservation they are found in virtually identical woodland in much of Europe.

Other non-authentic additions to the Welsh countryside still have me puzzled. We have seen a boom in Canada geese (*Branta canadensis*) over the last two decades; they are by far the commonest goose seen at Ynyshir bird reserve ten miles or so down the road from me and more significantly I am finding an increasing number of pairs colonizing the mountain pools. Farmers don't like Canada geese because they eat crops and make a mess but are they replacing other birds in the mountains of Snowdonia? Personal observation suggests that they may be driving away some duck-like goosander (*Mergus merganser*) from upland pools and I'm seeing less common sandpipers (*Tringa hypoleucos*) but there is no published evidence that I have been able to find to suggest competition. We still don't really know and such questions are likely to multiply.

It is important to be quite precise here. Long-established ecosystems, functioning with their 'original' species, are ecologically precious and almost certain to have a wider diversity and richness of interactions than younger, more disturbed alternatives. They also fit closely our definition of an authentic ecosystem: as they become scarcer their conservation value will increase even more as reference ecosystems. But where ecosystems have already been significantly disturbed, which is by all measures the majority of the planet, we also need a definition that allows us some measure of understanding of disruption, resilience and likely ecological trajectories. My instinct, as an ecologist, is that an aging woodland in Wales, with sycamore, beech, Norway spruce and a few other even more exotic species mixed in with the native oak and birch, and with grey squirrels scampering through the treetops, is likely to have a higher level of authenticity than a wood made up entirely of native tree species but that is regularly managed to remove dead timbers and has had most of its epiphytic lichens and mosses knocked out by air pollution. But am I right? At the moment we have few tools to help us make a decision. Below, in the final section, a draft is presented to help make decisions about authenticity. The implications of these suggestions will be discussed below.

Assessing authenticity

Most assessments of naturalness are either rather complex studies of integrity, assessed against a chosen baseline, or are supremely simple in that any more-or-less natural vegetation is regarded as natural. We saw this in many of the global or regional assessments of extent of natural ecosystems. I'm not blaming the researchers: there often are no tools to make any more subtle distinctions. But at the same time I think we need to start developing such tools. Because the naturalness of an ecosystem is composed of so many constituent elements, a simple 'score' is not going to work – in other words it would be hard to find a way of measuring naturalness that said a Welsh oak wood scored three and French beechwood scored four. Instead I think we need to break authenticity down into its constituent parts and provide a weighting for each: so for example we might measure the following (an indicative list only):

- Natural species composition
- Migrant species composition
- Invasive species
- Chemical composition
- Vegetation pattern
- Functioning food web
- Functioning ecological processes
- Regeneration process
- Resilience
- Area
- Connectivity

A simple scoring system for each could provide a graphic way of comparing ecosystems, and possibly shorthand for identifying aspects of ecology that were more or less natural. In Tables 7.2–7.4 these principles are applied in a qualitative way to three ecosystems discussed in this book.

TABLE 7.2 Assessing authenticity in Serengeti National Park: Tanzania

Constituent	Negative rating	Positive rating
Natural species composition		Most expected species present, wild dog has disappeared
Migrant spp. composition		The migration still operates naturally; one of the three largest in the world
Invasive species	A few plants	
Chemical composition		Good, clean air and lack of pollution in the Mara River
Vegetation pattern		Relatively natural but mosaic changing
Functioning food web		Apparently natural functioning
Functioning ecological processes		Insufficient data, some concern about water flow in Mara River
Regeneration process		Unnatural fire management
Resilience		Apparently resilient but insufficient data
Area		Large enough to maintain stable populations
Connectivity		Well connected although one break in migration route

TABLE 7.3 Assessing authenticity in Attenborough Nature Reserve, England, UK

Constituent	Negative rating	Positive rating
Natural species composition		Relatively rich in UK but many missing
Migrant spp. composition		Important stopping place for many migratory water birds
Invasive species	Serious concerns with crayfish, molluscs, balsam and others	
Chemical composition	Significant air and water pollution	
Vegetation pattern	Managed grassland some nat. regeneration	
Functioning food web		Many elements present
Functioning ecological processes		Many missing component
Regeneration process		Natural regeneration but also artificial
Resilience		Insufficient data
Area		Too small
Connectivity	Isolated but important along River Trent	connectivity

TABLE 7.4 Assessing authenticity in Snowdonia National Park, Wales, UK

Constituent	Negative rating	Positive rating
Natural species composition		Relatively high but major losses & decline
Migrant spp. composition		Most migrant species still occurring, some losses
Invasive species	Rhododendron, conifer plantations	
Chemical composition	Better than some coastal	average air, & water polln.
Vegetation pattern	Much distortion and forest but also natural	even-aged mosaics
Functioning food web		Functioning with gaps
Functioning ecological processes		Some serious gaps
Regeneration process	Mainly artificial, little natural regeneration	
Resilience		Insufficient data
Area		Large area
Connectivity	Some efforts also serious	at connectivity but breaks

Something like this can only ever be indicative. But if and when we start taking issues of naturalness or authenticity more seriously, we will need an assessment system that both measures and presents information broken down into constituent elements. In the next two chapters, some of the practical management implications of applying a criterion of authenticity are discussed, first practically in Chapter 8 and then from a more philosophical perspective in Chapter 9.

CHAPTER 8

Managing for Authenticity

> **Key messages**
>
> • *Conservation management should understand and in most cases consciously prioritise authenticity as a goal.*
> • *In many cases, at a landscape scale, this will require a mixture of protection, management and restoration.*
> • *The overarching goal over large parts of the world should be to achieve authenticity within nature.*

The island of Borneo still carries an aroma of the exotic: impenetrable jungle, wild rivers and head hunters. Today this is largely a myth. Settlers and loggers have destroyed much of the forest for timber and oil palm and forced the indigenous Dayak people into ever smaller areas, so that over-burning for shifting agriculture has created vast areas of *alang alang* grass (*Imperata cylindrica*). Primary rainforest only remains in the so-called Heart of Borneo, currently the focus of a desperate rearguard action by conservation organizations to save the remnants of an ecosystem. The Kinabatangang River in Malaysian Sabah encapsulates the potential and tensions of this extraordinary place. Travelling upstream by boat the visitor gets the impression of dense rainforest: orang-utans and proboscis monkeys can still be seen in the trees. But for much of the river's course the rainforest is paper thin; a narrow strip of trees with oil palm close behind and in some areas the oil palm companies have (illegally) planted right up to the water's edge.

These changes put huge pressures on the ecology. A herd of a hundred jungle elephants still makes a twice yearly migration along the river but when they come to the oil palm they literally have to swim around to avoid being shot by the plantation workers. I've watched them swimming and got close enough to see the buckshot scars on the backside of an old male. My two visits have been in connection with a conservation project that WWF is carrying out, a complicated mix of protection and restoration to try to ensure the integrity of the corridor: negotiating with plantation owners and loggers, promoting ecotourism, working with local villagers, replanting key gaps in the rainforest. In Kinabatangang the natural is still, just, hanging on. Decisions taken over

FIGURE 8.1 The natural habitat alongside the Kinabatangang River in Sabah, Malaysia, is now so degraded that elephants literally have to swim some stretches to avoid being shot at by oil plantation workers

the next few years will determine whether it survives and creeps back again or finally withers away as in so many other parts of Borneo. Which leads to the focus of this chapter: What are the options open to those who want to protect or restore authenticity?

Until recently the debate has been influenced by a conscious or unconscious assumption that the state of naturalness can only be lost once: phrases like 'virgin rainforest' could hardly be more specific. If naturalness is a once-only phenomenon that can never be recovered then protection – in fact rather strict protection – is the only viable management option. But if we accept that authenticity is both less precisely defined and capable of fluctuating over time it follows that the state can be both lost and, at least to a certain extent, regained.

This suddenly opens up a much wider range of new options: still protection of course but also management and restoration. But while I believe we need to be far more positive about the potential for bringing authenticity back, I'm not suggesting we give carte blanche to management approaches that *require* restoration. Protection remains paramount: we have seen that it is all but impossible to restore something exactly as it was and that we can often still distinguish 'restored' areas even after a millennium.

As conservationists we need to facilitate ecosystems that are sustainable, which means that either they can keep going without further intervention from ourselves (*self regulating*) or that human intervention is of a type where there are reasonable grounds for believing that it will be sustained in the long term (*functioning*). We are a very long way from that situation at the moment: many nature reserves and even large national parks are quite intensively managed, many cultural landscapes depend on traditional management interventions that are disappearing and climate change is disrupting everything and maintaining ecosystems will likely require more intervention rather than less. So this is a very long term aim.

There is also a real risk – in fact unless we are lucky or very determined a real probability – that whatever emerges from the maelstrom of land conversion, climate change, ocean acidification and other pressures will be a set of nominally functioning ecosystems that are far poorer in terms of species and ecological interactions than we have at the moment. Habitat generalists tend to invade once ecosystems are disturbed (Marvier et al, 2004). Such impoverished ecosystems are also likely to be less stable and thus less able to withstand further pressures in the future. We risk entering a downward spiral of loss.

As conservationists we should be railing against such losses. But simply trying to keep things as they are may no longer be an option in many places: rainforests are likely to become dry forests; tundra will start supporting boreal forest, and so on. We are still in the early stages of working out how these changes might be managed and it is clear that not all of them will be managed in any very controlled manner. A visionary conservation aim in these circumstances might be to maintain functioning ecosystems, with a full complement of species and interactions, in places where conditions remain suitable: these are increasingly being referred to as climate refugia and modellers have already started to map where they are likely to be (e.g. Vos et al, 2008). In places where conditions change we have to accept that some species will disappear but a useful conservation aim could be to facilitate the development of a 'new' ecosystem that is rich rather than poor; or more precisely as rich as possible given the then-current climate and the previous ecological history.

Having always been one who supported making decisions based on ecosystems rather than species in debates about conservation targets I'm wondering whether under climate change we need to consider both: aiming for no net loss of ecosystems in places where the ecosystems survive and no net loss of species in places so disrupted that ecosystems themselves undergo radical changes. This could be shortened to 'no net loss of biodiversity' although the strategic distinction between the two approaches is still important.

To be ethically and philosophically rigorous we should probably be talking about no net losses to biodiversity *caused by humans*; extinctions are a natural part of evolution and evolutionary theory tells us to expect all species eventually to become extinct, whereas the current debate is about a vast human-induced acceleration of this loss. In practical terms the tiny number of species we might expect to go extinct naturally over the course of the next century is going to be dwarfed by the wave of extinctions caused by our own contribution.

The extent to which we will be able to achieve these aims will depend on a number of factors. First, how overwhelming the predicted changes due to climate change, pollution, human population increase and land conversion turn out to be in reality. Second, our technical ability to understand and manage for such changes: where 'technical' includes both skills within the western scientific canon and also the innate ability of many local communities to come up with solutions to maintain ecosystem functioning. And third (and perhaps most important of all) the willingness of society to make the economic, political and cultural investments needed to maintain authentic ecosystems. Because authenticity is no longer simply a matter of chance or nature; it now depends at least partly on conscious or unconscious choices by society. Some of the reasons why we might choose authentic ecosystems are discussed in the following chapter, looking in turn at protection, management and restoration.

Catch 22: Protected areas don't work but they are the only things that *do* work

Protected areas are booming; creation of national parks, nature reserves and wilderness areas has over the last few decades affected more than a tenth of the world's land surface, creating the largest and fastest conscious change of land management in history. The Convention on Biological Diversity (CBD) recognizes the *Programme of Work on Protected Areas* as its most successful activity in terms of meeting targets and making real progress on the ground – the programme has been far from perfectly implemented but a major step forward nonetheless (IUCN WCPA, 2010). Creation and management of protected areas has also been the *only* really successful biodiversity component of the Millennium Development Goals. Yet biodiversity continues to decline at an apparently accelerating rate (Butchart et al, 2010). Species are even sometimes disappearing from inside protected areas (e.g. Craigie et al, 2010). When this is coupled with the continuing trickle of depressing stories about people being ejected from their traditional lands to set up protected areas, some people have been persuaded to start arguing that protected areas don't work. Community activists in many countries are now overwhelmingly negative about protected areas, talking instead about community conservation and 'mainstreaming' biodiversity conservation, and national parks are presented as threats in much the same way as mining or oil palm development.

I think that this is missing the point. Protected areas are certainly not a panacea that will solve all our conservation problems; they need capacity and good management, unfortunately often both lacking today, and they need to exist within a wider environment also managed sympathetically to conservation needs. But the only reason some species still exist is because they have been conserved within protected areas. When countries or regimes with bad human rights records set up protected areas they often do so in ways that ignore human rights and when countries with inadequate governance or rule of law set up protected areas these sites often fall prey to poaching or other forms of degradation. An example might be the initial damage to protected areas in Iran following the revolution of 1979: Iranian parks and reserves had been strongly supported by the Shah's family and were therefore perceived as the creation of a tyrannical government. It is incumbent on institutions – conservation NGOs, aid agencies and human rights groups – to address such failings, not least because they undermine conservation efforts as well. But this doesn't mean the whole concept is flawed. Whether we are primarily driven by a concern for species, or ecosystems, or geodiversity, or ecological authenticity or even primarily by questions of ecosystem services or aesthetic considerations, some way of retaining areas of natural habitat remains a critical step in wider management strategies. Indigenous peoples, in particular, often have virtually identical aims as those promoting conservation, in terms of maintaining the integrity of ecosystems in the face of development pressures, and it is an appalling indictment of bad planning that the two groups have often ended up in conflict, despite a growing number of examples of successful Indigenous Protected Areas.

But if protected areas are going to work as well as they can, we need to be fully aware of their strengths and weaknesses. Repeated independent assessments by academic researchers, development organisations and NGOs all show that protected areas are the best – in many cases the only – management strategy that successfully conserves natural vegetation (see Box 8.1). The establishment of protected areas has also been responsible for maintaining populations of many animal species, including particular large species or those with critical and delicate habitat requirements (Balmford, in press).

Unfortunately this is not enough. Most protected areas are not sufficiently large on their own to support stable and genetically viable populations of all their constituent species in the long term. If left as isolated 'islands' in a sea of inhospitable habitat they eventually start to lose biodiversity (Burkey, 1989). Therefore when we look at individual species, and particularly animal species rather than vegetation, the evidence for success is more ambiguous. We have already described the grim, empty forests that can result from the bushmeat trade; but depressing though these places certainly are, as long as they retain the ecological framework of vegetation they might still be expected to rebuild animal populations if poaching control became more effective. Such recoveries have been seen on many occasions; for example the globally significant population of Asian rhinos in Kaziranga National Park, in Assam, India was built up from a tiny remnant group due to rigorous anti-poaching patrols.

Unfortunately, declines have also been seen in plenty of protected areas where immediate pressures such as poaching are apparently minor or absent. In a now classic study of mammal extinctions in the national parks of western North America, William Newmark (1995) showed that extinctions had exceeded colonizations since protected area establishment and that rate

---

BOX 8.1 Evidence of effectiveness of protected areas

Protected areas appear to work more effectively than other approaches in maintaining natural vegetation, although research has focused mainly on forests. Most research looks at deforestation but some considers degradation, for example:

- **Conservation International:** a study on threats facing 92 protected areas in 22 tropical countries concluded that most protected areas are successful in protecting ecosystems, linking success to quality of enforcement (Bruner et al, 2001).
- **WWF and The World Bank:** a survey of 330 forest protected areas around the world using a consistent methodology, found biodiversity condition consistently scoring high, although this was a self assessment system (Dudley et al, 2007).
- **University of Queensland:** a global meta-study assessed management effectiveness evaluations from over 2300 protected areas and found that 86 per cent met their own criteria for good management (Leverington et al, 2008).
- **Indiana University and Ashoka Trust for Research in Ecology and the Environment:** research found lower rates of land-clearing in protected areas compared to surrounding areas (Nagendra, 2008).
- **Duke University:** research across four tropical areas assessed natural vegetation changes. Overall, protected areas were effective; forest cover was often 'strikingly higher' than surrounding areas (Joppa et al, 2008).
- **World Bank:** a global review, using fire incidence as a surrogate for deforestation, showed that tropical protected areas, especially those conserved by indigenous peoples, lose less forest than other management systems (Nelson and Chomitz, 2009).
- **UNEP World Conservation Monitoring Centre:** forests in protected areas accounted for just 3 per cent of tropical forest losses from 2000 to 2005 in countries studied, which is far better than average (Campbell et al, 2008).
- **Stanford University and partners:** studies in the Amazon found that protected areas, indigenous reserves and national forests generally, but not invariably, afforded protection against logging (Asner et al, 2005).

---

of loss was inversely proportional to size of protected area. Ian Craigie and colleagues have recently shown alarming declines of large mammals in many of Africa's national parks (Craigie et al, 2010) and James Fitzsimmons and his collaborators at The Nature Conservancy have also found amphibians disappearing from many of Australia's protected areas (Fitzsimons et al, 2010). The theory of island biogeography, which predicts such losses in genetically isolated populations, is repeatedly proved true in protected areas. In addition poaching, the knock-on effects of climate change are also reducing numbers. Indeed, periodic waves of poaching have destroyed populations of economically valuable species like rhinoceros and elephant. One of the grimmer assignments I have had in the last few years, concurrent with writing this book, was to assess the lessons learned from experiences in Vietnam, where it now seems virtually certain that the last Asian rhinoceros in mainland southeast Asia was shot by poachers in April 2010 in Cat Tien National Park. Calling something a protected area does not guarantee protection. Protected areas also need

FIGURE 8.2 Cat Tien National Park, Vietnam, where one of the last remaining Javan rhinos was shot by poachers in 2010

support from a strong and well-implemented legal process, particularly for species that have value in the wildlife trade.

Protected areas therefore cannot operate effectively in a vacuum but instead need to be linked to other natural ecosystems by suitable habitats such as biological corridors and 'stepping stones' for migratory species. There is growing evidence that corridors can be effective, for instance in increasing richness of plant species (Damschen et al, 2006). Recognition of this was the intellectual stimulus for development of the CBD's *ecosystem approach*, for the development of connectivity conservation (Worboys et al, 2010) and a major driver for sustainable forestry, organic agriculture and other management systems more sympathetic to the needs of wild species.

But all this is *as well as* rather than *instead of* protected areas. Well-managed farmland and exploited forest can help to maintain ecological connectivity and support a proportion of wild species but they can't support everything. A focus on naturalness of whole ecosystems rather than the survival of individual components reinforces this point. Improving management in the wider landscape may reduce the amount of strictly protected land and water that is needed to maintain biodiversity, but if protected areas were entirely replaced by 'sustainable management' we would in the large majority of cases see a proportion of wild species become extinct. Many species require specialized habitats within natural ecosystems and will disappear if this habitat disappears; so will the myriad ecological interactions from a naturally functioning ecosystem. It is important to stress this; the arguments against protected areas are certainly not about to go away – there are too many vested interests who would like to grab hold of the resources that they contain – and the protected area community will continue to need all the help that they can get.

Authenticity in protected areas

Does the world's system of protected areas provide a reservoir of authentic ecosystems? The answer is that it probably does, although one that is still incomplete, but the relationship between protected areas like national parks and nature reserves with concepts like naturalness or authenticity remains complicated.

Most of the earliest national parks were set up primarily as recreational resources and to preserve exceptionally beautiful landscapes. Some of the first modern parks, like Yellowstone in the United States and Blue Mountains outside Sydney in Australia were explicitly aimed at recreation for the newly emerging middle classes; a similar process has recently emerged in countries like China and South Korea. A few years ago in Sichuan, China we drove for *14 miles* past hotels catering to one particular World Heritage site, virtually all of them built in the decade previously.

At the early stages of national park establishment, the whole concept of nature being under threat was scarcely recognized as a problem in many areas. Others, such as Kaziranga National Park mentioned earlier, were set up to protect particular species; in the current instance Lady Curzon, the wife of the British Viceroy, wanted to protect the Asian rhino and had the political clout to set aside a large area of floodplain for the recovery or a remnant population. Over time, wildlife protection as a whole grew to be an increasingly important motivation in establishing protected areas, although still mainly aimed at particular charismatic species at risk like lions and tigers. More recently a wider concept of biodiversity protection, encompassing species, ecosystems and genetic diversity, has also become important and is the concept behind methodologies such as gap analysis used to identify sites for protected areas (Margules and Pressey, 2000; Dudley and Parrish, 2006).

This, however, says nothing explicit about how *natural* these protected areas should be and we have already seen many examples of highly 'unnatural' protected areas in the course of this book. Critics point out that a desire or fantasy about natural ecosystems has often distorted management of protected areas in ways that are detrimental to both people and ecosystems. In *The Myth of Wild Africa*, Adams and McShane (1992, p58) write: 'Fences seek to preserve a pristine wilderness that never existed while they endanger cultures that long ago adapted to living with wild animals'.

IUCN explicitly recognizes this dichotomy:

> *We note that few if any areas of the land, inland waters and coastal seas remain completely unaffected by direct human activity … terms such as 'natural' and 'cultural' are approximations. We therefore use the terms as follows:* **Natural or unmodified areas** *are those that still retain a complete or almost complete complement of species native to the area, within a more-or-less naturally functioning ecosystem.* **Cultural areas** *have undergone more substantial changes … species composition and ecosystem functioning are likely to have been substantially altered. Cultural landscapes can however still contain a rich array of species and in some cases these may have become reliant on cultural management. Use of terms such as 'natural' and 'un-modified' does not seek to hide or deny the long-term stewardship of indigenous and traditional peoples where this exists; indeed many areas remain valuable to biodiversity precisely because of this form of management.* (Dudley, 2008, p12)

IUCN provides further guidance to management responses in protected areas by identifying a set of six different management categories (one of which is further subdivided), defined by management objective; some of these are explicitly aimed at cultural or managed landscapes. The names assigned are approximate; there are for instance 'national parks' listed in the World Database on Protected Areas in all six of the IUCN categories:

Category Ia – Strict nature reserves: to protect biodiversity and geological/geomorphological features, where human visitation, use and impacts are strictly controlled.

Category Ib – Wilderness areas: usually large unmodified or slightly modified areas, retaining their natural character and influence, without permanent or significant human habitation to preserve their natural condition.

Category II – National parks: large natural or near-natural areas to protect large-scale ecological processes, which also provide educational, recreational and visitor opportunities. These are the 'classic' national parks of North America and Africa.

Category III – Natural monuments: to protect a specific natural monument; this can be a landform, seamount, submarine cavern, geological feature or a habitat such as an ancient forest grove.

Category IV – Habitat/species management area: aims to protect particular species or habitats. Many will need regular, active interventions to address the requirements of particular species or to maintain habitats, but this is not a requirement of the category.

Category V – Protected landscapes/seascapes: where the interaction of people and nature over time has produced significant ecological, biological, cultural and scenic value, and where safeguarding the integrity of this interaction is vital to protecting and sustaining the area.

Category VI – Protected area with sustainable use of natural resources: ecosystems with associated cultural values and traditional natural resource management systems, where a proportion is under sustainable natural resource management.

The relationship between different categories and concepts of naturalness does not follow a simple progression. In theory, anything assigned to category I would be expected to have a high degree of authenticity and conversely category V is explicitly designed for places that have been substantially altered by human management but some of the other designations are less obvious. Adrian Phillips designed a diagram to illustrate the relationship between protected area category and naturalness, which is still reasonably accurate today:

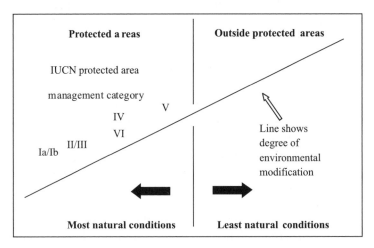

FIGURE 8.3 The relationship between protected area category and naturalness

Source: Bishop et al, 2004

Researchers using the Wildlife Conservation Society's Human Footprint Index and the World Database on Protected Areas found many discrepancies in this simple relationship (Leroux et al, 2010). Category Ia protected areas tended to have a higher footprint (i.e. were more impacted by human activities) than expected and VI lower; there were a relatively small number of protected areas overall with a low footprint, which is in line with what we have been seeing in terms of the scale of changes to ecosystems.

These designations are all approximate; categories are not decided by any strict set of criteria but rather reflect the primary aims of managers. The points to note in this regard are that there is a gradation within protected areas and, in practice, *all* categories can have a role in the protection and restoration of authenticity as it is being suggested here.

It is hard to give global statistics for protected area coverage by degree of authenticity even in the fairly crude terms summarized in the diagram. Almost 40 per cent of the protected areas in the World Database on Protected Areas have not been assigned a category (UNEP-WCMC, 2008). Of the rest, although category II protected areas cover around 5 million km^2, the generally 'less natural' categories IV–VI make up well over half of the total area. This suggests that the world's protected area network still gives relatively little emphasis on naturalness or authenticity as compared with other values; no surprise perhaps because in many countries these values have largely already been lost and everywhere require the stricter forms of protection that are generally resisted. This is particularly true for marine protected areas, where in many parts of the world the concept of strict protection has as yet proved politically impossible to introduce. For instance, despite its long history of protected areas the United States has virtually no marine reserves that ban commercial fishing that uses methods known to have impacts on marine biodiversity (Brailovskaya, 1998).

Management for naturalness: A contradiction in terms?

For the last 20 years there has been an active and sometimes acrimonious debate among conservationists about the extent to which managed habitats can also contain 'natural' values. This has been played out most publicly in the debate about forest management, pitting those who believe that well-managed forest can retain enough natural characteristics to be a useful component in conservation strategies (e.g. Franklin and Foreman, 1987) against those who think it is over-optimistic and diversionary to assume that managed forests can deliver substantial conservation benefits (Rice et al, 1997; Rice et al, 2001). This debate is still very much live and is not confined to forests, spilling over particularly into discussions about management of freshwaters; management of both these biomes is considered below.

Freshwaters

The Ramsar Convention, named after the Iranian city where it was first agreed in 1971, aims to encourage conservation of important wetlands around the world. Designation of a particular wetland as a Ramsar site is a compact between the government concerned and the convention and brings with it some obligations in terms of conserving a functioning ecosystem. But this doesn't mean that all Ramsar sites are nature reserves; many, probably most, are large inland or estuarine wetland areas that include a great deal of human activity. There is an unresolved debate about whether all Ramsar sites should automatically be considered as protected areas. We live on the edge of a Ramsar site in the Dyfi estuary in Wales; there are a scattering of nature reserves covering the richest wetland areas but also farms, forestry at the edges, rubbish dumps, caravan parks, villages and even some duck shoots; in addition part of the course of the river was changed when the railway was built altering flow patterns. Ramsar has pioneered the concept of 'wise use' – sustainable exploitation of wetlands in a way that does not destroy natural values, defined as 'the maintenance of their ecological character, achieved through the implementation of the ecosystem approach, within the context of sustainable development' (Hails and Peck, 2007). Ramsar does not refer to naturalness or an equivalent in its aims, although this is implicit in much of the management framework that it promotes.

A similar mixing of natural and human values is promoted in some other wetland designations, such as the Western Hemisphere Shorebird Reserve Network (WHSRN), a corridor of 69 shorebird migration sites stretching down the western coasts of North and South America from Alaska to Tierra del Fuego. As with Ramsar (and the networks share several sites), WHSRN aims to conserve the functioning of the natural ecosystem without necessarily eliminating all human uses.

Most freshwater conservation management therefore focuses on aspects of authenticity – clear water, natural flow regimes, elimination of invasive species – without actually referring to or defining a whole ecosystem approach in any comprehensive way. Moving towards the re-establishment of naturalness or authenticity needs to build on natural, type-specific reference conditions and focus on criteria for both processes and functions (Jungwirth et al, 2002); this is still a long way off for most wetlands.

Forests

The debate about whether or not 'natural' forests can be managed could fill several books rather than a couple of paragraphs. It includes consideration of a plethora of techniques aimed at maintaining functional aspects and key species from natural ecosystems within a managed forest estate. Most focus on minimizing the damage from logging operations in tropical forests (*reduced impact logging*); maintaining aspects of natural forest functions in managed forests (*new forestry* and similar approaches); and large-scale planning to maintain a network of more natural forests within a managed forest or plantation estate. Such measures can undoubtedly reduce ecological losses caused by forestry, although success depends on many factors including the individual commitment of managers. Studies in Borneo, for instance, found that reality often does not match up to theory in natural forest management (Meijaard et al, 2006). On the other hand, a recent review of a hundred or so studies of selective logging impacts on fauna found that biodiversity was in general retained (Putz et al, in review). Clearly many factors will impact on the net result, including forest type and quality of management.

Frameworks such as the High Conservation Value Forest (HCVF) concept provide a means of both defining and measuring sustainable forest management. HCVF was developed by the Forest Stewardship Council (FSC) and is encapsulated in six indicators relating to (1) biodiversity; (2) landscape-scale forests; (3) rare or endangered ecosystems; (4) ecosystem services; (5) supply of basic needs for local communities; and (6) cultural values (Jennings et al, 2003): at least three of these – biodiversity, landscape-scale ecosystems and rare/endangered ecosystems – relate to aspects of naturalness. The underlying concept was that any forest certified by the FSC and identified as HCVF has to be managed in a way that does not reduce any High Conservation Values identified. It would be fair to say that exactly what this means in practice has still not entirely been resolved. FSC has made it clear that in the case of HCVs related to ecosystems this should include no loss of populations of threatened species, viable populations of locally endemic and other species (although their populations may fluctuate), and retention of species composition, structure and size distribution. But exactly how this can be achieved within a managed system – and particularly within a system managed hard enough to turn a decent profit, remains unclear.

Can ecosystems be managed and remain authentic?

There is a philosophical question at the heart of this: If you're someone who believes that humans are separate from nature then clearly any intervention will reduce authenticity, but if you believe humans can play a role *within* natural ecosystems then equally clearly some interventions should be capable of accommodation without losing integral values. More broadly, retaining or regaining a *part* of naturalness may be possible even in quite altered ecosystems.

Sweeping generalizations are likely to be misleading; what may work in one ecosystem or at one particular time may be totally inappropriate elsewhere. Management for authenticity would generally aim to retain a full complement of species and mimic natural processes, particularly natural disturbance regimes (e.g. Angelstam, 1998), while recognizing the influence of both past history and surrounding land uses. Many individual elements are already well known and are summarized in Table 8.1 below.

These individual steps are well understood on a theoretical level, though their efficacy is still often the subject of debate. Developing an elegant ecological concept into a successful ecological tool usually involves a laborious period of testing, tends to be specific to certain times and places and is hard to generalize: in many cases we know the theory of sustainable management but have yet to translate it into a reality that is fully tested and understood. Proving that some intervention does or does not work is often a laborious

TABLE 8.1 Management to reflect elements of authenticity within ecosystems

Management aim	Examples
Retention of key components of the natural ecosystem	Protecting key species within managed habitats, for example through leaving unsprayed strips at the edges of agricultural land
	Setting aside critical microhabitats (ponds, dead wood, raised bogs, fire refugia)
Maintenance of natural patterns (e.g. vegetation mosaics)	Planning felling cycles in forests to ensure a mixed age stand
	Adjusting grazing to maintain natural vegetation mosaic
	Avoiding hard edges or transitions between habitats in cases where there would naturally be a gradual transition
Retention or mimicry of key processes	Keeping or restoring natural flow regimes in river systems (for instance by opening up flood plains to periodic inundation)
	Retaining safe habitat for fish breeding through temporary fishing set-asides
Avoiding fragmentation and maintaining connectivity	Maintenance and/or creation of biological corridors
	Protecting critical ecological 'stepping stones' at a landscape scale, of habitat suitable to provide stopping off or feeding places for regular or irregular movement of species

process. For instance, at the time that 'new forestry' started to be promoted as a way of addressing loss of natural forests, one of the key concepts was to leave a few standing stumps after felling to die and decay, thus mimicking some of the conditions in an old-growth forest (Franklin and Foreman, 1987). But it was largely a matter of theory. When Anders Lindhe set out to prove whether leaving a few standing tree trunks in felled forest areas actually provided useful breeding habitat for beetles, he embarked on a seven-year odyssey of research, along the way identifying almost 50,000 different beetle specimens collected from spruce, birch, aspen and oak in managed Swedish forests. He eventually found 316 saproxylic beetle species, including 40 species on the IUCN red list and showed that different tree species were more or less suitable, with spruce harbouring the most species, particularly on high stumps exposed to the sun (Lindhe and Lindelöw, 2004). Many other management actions still lack this kind of meticulous study.

Virtually all such management modifications come at a cost, in terms of either direct investment or opportunity costs through setting aside land that might otherwise be used for productive purposes. Land and water managers are faced with a complicated set of trade-offs and some critics of sustainable management approaches argue that it is better simply to sacrifice some areas to production and set aside others completely for protection. The strengths and weaknesses of these different strategies will vary from one place to another and be influenced both by the type of ecosystem involved and the willingness of land managers to prioritize retention of natural processes within their operations. In practice such approaches can only ever recreate or retain some particular elements of natural ecosystems functioning, although such partial ecosystems can nevertheless be valuable in linking or buffering more natural ecosystems.

Management for authenticity takes a further leap into the dark when likely climate changes are factored into the discussions (and in these cases active management may also become increasingly important for protected areas as well). Management might start – is already starting in those countries that are taking climate adaptation seriously – with some small steps, like increasing the area of core reserves, maintaining connectivity to allow vertical and latitudinal movement of species as conditions change and allowing room for inland migration of coastal habitats as sea levels rise (for instance Dunlop and Brown, 2008). If the more extreme predictions turn out to be correct, the level of interventions will quickly increase, potentially to actions such as translocation of species or even whole habitats and identification and strict protection of climate refugia. In the worst case scenarios of ocean acidification for example, scientists and conservationists might be looking towards artificial maintenance of lower pH in selected 'ark' habitats that can be more-or-less isolated from the wider changes in the ocean, or even setting up artificial habitats to maintain a proportion of species associated with specific habitats such as coral reefs until such time as pH levels decline again. Such doomsday scenarios are so extreme that they are scarcely even talked about as yet but the next generation of conservationists may be forced to confront in reality what at present seems like fantasy.

Management under climate change will create a range of ethical questions as well. If the entire habitat of a particular species disappears, as is likely to be the case for some endemic small island species or those confined to isolated mountain tops, should we create a home for them elsewhere or simply accept that they face extinction? How does *ex situ* breeding fit into such debates? In a world of stretched resources questions like these are only likely to be asked for larger and more interesting species; others will quietly fade away, many without ever having been recognized or described by scientists.

Getting back to naturalness: The role of restoration

When the early white settlers of New Zealand arrived at the Coramandel Peninsula and gazed up at the dense, apparently impenetrable forests that covered the mountains, they somehow conceived a vision of replacing them with rolling, grass-covered hills and sheep pasture. Ecological transformation at this scale, with the limited tools then available, must have been a little like science fiction writers imagining terra-forming Mars. But over the next few years they did create their sheep pastures, clearing huge areas of kauri (*Agathis australis*) forest, in the process felling many ancient trees that were sacred to the

FIGURE 8.4 Despite a ruthless battering by white settlers, the forests of the Coromandel Peninsula in New Zealand are creeping back to life, huddled around the few remaining remnants of the gigantic kauri trees that used to dominate the landscape

Maori (Lewington and Parker, 1999), and dramatically transforming an entire landscape. Not only felling: someone discovered that the resin from kauri was valuable and it was collected by the brutal process of burning trees, ground vegetation and even firing the soil itself in a dramatic scorched earth policy of one-time extraction (Jowitt, 1991). Early sepia photographs show a blackened, smoking landscape of the type we now associate with exploited areas of the Amazon. Miners further transformed the scene, blasting tracks out along the edges of mountains and digging into the newly exposed rock. Although we might shudder at what they did the sheer chutzpah was impressive.

But as it turned out, sheep farming was never particularly successful in many parts of Coramandel and the mines ran out or failed to meet their promise, so that some areas were fairly quickly abandoned, albeit damaged almost beyond recognition and host to a disruptive group of invasive European plants and animals. But the land still retained the seeds of its own recovery. A handful of kauri trees remained; some were set aside or maybe the settlers never got around to clearing them, in other places trees seem to have hung on somehow, fire-blackened but unbowed, on steep slopes where everything else had vanished. These remnant patches are now considered precious; the first time I visited, I walked a whole day through regenerating forest to reach the most ancient trees, miles from the nearest drivable track. In time, some of these areas were protected from further exploitation and a patchwork of reserves and national parks were set up to conserve the fragments that were left and allow the natural ecology, as far as possible, to restore itself. Today that healing process is evident in dense stands of young kauri and other native tree species, endemic birds calling in the young forests, streams of clear water and a booming tourist industry based on the natural beauty. To the casual visitor, large parts of the national parks probably seem completely natural and restoration efforts in the Coramandel could be held up as an example of nature rebuilding itself from conditions of extreme damage. Not completely though: the flora of the forest edges is at first sight almost completely European. In addition, introduced possums (*Trichosurus vulpecula*) are still a huge threat to native bird species and I saw many possum corpses poisoned in desperate government efforts to reduce numbers. I have also sat in a bar in Thames, the local town, chatting to men who made a living of a sort hunting feral pig and deer in the forests. Coramandel is coming back, but not exactly as it once was.

Which introduces some critical questions that face anyone interested in restoring naturalness, particularly if they are living in degraded or altered ecosystems: first, is restoration even possible? If so how? Exactly what are we restoring to; what is the baseline? And – particularly critical at a time of dramatic environmental change – how are we supposed to restore an ecosystem if the conditions that created it have already changed? Choices need to be made about whether restoration is needed and justified, and also what *kind* of restoration we are aiming for: as in other issues relating to authenticity of ecosystems, the role of human choice in restoration is critical, but often unrecognized (Allison, 2007).

Many conservationists are deeply suspicious of restoration (e.g. Katz, 1992). They argue that complete restoration of an ecosystem is impossible, or takes place over such a huge timescale as to be impractical; at best you'll get a pale imitation with fewer native species and simplified ecosystem functioning. They point out that restoration of a damaged ecosystem is massively more expensive than ensuring it remains intact in the first place. Most bitterly of all, they claim that the promise of restoration is simply used as a sweetener by individuals or companies who want to cause environmental damage in the pursuit of profit. Restoration is also seen as a diversion, squandering huge amounts of time and money into clawing back second-rate habitats with impoverished nature in rich countries, rather than tackling the far more valuable task of protecting richer and more pristine nature in the poor countries where it still exists. The need to focus down on what is most important has been the driving force behind efforts to prioritize conservation and the antipathy to restoration projects is, I think, one manifestation.

This viewpoint contains enough truth to be worth remembering as a checklist of potential problems with restoration projects. But it is already out of date. A major part of this book has been arguing that natural ecosystems have been distorted almost everywhere, so the idea that large areas of pristine wilderness remain is already a myth for most countries and the need for restoration is well established. This is not only true for the long-term cultural landscapes of Europe, southeast Asia and the flatlands of North America but also in many of the places that conservationists have identified as still containing important biodiversity values. A few years ago, Stephanie Mansourian and I looked at the potential for forest restoration in WWF's 'Global 200' (G200) a compilation of 238 ecoregions that were judged by the WWF Conservation Science Programme to be of global significance for the richness and endemism of their plant and animal species. We found that 22 per cent of the 87 Global 200 forest ecoregions had already lost at least 85 per cent of their forests – sometimes only 1–2 per cent of the forest being left, yet the G200 are generally among the less disturbed of the world's 800 or so terrestrial ecoregions. Any global assessment of restoration needs would be even larger. Deforestation is also identified as a key threat to water quality in 59 per cent of freshwater ecoregions in the Global 200 and at least 20 per cent of these have riparian forests at risk. Furthermore three quarters of G200 mangrove ecoregions are under threat and at least a fifth of the G200 marine ecoregions are damaged by sedimentation from deforestation and would thus benefit from restoration (Dudley and Mansourian, 2003). Such statistics are supported by other analyses. Assessment of data from Birdlife International's 'Endemic Bird Areas' study (Stattersfield et al, 1998) found 40 per cent already threatened by biodiversity losses due to forest loss. Similar analysis for biomes such as grasslands, freshwater ecosystems and some coastal habitats would almost certainly find even greater proportions of lost or degraded habitat. Many ecosystems are already at a stage where long-term survival of species and ecosystem functioning is seriously in doubt and therefore restoration is urgently required now, rather than at some theoretical point in the future.

Restoration can be fearfully expensive, as demonstrated by the size of investment that the better (and wealthier) mining companies pour into cleaning up their sites, but it doesn't always have to be. Simple policy changes that remove particular pressures can sometimes allow ecosystems to regain much of their function without further human effort and in other cases fairly small investments of money and effort can quickly yield large dividends. The latter has been seen quite frequently in the case of mangrove restoration for instance.

But restoration is also becoming increasingly vital as a tool for responding to ecological crises and changes. In fact if I was a gambler, I would stake heavily on the proposal that restoration techniques will become *the* necessary skill for ecologists in the future. The combination of existing damage, likely future damage and the accelerating pressures from climate change will mean that restoration and ecological rebuilding will become essential skills: not just for conservationists, but for farmers, local councils, water engineers, forest managers – in fact anyone who is involved in any type of ecosystem service or natural resource management. Restoration is not only a biological issue but also one with strong social implications (Aronson et al, 2010). Given that as noted above most 'managed' restoration is also expensive, this is also likely to be an increasing burden on both the tax-payer and on business, investors and individuals. Streamlining restoration, increasing the role of communities and volunteers and integrating restoration techniques into everyday management will all be of growing importance into the future.

Restoration does not just mean planting things or reintroducing species, although both of these may be needed. And it is, or should be, a time-limited process rather than an end in itself; some restoration specialists dislike the term 'restoration' and prefer to see their inputs as one aspect of management. Bengtsson and his collaborators (2003) talk about the importance of *ecological memory* as a prerequisite for recovery after large-scale, human-induced distur-bance, with ecological memory being composed of species, interaction and structures. They argue that protected areas alone cannot hope to protect nature in the face of large-scale changes and argue that static reserves need to be comple-mented with 'dynamic reserves' like ecological fallows and dynamic successional reserves mimicking natural disturbance regimes. Such reserves might be in exist-ence for a set period of time to allow recovery after a catastrophic event such as a major fire, or to help facilitate ecological shifts under conditions of climate change. Governments might, for example, pay compensation for a number of years to landowners to allow movement of species from one reserve to another at a higher altitude, or further inland. Scientists are starting to develop tools to identify likely climate change pressure points at landscape scale, where special responses will be needed (Vos et al, 2008). Restoration therefore needs to look beyond the site and at the role of restoration at a landscape or seascape scale (Mansourian et al, 2005, Rietbergen-McCracken et al, 2008) and should involve careful planning (e.g. Vallauri et al, 2005).

Conclusions

WWF uses the phrase 'protect, manage, restore' to describe its approach to forest conservation. Managing for authenticity in nature needs these three components as well. But in addition it needs a clear vision of what type of authenticity is being managed for and which particular vision of an authentic landscape or seascape that we aspire to. Are we searching for an Arcadian vision, where humanity and nature meet in a well-ordered 'halfway house' that we determine and manage, or are we seeking to step aside and let the rest of nature run free? This is at least partly a matter of choice: our choice. The role of choice in authenticity is tackled in the penultimate chapter.

CHAPTER 9

Into the Future: Making Choices about Natural Ecosystems

> **Key messages**
>
> - *Conservation planners and managers are constantly making choices about naturalness, but these often go unrecognised or are suppressed.*
> - *There is often not one single type of naturalness or authenticity possible but rather a range of choices; selecting the optimal ecosystem composition and functioning is a critical aspect of conservation planning and implementation.*
> - *We need to make choices about authenticity in ecosystems much more consciously and with better information available than has been the case to date.*

I'd like to start drawing to a close with two conversations. The first takes place in Győr, Hungary, where I'm having dinner at a riverside restaurant with Zoltan Kun and colleagues from the Pan Parks network, while they explain their strategy for wilderness protection in Europe. I've known Pan Parks since it was set up, but this is the first time I have had the chance to hear about their vision in detail. Pan Parks runs a certification system, aiming to recognize protected areas in Europe that provide outstanding wildlife and visitor experience. One critical requirement of the standards is that any Pan Park must have a core area of at least 10,000 hectares that is totally protected: no agriculture, grazing animals, tourist infrastructure or hunting: just a few footpaths and wild nature (Vancura et al, 2008). After years of effort Pan Parks has certified 11 sites in Scandinavia, Central and Eastern Europe and northern Portugal. The whole concept has been quite controversial; many people think the idea of setting aside wilderness in Europe is crazy; actually more than that, people find untouched ecosystems slightly frightening and primitive, something we have moved away from. But others have got really excited about the idea of European wilderness. If Zoltan reaches his aim of 25 Pan Parks he will have recovered and protected a total area of authentic ecosystems in Europe roughly the size of Budapest.

The second conversation takes place sitting outside our tents on the top of a mountain in the Ram Plateau in Canada, which I mentioned in the Introduction. I'm talking with a group of leading wilderness and protected area specialists from North America. We came here by helicopter a couple of days back and we're still pretty much on the edge of the main wilderness area, but it would be a 70 mile trek out of here to the nearest tiny settlement, even if we could find our way down from the plateau. This evening, we are talking about aspirations for wilderness protection in Canada. The expansion of the Nahanni National Park, the reason for our trip, has increased it to not much less than the size of Switzerland, a country you could fit an awful lot of Budapest-sized cities into. And Nahanni is by no means the largest wilderness area in Canada, which already has 82 million hectares under permanent protection; two thirds of the area protected is in a few massive protected areas that exceed 300,000ha (Lee and Cheng, 2010). In fact Canadian conservationists now aspire to setting aside half the country into protected areas and provinces like Quebec have already made this commitment; a colossal change in perspective in little more than a generation. To make the comparison more graphic, Canada is roughly the same size as Europe, west of the Ural Mountains, so that half of Canada is equivalent to half of Europe. We're a long way from the restaurant in Győr.

And this distance is itself at the heart of many of the confusions and disagreements sketched out in the book. For the last century, the major centres of global thought, passion and development about conservation (although not always the places with the best practice) have been in western Europe and in the mainly English-speaking former colonies in North America, Australia, New Zealand and South Africa. The status of ecology, degrees of naturalness, physical conditions and political possibilities are dramatically different between Europe and the rest. Furthermore, neither of these groups of countries much resembles the conditions found in tropical countries, although this has never stopped Western experts from saying how conservation should be run there. Conservationists have been struggling to reconcile wildly different worldviews into a single coherent global philosophy without realizing that we are sometimes talking almost completely different languages. And we then have to sell our message to a wider audience, with even more different worldviews. All too often the sense gets scrambled.

Some years ago I was in a small town in Finnish Karelia, at a public meeting to discuss growing tension between old-growth forest conservation and forest jobs – a debate I've seen time and again around the world. The question was whether or not a particular tract of old forest should be felled. Due to the presence of a few foreigners, and the linguistic ability of the Finns, the meeting was in English. The timber industry presentation was led by a pretty, soft-spoken woman who described the deep love all the townspeople had for their forests, the critical need for jobs to stop rural economic collapse, the presence of protected areas to ensure the survival of all species, the care with which the forests would be restored. The environmentalists were younger, scruffier, male and much angrier: at the end of an impassioned attack on the industry the spokesperson shouted: 'What are we talking about jobs for? There are *lichens at risk*!' There may well have been. The ethical case for biodiversity conservation has already been made and on occasions taking the survival of other species seriously will undoubtedly mean sacrifices. But these need to be negotiated with a bit more panache than on that occasion (to be fair, they usually are in Finland). I want to look at how the various ideas discussed earlier play out in practice and at how we approach making choices about the naturalness of ecosystems.

Levels of change

To recap: we live in a changed world, or more precisely a world that we have changed ourselves and where stewardship of ecosystems is now forced upon us both as a necessity and an obligation. The remaining natural world can be divided into three often overlapping types:

1 *Fairly unchanged*: Significant areas remain but (the Antarctic apart) they are a fraction of the whole.
2 *Changed*: The large majority of the land surface and much of the ocean, with 'change' covering a very wide spectrum of states.
3 *Changing*: Also a very large proportion, almost everything if the impacts of climate change are included in the equation.

Choosing the degree of authenticity in ecosystems

Ecosystem management needs to address all three situations and their combinations. In most parts of the world we can't begin to do this on a species by species basis because we have neither the knowledge nor the resources. People who work in well studied, rich countries sometimes don't realize quite how stark the differences can be. On the bookshelf behind me as I write is Arthur Chater's monumental *Flora of Cardiganshire* (2010), a magnificent 930-page volume that maps every flowering plant species at a 1km square scale throughout the sub-county to the south of where I live. The first edition sold out within a few months of publication and it is going to be a legendary volume among enthusiasts for the sheer scale and detail, but many other parts of the UK are also now mapped in this detail. In a rich country with low biodiversity and many naturalists it is possible to achieve an extraordinary level of understanding and management: the UK has individual Biodiversity Action Plans for almost 20 molluscs for instance. Similar detail can be found throughout much of northwest Europe.

But in other areas, including some of the world's richest biodiversity areas, many countries are still compiling very basic lists of even the mammals and birds that exist, let alone mapping their distribution. I spent the last months of 2010 working with the Vietnam Conservation Fund, a sinking fund aimed to build capacity in the country's protected areas; here the surveys that the Fund was sponsoring are still finding primates in entirely new parts of the country and it is only a few years since the saola (*Pseudoryx nghetinhensis*) was discovered, a whole new species of antelope. A survey sponsored by the fund in one Vietnamese protected area 'discovered' elephants in the park. Hundreds or probably thousands of new species will have been described worldwide during the time it has taken me to write this book. Conservation in places with huge knowledge gaps is necessarily much more broad-brush in its approach. We need to conserve whole ecosystems because we don't know yet what they contain.

The question is how to achieve this in a world that is largely changed and still changing fast. The wild and the tamed: the wilderness celebrated by Muir and the cultural landscapes beloved by Thoreau and Gilbert White. If, as the Wildlife Conservation Society suggest (Sanderson et al, 2002), we have had stewardship forced upon us, what does this mean? One important implication, which often goes unrecognized, is that we now have both the power and the obligation to make conscious choices about the composition and functioning of natural ecosystems; in other words *we set our own baseline of authenticity*. The practical and ethical implications of this have scarcely been addressed.

Well on the way through writing this book I learned about what sounds like a fascinating workshop, looking at the shortcomings of naturalness as a foundation for protected area management: 'naturalness is no longer the umbrella under which all protected area values comfortably sit' (Cole et al, 2008, p40; Cole and Young, 2010). Participants found that national parks such as Bandelier National Monument in New Mexico were continuing to degrade despite protection and had changed so fundamentally that removing the original pressure was no longer enough to return to equilibrium; instead they increasingly require intervention. The concept of naturalness gave little indication to managers about whether or not to intervene (for instance to protect a particular species). Participants disagreed about the way forward: some favoured redefining naturalness, whereas others felt that the concept was fatally flawed and examined alternatives, including ecological integrity and resilience. Some felt that there should be more intervention, others argued for a hands-off approach. They recognized a strong overlap between the concepts of historical fidelity, ecological integrity, resilience and biodiversity conservation but also that none were exactly the same as the others. These were suggested as part of a suite of principles for managing protected areas, along with autonomy of nature and managing with humility (Hobbs et al, 2009). A methodology to guide interventions in protected areas was proposed (Higgs and Hobbs, 2010).

The meeting took place in North America where naturalness has long been a principle guiding national parks management; discussion would have been different in Europe where promotion of naturalness is still seen as a radical concept, which has often explicitly been rejected and I've been arguing needs reinvigoration again.

But in practice we are making changes all the time whenever we intervene in ecosystems, even if our intervention is to set them aside or even if we are clearing up a mess we made earlier. Reintroducing the white-tailed sea eagle (*Haliaeetus albicilla*) into Britain has been a conservation success, but it has caused a rapid dip in populations of puffins (*Fratercula arctica*) in some areas: cute looking seabirds that many people hold in high regard. Debates about the reintroduction of wolves into Scotland to control deer (Manning et al, 2009) are fraught with questions about the wider ecological implications, yet wolves were originally British species. The Ecuadorian government has made huge efforts to eradicate feral goats from the Galapagos Islands, but this has led to problems for nesting waved albatross (*Phoebastria irrorata*) because goats had replaced the original herbivores as grazers (Anderson et al, 2002). Protection for the cormorant (*Phalocrocorax carbo*) in Europe has caused an acrimonious debate between anglers, ornithologists and freshwater biologists; cormorant populations have boomed and the birds are now spreading, spoiling sport fishing but also driving endemic fish species to extinction. Questions about how to respond have gone on for a decade or more but the truth is we don't really understand what is happening although additional food from aquaculture is thought to be a component in the apparently unstoppable rise of the cormorant. Scott Jones and others have spent years trying to manage the conflicts that arise (Carss et al, 2003). Note that these cases are not disturbances caused by introducing alien species or causing habitat degradation but by replacing individual species lost earlier or protecting species hitherto in decline. Things become even more complicated when we start altering whole ecosystems through controlling fire, altering river patterns and changing the chemical composition of air or water. There may be many forms of authenticity; with different compositions, different processes.

From a conservation perspective, my instinct is to maintain ecosystems in as close to their original state as possible, but I'm aware that not everyone shares this view, and that even many in the conservation community do not. In any case, who is to decide which is the most natural? There is no simple answer to this question in many cases; or if there is, we don't know it yet. Once overtly cultural landscapes are considered, the degree of choice made by managers increases even more: in the Mediterranean for instance, or in much of the Andes, in the huge areas of rice paddy across much of Asia and the grazing lands of South America.

So to some extent we clearly can and do make choices about levels of authenticity in natural and semi-natural ecosystems. While we are not by any means entirely in control, we do have a range of options; in deciding what level of authenticity to aim for in protected areas for instance or in choosing

FIGURE 9.1 Throughout the world, a boom in cormorant numbers is causing controversy, with animal rights groups opposing a cull, angling groups and freshwater biologists dismayed by the impact on aquatic ecosystems and ecologists still puzzled to explain the speed and extent of the growth

whether or not to incorporate ecosystem services into planning: such as building a sea wall or restoring a mangrove.

For the first time, conscious decisions are being made about levels of naturalness or authenticity in ecosystems. There is a gradual increase in the idea of 'letting ecosystems go' in places where they have long been managed: in parts of Europe for instance as the vignette that started the chapter showed; in the prairies of North America, the central wilderness of Tasmania and the native forests of New Zealand. In the UK the John Muir Trust is buying and managing land in Scotland for its wilderness value and a new campaign is focusing on re-wilding large areas of Europe, with pilot areas in the Danube delta, Eastern and Southern Carpathians, Velebit (Croatia) and Western Iberia (Sylven et al, undated). Landowners are deliberately stepping back from management and seeing what happens. This is enormously significant; many of these ecosystems are being left without immediate human influence for the first time in hundreds or thousands of years.

But that is one kind of choice. In other parts of the world, governments and others are investing money to maintain cultural landscapes after the immediate utilitarian reasons for their existence have gone, with at least some of the justification being because of the nature they contain. Here people are making a different kind of choice about naturalness; that particular cultural landscapes need to be conserved to maintain a mix of species that society has become used to and wants to remain. We need to experiment more consciously and systematically than we have done to date with different strategies, different levels and types of intervention, different end goals.

Strategies

The level of authenticity chosen also informs our choices about conservation. There are compelling reasons for keeping enough of the remaining natural or near-natural ecosystems with a minimum of disturbance to ensure long-term survival of biodiversity: in most cases we don't know enough to meddle very effectively and any changes we make will probably result in losses. In these 'unchanged' systems conservation emphasis should give high priority to protection. However in 'changed' or 'changing' systems everything is more complicated and here there is and will continue to be an active debate about what authenticity means, in much the same way as we saw for buildings and archaeological sites.

In these changed landscapes I think we need to add to our thinking: how much authenticity we want or are prepared to accept and what 'sort' of authenticity? Do we want all aspects of the ecosystem to be authentic or just some elements? Is the composition of species more important than the ways in which they interact? Is it worth restoring an original mix of species even if it risks upsetting the current mix or reduces the total number of species in the ecosystem? Do we need to trade off the natural regeneration processes against the social and economic upset that they cause? Does it matter that a few new species have moved in to replace the old? The answers will depend on time, place and what people want, but at the moment we don't usually even ask these questions. They will become even more important as ecosystems vary more dramatically under climate change.

Making the case

Those who may think maximizing naturalness and authenticity in ecosystems is important for conservation have the responsibility to make a case. An appreciation of natural landscapes often literally needs to be relearned, but people are frequently more open to this than we sometimes assume. At a period when the debate about forest management was most intense in Sweden, with conservationists head to head with foresters about the protection of old-growth forest and a growing divide within the country, the Swedish Forestry Board launched the *Rikare Skog* ('Richer Forest') programme to help forest owners and others learn about forest wildlife and ecosystems (Persson and Manus, 1990). The programme was based around a simple illustrated book, supplied free to anyone who asked, used in weekly group learning sessions during the long, dark winter months. The programme was hugely popular and made some important changes in attitude; foresters that had grown up believing good forestry meant clearing away anything but the growing trees began to learn the values of deadwood and undergrowth and the full forest cycle. In a country where much forestry on private lands is carried out for aesthetic purposes, the aesthetics started to change.

Interest in nature, in the broadest sense, is latent somewhere inside many of us and can be rekindled very quickly given the right set of conditions. The Republic of Korea has been one of the most spectacular of the Asian Tiger economies. Thirty years ago South Korea had a GDP not dissimilar to Kenya or Tanzania, now average wages in the country are about the same as Australia; within a generation the country has shaken free from the 'Third World' and assumed a place at the table of rich nations. Not only that: after the damage received during the Second World War and the civil war the ecology was in crisis; in particular most of the forests had disappeared as a result of conflict and a desperate search for fuel. Since then, the Korean government has undertaken one of the most spectacular reforestation programmes in history (Eckholm, 1979) so that the majority of the land is now covered with maturing forest. Korea has also developed a flourishing protected area system that covers some

FIGURE 9.2 South Korea has gone from being one of the most deforested countries on the planet to one with a rich forest estate over a period of around forty years; although currently even-aged it is planned that forests within national parks like Jirisan, pictured here, will eventually gain natural age distribution and characteristics

16,000 square kilometres. The national parks and other reserves set aside are hugely popular with the mainly urbanized society of Korea; in 2007 there were 38 million visitors to national parks alone, 99 per cent of which are tourists from within the country (KNPS, 2009). A generation after people scrabbled around on the land to supply basic livelihood needs, their urban sons and daughters are spending holidays appreciating nature in another way. South Korea is far from unique in its flowering of interest in the natural world.

Concluding remarks

I hope people reading this book will agree that the authenticity of natural ecosystems remains important, not just because of some current fashion in conservation but for the intrinsic values represented by life on Earth. By our own actions, we have unwittingly created a situation where we are now necessarily stewards of much of this life. In many cases, we have the power to make choices about naturalness in ecosystems, albeit choices that will be pushed and pulled in many different directions by the wave of change currently sweeping over the planet. Decisions about how or if we manage for naturalness will vary around the world and also over time. But it is important that we recognize that we have a choice and build up the knowledge and skills necessary to make informed decisions about these choices.

The concept of authenticity provides a common framework that covers both near-pristine ecosystems and dramatically changed or changing ecosystems. I believe that a common framework of this type is important to help us think logically about the ways in which ecosystems with dramatically different levels of authenticity can be approached. I hope it might help conservationists (and other managers of land and water) with differing priorities to find common ground.

One framework certainly does not mean one type of management response, but it does imply a common set of questions to consider. In the case of authenticity, this includes considering the historic, geographic and climatic conditions (current and predicted) when deciding on a particular strategy for management. It also means making choices and I think that we should be doing these consciously rather than by default. That way at least we can have an educated discussion about the options.

But prioritizing authenticity needs some conscious choices by society and some explicit actions. The final chapter outlines five important steps in developing this process.

CHAPTER 10

A Manifesto for Authenticity

Two historically unprecedented changes lie behind almost every topic discussed in this book: a rise in global temperature at a rate hitherto not experienced by life on the planet coupled with a similarly unique decrease in biodiversity. As we have discussed, the two influence each other. Climate change will further accelerate biodiversity loss and it is becoming increasingly clear that loss of biodiversity can decrease the resilience of ecosystems to withstand climate change. Any wider discussion of naturalness has to be placed against this backdrop.

The world is making slow progress towards addressing threats that some of us believe are among the gravest we have ever faced. In October 2010, the tenth Conference of Parties of the Convention on Biological Diversity, meeting in Nagoya, Japan, agreed a global strategy and targets for biodiversity protection that are being hailed by some as a triumph and by others as a disaster. They include a rapid increase in area of land and ocean under protection. Negotiations under the UN Framework Convention on Climate Change on the other hand appear to be stalled: the climate change deniers have pulled off some spectacular media triumphs and captured whole political movements, like the Tea Party in the United States and much conservative thinking in Australia. Climate change is slipping down the list of peoples' priorities and industry, particularly the oil industry, is staging some spectacular coups in efforts to maintain and increase levels of pollution. While some tentative steps forward were made in 2010, the situation remains fragile.

One reason why we are failing in our attempts to address the concrete and urgent environmental problems facing the planet is that our responses tend to be fragmented and in conflict. On a micro-scale, projects and organizations do not confer (in fact they compete for the same funds). Too many people involved in rural development do not talk to people involved in wildlife conservation and vice versa; neither of them talks to industry players, who also often fight among themselves. There are exceptions, but the general pattern remains, and repeats itself on a larger scale in local and national governments and in intergovernmental processes. Part of this, at least some of the time, is a result of the kinds of personal ambitions, vanities and weaknesses that it is hard to address through general policy initiatives, but there is a larger disconnect in place.

FIGURE 10.1 A fence line on a mountain slope in the Snowdonia National park, Wales, showing the difference between habitat grazed by sheep on the left and regenerating moorland and woodland on the right

A focus on natural or authentic ecosystems could provide some of the glue to stick different parts of the puzzle together and help to develop a more rational and coherent approach to a number of the critical challenges facing us. Below is a first draft of a 'manifesto for authenticity': some important steps to help bring the concepts of naturalness in ecosystems into the centre of debate and make some progress towards addressing these challenges. Unlike other parts of the book, which are relatively timeless, this deliberately focuses on needs and opportunities that will occur within a few years of publication and begins to pave out a route for how some of the ideas discussed above could be put into action.

1 Carry out a comprehensive assessment and gap analysis for natural ecosystem protection and management

We are still a long way from having a thorough understanding of how much natural ecosystem exists and how much we need; to conserve the world's biodiversity for instance, or to provide sufficient water for the projected world population; to secure genetic resources and to contribute to climate response strategies. Such a study would need to be tackled sector by sector and the results amalgamated and compared. A target date for completion of a global protected areas gap analysis could be the next World Parks Congress in 2014; other sectors could find similar timelines and forums. A key element of such a research programme would be to address the question of how natural an ecosystem needs to be to address particular functions: the authenticity of a forest for water catchment protection could be much lower than one needed for biodiversity conservation and genetic resource management for instance. The gap analysis should contain proposals and scenarios for how countries or regions might address the identified needs. The obvious intergovernmental bodies to coordinate such work would be the United Nations Environment Programme, Secretariat of the Convention on Biological Diversity and the UN Framework Convention on Climate Change. Many research institutions would need to be involved, following the models of the Intergovernmental Panel on Climate Change, along with non-governmental organizations such as IUCN.

2 Develop authenticity as a target of national and global conservation strategies

Maintenance and protection of natural ecosystems is often inferred rather than stated in national conservation strategies, National Biodiversity Strategies and Action Plans (NBSAPs) and other such strategies. In some parts of the world, particularly Europe, the focus is often deliberately on cultural landscapes and naturalness is tacitly or explicitly regarded as irrelevant or irretrievable. This bias is not necessarily desirable. Along with biodiversity conservation, which often requires a high degree of intervention aimed at the protection of named species, we also need a focus on more general recognition of natural or near-natural ecosystems, for protection of those minor species and inter-relationships that often remain poorly understood or unknown and for the wider values that such places represent. Tools and approaches aimed at naturalness and authenticity are required alongside those aimed at species. Developing naturalness as a target within the plans developed to implement the CBD's new ten-year strategy would be a valuable steps towards greater recognition of these values.

3 Develop a better understanding of the resilience of natural ecosystems under conditions of climate change

The role of natural ecosystems in responding to climate change has only recently been fully acknowledged, yet it provides an important new incentive for their preservation and management. The extent to which fully natural ecosystems can confer added resilience is still largely speculative although there have been some interesting initial studies; some of these were discussed in Chapter 5. The robustness of science around these issues needs to be a priority; there are compelling reasons for the CBD and the United Nations Framework Convention on Climate Change (UNFCCC) to work more closely together on adaptation strategies that mix biodiversity conservation and climate change responses. A special task force of the Intergovernmental Panel on Climate Change needs to focus on issues of resilience and this should also be a focus of collaborative work between the UNFCCC and the CBD.

4 Provide adequate social safeguards for change

The climatic and environmental changes currently taking place bring similar huge changes to human communities and we know that in the past some conservation responses have made things worse rather than better for local communities, as discussed in Chapter 4. A massive increase in commitment to protecting and restoring natural habitats will only be ethically acceptable – and feasible – if planned with and accepted by people living in such areas. While this has not always been the case in the past, there are many good reasons for working together. The fact that indigenous peoples traditionally control large areas of land in some parts of the world has long been a source of tension: responses have varied from brutal conquest to quasi-legal occupation and legal and policy challenges. There is common cause between the desire of indigenous communities to stay on their land and the desire of the conservation community to keep such lands in a natural state for the regional and global services they provide; this is one reason why Australian Aboriginal communities have voluntarily set aside 20 million hectares of their land into indigenous protected areas in the last decade. Similar changes are taking place in the Amazon, Canada and many places where tribal people are fighting to retain traditional lands. Such agreements are always trade-offs: indigenous communities retain use rights that conservationists might ideally like to see disappear and the communities also lose some rights (for instance to clear land for oil palm plantations). The plethora of payment for ecosystem service schemes, compensation packages and joint agreements being developed around the world provide the tools and an increasingly robust framework for such agreements, which will be needed on a far larger scale than hitherto. Steps towards better cooperation between conservation organizations and indigenous peoples groups could be a major output for both the World Conservation Congress in 2012 and the World Parks Congress in 2014.

5 Developing a cross-sector global strategy towards the values, benefits, likely futures and requirements of authentic ecosystems.

The culmination of much of the above should be a comprehensive global strategy that addresses the needs of and benefits from authentic ecosystems.

Such a strategy would be a major enterprise, with proper funding, targets and processes. It would necessarily look beyond biodiversity conservation and embrace the multiple ecosystem services described in Chapter 5, including climate mitigation and adaptation, and also cultural, spiritual and aesthetic needs; and to consider both the costs and benefits of different scenarios. It should start with some of the obvious institutions, initially the CBD and the UNFCCC but also bodies such as the United Nations Environment Programme (UNEP) and the United Nations Development Programme (UNDP), major NGOs and donor/lender organizations such as the World Bank and bilateral landing agencies. Many of these bodies already work together. But a global approach should go far further and include other institutions that rely on natural ecosystems: health organizations, disaster relief agencies, crop breeding and pharmaceutical companies, military strategists, fishery agencies, forest product companies and the world's huge tourist industry. The role of faith groups and religions is also critical. These and other bodies all have a stake in nature but their collaboration, if it happens at all, tends to be ad hoc and one-to-one. Changing that process is an urgent requirement that could, for example, be a major output agreed at the *Rio Plus 20* meeting in 2012.

And so to the end. A gravel pit nature reserve or a Canadian wilderness? I hope if you've got this far you know that I don't think the answer is either one or the other, but both. As ecological authenticity decreases, it becomes more precious as a commodity, with its value rising all the time as we learn more about the way that natural ecosystems respond to stress. Understanding, managing and learning to cherish authenticity will become essential elements in confronting the scary ecological future that confronts us. I hope I've raised some questions; it will need effort from many more people to supply all the answers.

References

Abbey, E. (1975) *The Monkey Wrench Gang*, Lippincott Williams & Wilkins, Philadelphia, PA

Adams, J. and McShane, T. O. (1992) *The Myth of Wild Africa*, California University Press, Berkeley, CA

Adger, W. N., Arnell, N. W. and Tompkins, E. L. (2005) 'Successful adaptation to climate change across scales', *Global Environmental Change*, vol 15, pp77–86

Aide, T. M. and Grau, H. R. (2004) 'Globalization, migration, and Latin American ecosystems', *Science*, vol 305, no 5692, pp1915–1916

Airoldi, L., Balata, D. and Beck, M. W. (2008) 'The gray zone: Relationship between habitat loss and marine diversity and their applications in conservation', *Journal of Experimental Marine Biology and Ecology*, vol 366, pp8–15

Aksenov, D. E., Dobrynin, D., Dubinin, M., Egorov, A., Isaev, A., Karpachevskiy, M., Laestadius, L., Potapov, P., Purekhovskiy, A., Turubanova, S. and Yaroshenko, A. (2002) *Atlas of Russia's Intact Forest Landscapes*, Biodiversity Conservation Center, Greenpeace Russia, International Socio-Ecological Union and World Resources Institute, Moscow

Aksenov, D. E., Dubinin, M. Yu., Karpachevskiy, M. L., Liksakova, N. S., Skvortsov, V. E. Yu., Smirnov, D. Yu. and Yanitskaya, T. O. (2006) *Mapping High Conservation Value Forest of Primorsky Krai, Russian Far East*, Global Forest Watch Russia, Moscow and Vladivostok

Al-Awadhi, J. M., Omar, S. A. and Misak, R. F. (2005) 'Land degradation indicators in Kuwait', *Land Degradation and Development*, vol 16, pp163–176

Alberts, H. C. and Hazen, H. D. (2010) 'Maintaining authenticity and integrity at cultural World Heritage sites', *The Geographical Review*, vol 100, n. 1, pp56–73

Allison, S. K. (2007) 'You can't not choose: Embracing the role of choice in ecological restoration', *Restoration Ecology*, vol 15, no 4, pp601–605

Alongi, D. M. (2008) 'Mangroves forests: Resilience, protection from tsunamis and responses to climate change', *Estuarine and Coastal Shelf Science*, vol 76, pp1–13

Altesor, A., Oesterheld, M., Leoni, E., Lezama, F. and Rodríguez, C. (2005) 'Effect of grazing on community structure and productivity of a Uruguayan grassland', *Plant Ecology*, vol 179, no 1, pp83–91

Altesor, A., Piñeiro, G., Lezama, F., Jackson, R. B., Sarasola, M. and Paruelo, J. M. (2005a) 'Ecosystem changes associated with grazing in subhumid South American grasslands', *Journal of Vegetation Science*, vol 17, pp323–332

Alves, R. R. N. and Rosa, L. M. L. (2007) 'Biodiversity, traditional medicine and public health: Where do they meet?', *Journal of Ethnobiology and Ethnomedicine*, vol 3, p14

Anderson, D. M., Glibert, P. M. and Burkholder, J. M. (2002) 'Harmful algal blooms and eutrophication: Nutrient sources, composition, and consequences', *Estuaries*, vol 25, no 4b, pp704–726

Anderson, J. E. (1991) 'A conceptual framework for evaluating and quantifying naturalness', *Conservation Biology*, vol 3, no 3, pp347–352

Angelstam, P. K. (1998) 'Maintaining and restoring biodiversity in European boreal forests by developing natural disturbance regimes', *Journal of Vegetation Science*, vol 9, pp593–602

Angermeier, P. L. (1994) 'Does biodiversity include artificial diversity?', *Conservation Biology*, vol 8, pp600–602

Angermeier, P. L. and Karr, J. R. (1994) 'Biological integrity verses biological diversity as policy directives', *Bioscience*, vol 44, no 10, pp690–697

Anon (1994) *Indicators for the Sustainable Management of French Forests*, Ministère de l'agriculture et de la pêche, Paris

Anon (2001) *Cader Idris*, Exhibition catalogue from the Royal Cambrian Academy, Conwy

Anon (2009) *The State of the UK's Birds 2008*, RSPB, BTO, WWT and Joint Nature Conservation Committee, Sandy, Bedfordshire, UK

Aplet, G., Thompson, J. and Wilbert, M. (2000) 'Indicators of wildness: Using attributes of the land to assess the context of wilderness', USDA Forest Service Proceedings RMRS-P-15-Vol 2, pp89–98

Araújo, M., Cabeza, M., Thuiller, W., Hannah, L. and Williams, P. H. (2004) 'Would climate change drive species out of reserves? An assessment of existing reserve-selection methods', *Global Change Biology*, vol 10, pp1618–1626

Archer, M. and Beale, B. (2004) *Going Native*, Hodder, Adelaide, Australia

Arnold, M., Kohlin, G., Persson, R. and Shepherd, G. (2003) *Fuelwood Revisited: What Has Changed in the Last Decade?*, CIFOR Occasional Paper No 39, Center for International Forestry Research, Bogor, Indonesia

Aronson, J., Blignaut, J. N., Milton, S. J., le Maitre, D., Esler, K., Limouzin, A., Fontaine, C., de Wit, M. W., Mugido, W., Prinsloo, P., van der Elst, L. and Lederer, N. (2010) 'Are socio-economic benefits of restoration adequately quantified? A meta analysis of recent papers (2000–2008) in Restoration Ecology and 12 other scientific journals', *Restoration Ecology*, vol 18, pp43–154

Asner, G. P., Knapp, D. E., Broadbent, E. B., Oliveira, P. J. C., Keller, M. and Silva, J. N. (2005) 'Selective logging in the Amazon', *Science*, vol 310, pp480–482

Atauri, J. A. and de Lucio, J. V. (2001) 'The role of landscape heterogeneity in species richness distribution of birds, amphibians, reptiles and lepidopterans in Mediterranean landscapes', *Landscape Ecology*, vol 16, pp147–159

Bagader, A. A., Al-Chirazi El-Sabbagh, A. T., As-Sayyid Al-Glayand, M. and Izzi-Deen Samarrai, M. Y. (1994) *Environmental Protection in Islam* (2nd edn), IUCN Environmental Policy and Law Paper No 20, IUCN, Gland, Switzerland

Baker, T. R., Phillips, O. L., Malhi, Y., Almeida, S., Arroyo, L., Di Fiore, A., Erwin, T., Killeen, T., Laurance, S. G., Laurance, W. F., Lewis, S. L., Lloyd, J., Monteagudo, A., Neill, D., Patiño, S., Pitman, N., Silva, J. N. M. and Vásquez Martínez, R. (2004) 'Variation in wood density determines spatial patterns in Amazonian forest biomass', *Global Change Biology*, vol 10, pp545–562

Balmford, A. (in press) *The Glass Half-full: Stories of Hope for Wild Nature*, University of Chicago Press, Chicago, IL

Balustein, A. R. and Wake, D. B. (1995) 'The puzzle of declining amphibian populations', *Scientific American*, vol 272, no 4, pp56–61

Barnett, R. (ed) (2000) *Food For Thought: The Utilization of Wild Meat in Eastern and Southern Africa*, TRAFFIC East/Southern Africa, Nairobi

Barr, B. W. and Lindholm, J. (2000) 'Conservation of the sea: Using lessons from the land', *George Wright Forum Journal*, vol 17, no 3, pp77–85

Barreto, P., Souza, C. Jnr, Noguerón, R., Anderson, A. and Salomão, R. (2006) *Human Pressure on the Brazilian Amazon Forests*, World Resources Institute, Global Forest Watch and Imazon, Washington DC

Bates, B., Kundzewicz, Z. W., Wu, S. and Palutikof, J. (eds) (2008) *Climate Change and Water*, Intergovernmental Panel on Climate Change, WMO and UNEP, Geneva

Battisti, A., Stastny, M., Netherer, S., Robinet, C., Schopf, A., Roques, A. and Larsson, S. (2005) 'Expansion of geographic range in the pine processionary moth caused by increased winter temperatures', *Ecological Applications*, vol 15, pp2084–2096

Bauer, H. J. (1985) *Welche Ursachen führten zur Gefährdung und Ausrottung von Arten?*, in Deuttscher Rat für Landesplege, *Warum Artenschutz?*, Heft 46, Bonn. Quoted in Baldock, D. (1990) *Agriculture and Habitat Loss in Europe*, WWF International CAP Discussion Paper No 3, WWF International, Gland, Switzerland

Bax, N., Williamson, A., Aguero, M., Gonzalez, E. and Geeves, W. (2003) 'Marine invasive alien species: A threat to global biodiversity', *Marine Policy*, vol 27, pp313–323

BBC (2007) News website, 21 May

Beattie, A. J. (2003) 'New products and industries from biodiversity', in Hassan, R., Scholes, R. and Ash, N. (eds) *Ecosystems and Human Well-being: Current State and Trends. Findings of the Condition and Trends Working Group*, Island Press, Washington DC

Beebee, T. J. C. (1979) 'Habitats of the British amphibians (2): Suburban parks and gardens', *Biological Conservation*, vol 15, no 4, pp241–257

Behling, H., DePatta Pillar, V. and Girardi Bauermann, S. (2005) 'Late Quaternary grassland (Campos), gallery forest, fire and climate dynamics, studied by pollen, charcoal and multivariate analysis of the São Francisco de Assis core in western Rio Grande do Sul (southern Brazil)', *Review of Palaeobotany and Palynology*, vol 133, pp235–248

Beinart, W. and Coates, P. (1995) *Environment and History: The Taming of Nature in the USA and South Africa*, Routledge, London and New York

Bélair, C., Ichikawa, K., Wong, B. Y. L. and Mulongoy, K. (eds) (2010) *Sustainable Use of Biological Diversity in Sicio-Ecological Production Landscapes: Background to the 'Satoyama Initiative for the benefits of biodiversity and human well-being'*, CBD Technical Series number 52, CBD Secretariat, Montréal

Belcher, B., Ruíz-Pérez, M. and Achdiawan, R. (2005) 'Global patterns and trends in the use and management of commercial NTFPs: Implications for livelihoods and conservation, *World Development*, vol 33, no 9, pp1435–1452

Béné, C., Macfadayen, G. and Allison, E. H. (2006) 'Increasing the contribution of small-scale fisheries to poverty alleviation and food security'. *Fisheries Technical Papers*, vol 481, FAO, Rome

Bengtsson, J., Angelstam, P., Elmqvist, T., Emanuelsson, U., Folke, C., Ihse, M., Moberg, F. and Nyström, M. (2003) 'Reserves, resilience and dynamic landscapes', *Ambio*, vol 32, no 6, pp389–396

Bennett, E. L. and Robinson, J. G. (2000) *Hunting of Wildlife in Tropical Forests: Implications for Biodiversity and Forest Peoples*, Biodiversity Series – Impact Studies, World Bank, Washington DC

Berdén, M., Nilsson, I. S., Rosén, K. and Tyler, G. (1987) *Soil Acidification: Extent, Causes and Consequences: An Evaluation of Literature Information and Current Research*, National Swedish Environment Protection Board Report 3292, Solna

Berghöfer, A. and Dudley, N. (2011) 'Protected areas', in H. Wittmer and H.Gundimeda (eds) *The Economics of Ecosystems and Biodiversity in Local and Regional Policy and Management*, an output of TEEB: The Economics of Ecosystems and Biodiversity, Earthscan, London

Bertolino, S. and Genovesi, P. (2003) 'Spread and attempted eradication of the grey squirrel (*Sciurus carolinensis*) in Italy, and consequences for the red squirrel (*Sciurus vulgaris*) in Eurasia', *Biological Conservation*, vol 109, pp351–358

Bevilacqua, M., Cárdenas, L., Flores, A. L., Hernández, L., Lares, E., Mansutti, A., Miranda, M., Ochoa, J., Rodríguez, M. and Selig, E. (2002) *The State of Venezuela's Forests: A Case Study from the Guayana Region*, World Resources Institute, Washington DC

Bhagwat, S. A. and Palmer, M. (2009) 'Conservation: The world's religions can help', *Nature*, vol 461, p37

Bhagwat, S. A., Dudley, N. and Harrop, S. R. (2011) 'Religious following in biodiversity hotspots: Challenges and opportunities for conservation and development', *Conservation Letters*, DOI: 10.1111/j.1755-263X.2011.00169.x

Bikié, H., Collomb, J. G., Djomo, L., Minnemeyer, S., Ngoufo, R. and Nguiffo, S. (2000) *An Overview of Logging in Cameroon*, Global Forest Watch and World Resources Institute, Washington DC

Bilenca, D. and Minarro, F. (2004) *Identification de Areas Valiosas de Pastizal en las Pampas y Campos de Argentina, Uruguay y sur de Brasil*, Fundacion Vida Silvestre, Buenos Aires

Bishop, K., Dudley, N., Phillips, A. and Stolton, S. (2004) *Speaking a Common Language: The Uses and Performance of the IUCN System of Management Categories for Protected Areas*, Cardiff University, IUCN and UNEP-WCMC, Gland, Switzerland, Cardiff and Cambridge, UK

Blackbourn, D. (2006) *The Conquest of Nature: Water, Landscape and the Making of Modern Germany*, W. W. Norton, New York and London

Bobiec, A., van der Burgt, H., Zuyderduyn, C., Haga, J. and Vlaanderen, B. (2000) 'Rich deciduous forests in Bialowieza as a dynamic mosaic of developmental phases: Premises for nature conservation and restoration management', *Forest Ecology and Management*, vol 130, nos 1–3, pp159–175

Bond, I., Grieg-Gran, M., Wertz-Kanounnikoff, S., Hazlewood, P., Wunder, S. and Angelsen, A. (2009) *Incentives to Sustain Forest Ecosystem Services: A Review and Lessons for REDD*, International Institute for Environment and Development, London

Bond-Lamberty, B., Peckham, S. D., Ahl, D. E. and Gower, S. T. (2007) 'Fire as the dominant driver of central Canadian boreal forest carbon balance', *Nature*, vol 450, pp89–93

Borrini-Feyerabend, G. and Dudley, N. (2005) 'Elan Durban: Nouvelles perspectives pour les Aires Protégées à Madagascar', IUCN World Commission on Protected Areas and IUCN Commission on Environmental, Economic and Social Policy, Gland, Switzerland

Borrini-Feyerabend, G., Pimbert, M., Farvar, M. T., Kothari, A. and Renard, Y. (2004) *Sharing Power: Learning-by-doing in Co-Management of Natural Resources throughout the World*, Earthscan, London

Bowyer, C., Tucker, G., By, H. and Baldock, D. (2010) *Operationalising Criteria to Protect Highly Biodiverse Grasslands under the Renewable Energy Directive* (2009/28/EC), Institute for European Environmental Policy, London

Boyland, M. and Bunnell, F. L. (2002) *Vertebrate Use of Dead Wood in the Pacific Northwest*, University of British Columbia, British Columbia

Bradshaw, S. D., Dixon, K. W., Hopper, S. D., Lambers, H. and Turner, S. R. (2011, in press) 'Little evidence for fire-adapted plant traits in Mediterranean climate regions', *Trends in Plant Sciences*

Brailovskaya, T. (1998) 'Obstacles to protected marine biodiversity through marine wilderness preservation: Examples from the New England region', *Conservation Biology*, vol 12, no 6, pp1236–1240

Brander, K. M. (2007) 'Global fish production and climate change', *PNAS*, vol 104, no 50, pp19709–19714

Briggs, J. M., Knapp, A. K. and Brock, B. L. (2002) 'Expansion of woody plants in tallgrass prairie: A fifteen year study of fire and fire-grazing interaction', *American Midland Naturalist*, vol 147, no 2, pp287–294

Brodie, J. F. (2008) *A Review of American Bison* (Bos bison) *Demography and Population Dynamics*, Working Paper No 35, Wildlife Conservation Society, New York

Brody, H. (1987) *Living Arctic: Hunters of the Canadian North*, Faber and Faber, London

Brookes, T. M., da Fonseca, G. A. B. and Rodrigues, A. S. L. (2004) 'Protected areas and species', *Conservation Biology*, vol 18, pp616–618

Brown, J., Mitchell, N. and Beresford, M. (eds) (2005) *The Protected Landscape Approach: Linking Nature, Culture and Community*, IUCN, Areas, Gland, Switzerland

Brown, J. W., van Coeverden de Groot, P. J., Birt, T. P., Seutin, G., Boag, P. T. and Friesen, V. L. (2007) 'Appraisal of the consequences of the DDT-induced bottleneck on the level and geographic distribution of neutral genetic variation in Canadian peregrine falcons, *Falco peregrinus*', *Molecular Ecology*, vo. 16, pp327–343, doi: 10.1111/j.1365-294X.2007.03151.x

Bruner, A. G., Gullison, R. E., Rice, R. E. and da Fonseca, G. A. B. (2001) 'Effectiveness of parks in protecting tropical biodiversity', *Science*, vol 291, pp125–129

Bryant, D., Nielsen, D. and Tangley, L. (1997) *The Last Frontier Forests: Ecosystems and Economies on the Edge*, World Resources Institute, Washington DC

Bubb, P., May, I., Miles, L. and Sayer, J. (2004) *Cloud Forest Agenda*, UNEP World Conservation Monitoring Centre, Cambridge

Bullard, E. R. (1979) *Orkney: A Checklist of Vascular Plants, Flowering Plants and Ferns* (new edn), Stromness, Orkney Islands

Burgiel, S. W. and Muir, A. A. (2010) *Invasive Species, Climate Change and Ecosystem-based Adaptation: Addressing Multiple Drivers of Global Change*, Global Invasive Species Programme (GISP), Washington DC and Nairobi

Burke, L., Kura, Y., Revenga, C., Spalding, M. and McCalliser, D. (2000) *Pilot Analysis of Global Ecosystems: Coastal Ecosystem*, World Resources Institute, Washington DC

Burkey, T. V. (1989) 'Extinction in nature reserves: The effects of fragmentation and the importance of migration between reserve fragments', *Oikos*, vol 55, pp75–81

Butchart, S. H. M., Walpole, M., Collen, B., van Strien, A., Scharlemann, J. P. W., Almond, R. E. A., Baillie, J. E. M., Bomhard, B., Brown, C., Bruno, J., Carpenter, K. E., Carr, G. M., Chanson, J., Chenery, A. M., Csirke, J., Davidson, N. C., Dentener, F., Foster, M., Galli, A., Galloway, J. N., Genovesi, P., Gregory, R. D., Hockings, M., Kapos, V.,

Lamarque, J. F., Leverington, F., Loh, J., McGeoch, M. A., McRae, L., Minasyan, A., Hernández Morcillo, M., Oldfield, T. E. E., Pauly, D., Quader, S., Revenga, C., Sauer, J. R., Skolnik, B., Spear, D., Stanwell-Smith, D., Stuart, S. N., Symes, A., Tierney, M., Tyrrell, T. D., Vié, J. C. and Watson, R. (2010) 'Global biodiversity: Indicators of recent declines', *Science*, vol 328, pp1164–1168

Butzer, K. (1990) 'The Indian legacy in the American landscape', in Conzen, M. P. (ed) *The Making of the American Landscape*, Routledge, London, pp27–50

Caldecott, J. and Wickremasinghe, W. R. M. S. (2005) *Sri Lanka: Post-Tsunami Environmental Assessment*, United Nations Environment Programme, Geneva

Callicot, J. B. (2000) 'Contemporary criticisms of the received wilderness idea', USDA Forest Service Proceedings RMRS-P-15-Vol 1, pp24–31

Campbell, A., Kapos, V., Lysenko, I., Scharlemann, J., Dickson, B., Gibbs, H., Hansen, M. and Miles, L. (2008) *Carbon Emissions from Forest Loss in Protected Areas*, UNEP World Conservation Monitoring Centre, Cambridge

Campese, J., Sunderland, T., Greiber, T. and Oviedo, G. (eds) (2009) *Rights-based Approaches: Exploring Issues and Opportunities for Conservation*, CIFOR and IUCN, Bogor, Indonesia

Carey, C., Dudley, N. and Stolton, S. (2000) *Squandering Paradise?*, WWF International, Gland, Switzerland

Carpenter, K. E., Abrar, M., Aeby, G., Aronson, R. B., Banks, S., Bruckner, A., Chiriboga, A., Cortés, J., Delbeek, J. C., DeVantier, L., Edgar, G. J., Edwards, A. J., Fenner, D., Guzmán, H. M., Hoeksema, B. W., Hodgson, G., Johan, O., Licuanan, W. Y., Livingstone, S. R., Lovell, E. R., Moore, J. A., Obura, D. O., Ochavillo, D., Polidoro, B. A., Precht, W. F., Quibilan, M. C., Reboton, C., Richards, Z. T., Rogers, A. D., Sanciangco, J., Sheppard, A., Sheppard, C., Smith, J., Stuart, S., Turak, E., Vernon, J. E., Wallace, C., Weil, E. and Wood, E. (2008) 'One-third of reef-building corals face elevated extinction risk from climate change and local impacts', *Science*, vol 321, pp560–563

Carpenter, S. E., Bennett, E. M. and Peterson, G. D. (2006) 'Scenarios for ecosystem services: An overview', *Ecology and Society*, vol 11, no 1, p29

Carrere, R. (2001) *Monte Indígena: Mucho mas que un conjunto de arboles*, Ediciones de Brecha and Nordan Comunidad, Montevideo

Carson, R. (1962) *Silent Spring*, Houghton Mifflin, Boston MA

Carss, D., Jones, S. and Marzano. M. (2003) 'Negotiating peace with cormorants', *Planet Earth*, Spring 2003, p22

Carter, P., Sadler, P. and Wightman, J. (2005) *Attenborough Wildlife 2005*, Nottinghamshire Wildlife Trust, Nottingham

Castellanos, C. (2008) 'Applying the enhancing our heritage toolkit to cultural World Heritage sites', in Hockings, M., James, R., Stolton, S., Dudley, N., Mathur, V., Makombo, J., Courrau, J. and Parrish, J. D. (eds) *Enhancing Our Heritage Toolkit: Assessing Management Effectiveness of Natural World Heritage Sites*, World Heritage Papers 23, UNESCO, UN Foundation and IUCN, Paris, pp87–92

Caughley, G., Grigg, G. C., Caughley, J. and Hill, G. J. E. (1980) 'Does dingo predation control the densities of kangaroos and emus?', *Australian Wildlife Research*, vol 7 pp1–12

CBD (Convention on Biological Diversity) (1997) *Recommendations for a Core Set of Indicators of Forest Biological Diversity*, UNEP/CBD/SBSTTA/3/9, 10 July 1997, paper for the Subsidiary Body on Scientific, Technical and Technological Advice, Third Meeting, Montréal, Canada, 1–5 September 1997

Chapin, F. S. III, Reynolds, H. L., D'Antonio, C. M. and Eckhart, V. M. (1996) 'The functional role of species in terrestrial ecosystems', in Walker, B. H. and Steffen, W. L. (eds) *Global Change and Terrestrial Ecosystems*, University of Cambridge, Cambridge, UK

Chapple, C. K. (1998) 'Hinduism, Jainism, and ecology', *Earth Ethics*, vol 10, no 1, pp16–18

Chater, A. O. (2010) *Flora of Cardiganshire*, published by A. O. Chater, Aberystwyth.

Chatwin, B. (1987) *The Songlines*, Jonathan Cape, London

Chiarello, A. G. (2000) 'Density and population size of mammals in remnants of Brazilian Atlantic Forest', *Conservation Biology*, vol 14, no 6, pp1649–1657

Choi, B. S. (2007) 'Nature in Korea', in Heo, H. Y. (ed) *The Biodiversity and Protected Areas of Korea*, Ministry of Environment and Korea National Park Service, Seoul

Chomitz, K. M. and Kumari, K. (1998) 'The domestic benefits of tropical forests: A critical review', *The World Bank Research Observer*, vol 13, no 1, pp13–35

Chown, S. L., Slabber, S., McGeoch, M. A., Janion, C. and Petter Leinaas, H. (2007) 'Phenotypic plasticity mediates climate change responses among invasive and indigenous arthropods', *Proc. R. Soc. B*, vol 274, pp2531–2537, doi:10.1098/rspb.2007.0772

Christiansen, N. L., Bartuska, A. M., Brown, J. H., Carpenter, S., D'Antonio, C., Francis, R., Franklin, J. F., MacMahon, J. A., Noss, R. F., Parsons, D. J., Peterson, C. H., Turner, M. G. and Woodmansee, R. G. (1996) 'The report of the Ecological Society of America Committee on the Scientific Basis for Ecosystem Management', *Ecological Applications*, vol 6, no 3, pp665–691

CIFOR and FAO (2005) *Forests and Floods: Drowning in Fiction or Thriving on Facts?*, RAP Publication 2005 03, Forest Perspectives 2, FAO and CIFOR, Rome and Bogor, Indonesia

Clark, J. (1992) 'The future of native forest logging in Australia', Centre for Resource and Environmental Studies Working Paper 1992/1, The Australian National University, Canberra

Clark, K. (1949) *Landscape into Art*, Penguin Books, Harmondsworth

Clergeau, P., Fourcy, D., Reeber, S. and Yésou, P. (2010) 'New but nice? Do alien sacred ibises *Threskiornis aethiopicus* stabilise nesting colonies of native spoonbills *Platalea leucorodia* at Grand-Lieu Lake, France?', *Oryx*, vol 44, no 4, pp533–538

Clesla, W. M. and Donaubauer, E. (1994) *Decline and Dieback of Trees and Forests: A Global Overview*, FAO Forestry Paper 120, UN Food and Agriculture Organisation, Rome

Colchester, M. and Argumedo, A. (2003) *Peru: Visit to a 'Potato Park'*, document prepared for the IUCN World Parks Congress, www.wrm.org.uy/bulletin/73/Peru.html (accessed 22 January 2011)

Colchester, M. and Erni, C. (eds) (1999) *Indigenous Peoples and Protected Areas in South and Southeast Asia: From Principles to Practice*, Proceedings of the conference at Kundasang, Sabah, Malaysia, 14–18 December 1998, IWGIA Document No 97, International Work Group for Indigenous Affairs and Forest Peoples Programme, Copenhagen and Moreton-in-Marsh, UK

Cole, D. and Yung, L. (eds) (2010) *Beyond Naturalness: Rethinking Park and Wilderness Stewardship in an Era of Rapid Change*, Island Press, Washington DC

Cole, D. N., Yung, L., Zavaleta, E. S., Aplet, G. H., Chapin III, F. S., Graber, D. M., Higgs, E. S., Hobbs, R. J., Landres, P. B., Millar, C. I., Parsons, D. J., Randall, J. M.,

Stephenson, N. L., Tonnessen, K. A., White, P. S. and Woodley, S. (2008) 'Naturalness and beyond: Protected area stewardship in an era of global environmental change', *George Wright Forum*, vol 25, no 1, pp37–56

Colfer, C. J. P., Sheil, D., Kaimowitz, D. and Kish, M. (2006) 'Forests and human health in the tropics: Some important connections', *Unasylva*, vol 57, no 224, pp3–10

Collomb, J. G., Mikissa, J. B., Minnemeyer, S., Mundunga, S., Nzao Nzao, H., Madouma, J., Mapaga, J. D., Mikolo, C., Rabenkogo, N., Akagah, S., Bayani-Ngoye, E. and Mofouma, A. (2000) *A First Look at Logging in Gabon*, World Resources Institute, Washington DC

Condry, W. (1954) *Thoreau*, H. F. and G. Witherby Ltd, London

Condry, W. (1966) *The Snowdonia National Park*, Collins, London

Condry, W. (1970) *Exploring Wales*, Faber and Faber, London

Condry, W. (1981) *The Natural History of Wales*, Collins, London

Conry, P. J. (1988) 'High nest predation by brown tree snakes on Guam', *The Condor*, vol 90, pp478–482

Conway, G. R. and Pretty, J. N. (1991) *Unwelcome Harvest: Agriculture and Pollution*, Earthscan, London

Cooke, S. J. and Cowx, I. G. (2004) 'The role of recreational fishing in global fish crises', *Bioscience*, vol 54, no 9, pp857–859

Cowling, R. M., Knight, A. T., Faith, D. P., Ferrier, S., Lombard, A. T., Driver, A., Rouget, M., Maze, K. and Desmet, P. G. (2004) 'Nature conservation requires more than a passion for species', *Biodiversity Conservation*, vol 18, no 6, pp1674–1676

Cox, R. M. (1992) 'Air pollution effects on plant reproductive processes and possible consequences to their population ecology', in Barker, J. R. and Tingey, D. T. (eds) *Air Pollution Effects on Biodiversity*, Van Nostrand Reinhold, New York

Craigie, I. D., Baillie, J. E. M., Balmford, A., Carbon, C., Collen, B., Green, R. and Hutton, J. M. (2010) 'Large mammal population declines in Africa's protected areas', *Biological Conservation*, doi:10.1016/j.biocon.2010.06.007

Crick, H. Q. P. (2004) 'The impact of climate change on birds', *Ibis*, vol 146 (Supplement 1), pp48–56

Crist, E. (2004) 'Against the social construction of nature and wilderness', *Environmental Ethics*, vol 26, pp5–24

Cronon, W. (1983) *Changes in the Land: Indians, Colonists and the Ecology of New England*, Hill and Wang, New York

Crosby, A. W. (1986) *Ecological Imperialism: The Biological Expansion of Europe, 900–1900*, Cambridge University Press, Cambridge UK

Dafni, A. (2002) 'Why are rags tied to the sacred trees of the Holy Land?', *Economic Botany*, vol 56, no 4, pp315–327

Dahdouh-Guebas, F. and Koedam, N. (2006) 'Coastal vegetation and the Asian Tsunami', *Science*, vol 311, pp37–38

Damschen, E. I., Haddad, N. M., Orrock, J. L., Tewkesbury, J. J. and Levey, D. J. (2006) 'Corridors increase plant species richness at large scales', *Science*, vol 313, pp1284–1286

Danielsen, F., Sørensen, M. K., Olwig, M. F., Selvam, V., Parish, F., Burgess, N. D., Hiraishi, T., Karunagaran, V. M., Rasmussen, M. S. Hansen, L. B., Quarto, A. and Suryadiputra, N. (2005) 'The Asian Tsunami: A protective role for coastal vegetation', *Science*, vol 310, no 5748, p643

Dayton, P. K., Sala, E., Tegner, M. J. and Thrush, S. (2000) 'Marine reserves: Parks, baselines and fishery enhancement', *Marine Science*, vol 66, no 3, pp617–634

Dayton, P. K., Tegner, M. J., Edwards, P. B. and Riser, K. L. (1998) 'Sliding baselines, ghosts, and reduced expectations in kelp forest communities', *Ecological Applications*, vol 8, no 2, pp309–322

Delang, C. (2006) 'Not just minor forest products: The economic rationale for the consumption of wild food plants by subsistence farmers', *Ecological Economics*, vol 59, pp64–73

Denevan, W. M. (1992) 'The pristine myth: The landscape of the Americas in 1492', *Annals of the Association of American Geographers*, vol 82, no 3, pp369–385

Descimon, H., Bachelard, P., Boitier, E. and Pierrat, V. (2006) 'Decline and extinction of *Parnassius apollo* populations in France – continued', in Kühn, E., Feldmann, R. and Settele, J. (eds) *Studies on the Ecology and Conservation of Butterflies in Europe: Vol 1 General Concepts and Case Studies*, PENSOFT, Sofia, Bulgaria

Devlin, M. J. and Brodie, J. (2005) 'Terrestrial discharge into the Great Barrier Reef Lagoon: Nutrient behavior in coastal waters', *Marine Pollution Bulletin*, vol 51, pp9–22

Diamond, J. (1998) *Guns, Germs and Steel: A Short History of Everybody for the Last 13,000 years*, Vintage, London

Diamond, J. (2005) *Collapse: How Societies Choose to Fail or Succeed*, Viking Press, New York

Dillard, A. (1974) *Pilgrim at Tinker Creek*, Jonathan Cape, London

Dinerstein, E., Olson, D., Atchley, J., Loucks, C., Contreras-Balderas, S., Abell, R. Iñigo, E., Enkerlin, E., Williams, C. and Castilleja, G. (eds) (2000) *Ecosystem-based Conservation in the Chihuahuan Desert: A Biological Assessment*, WWF, Comisíon National para el Conocimiento y Uso de la Biodiversidad (CONABIO), The Nature Conservancy, PRONATURA Noreste, and the Instituto Tecnologico y de Estudios Superiores de Monterrey (ITESM), Washington DC and Mexico City

Donald, P. F., Green, R. E. and Heath, M. F. (2001) 'Agricultural intensification and the collapse of Europe's farmland bird populations', *Proceedings of the Royal Society London B*, vol 268, pp25–29

Douglas, E. M., Wood, S., Sebastian, K., Vörösmarty, C. J., Chomitz, K. M. and Tomich, T. P. (2007) 'Policy implications of a pan-tropic assessment of the simultaneous hydrological and biodiversity impacts of deforestation', *Water Resources Management*, vol 21, pp211–232

Drabløs, D. and Tollan, A. (eds) (1980) *Ecological Impact of Acid Precipitation*, Proceedings of an International Conference, Sandefjord, Norway, 11–14 March 1980, SNSF Project, Oslo

Duarte, C. M. (2002) 'The future of seagrass meadows', *Environmental Conservation*, vol 29, pp192–206

Dublin, H. T. (1995) 'Vegetation dynamics in the Serengeti-Mara ecosystem: The role of elephants,fire and other factors', in Sinclair, A. R. E. and Arcese, P. (eds) *Serengeti II: Dynamics, Management and Conservation of an Ecosystem*, Chicago University Press, Chicago, IL, pp71–90

Dudley, N. (1986) *Nitrates in Food and Water*, The London Food Commission, London

Dudley, N. (1986a) 'Acid rain and British pollution control policy', in Goldsmith, E. and Hildyard, N. (eds) *Green Britain or Industrial Wasteland*, Polity Press, Cambridge, UK

Dudley, N. (1986b) *How Does Your Garden Grow?*, The Soil Association, Bristol

Dudley, N. (1992) *Forests in Trouble: A Review of the Status of Temperate Forests Worldwide*, WWF International, Gland, Switzerland

Dudley, N. (1996) 'Authenticity as a means of measuring forest quality', *Biodiversity Letters*, vol 3, pp6–9

Dudley, N. (2003) 'L'importance de la naturalité dans les paysages forestiers', in Vallauri, D. (ed) *le Livre Blanc de la Forets de France*, WWF France, Paris

Dudley, N. (ed) (2008) *Guidelines for Applying Protected Area Management Categories*, IUCN, Gland, Switzerland

Dudley, N. (2008a) 'Back to the energy crisis: The need for a coherent policy towards energy systems', *Policy Matters*, issue 16, pp38–42, IUCN Commission on Environmental, Economic and Social Policy

Dudley, N. (2010) 'Protected areas as tools for REDD: An issues paper for WWF', WWF US, Washington DC

Dudley, N. and Aldrich, M. (2007) *Five Years of Implementing Forest Landscape Restoration: Lessons to Date*, WWF International, Gland, Switzerland

Dudley, N. and Gordon Clarke, J. (1983) *Thin Ice*, Marine Action Centre, Cambridge, UK

Dudley, N. and Mansourian, S. (2003) *Forest Landscape Restoration and WWF's Conservation Priorities*, WWF International, Gland, Switzerland

Dudley, N. and Parrish, J. (2006) *Closing the Gap. Creating Ecologically Representative Protected Area Systems: A Guide to Conducting the Gap Assessments of Protected Area Systems for the Convention on Biological Diversity*, Secretariat of the Convention on Biological Diversity, Montréal

Dudley, N. and Stolton, S. (eds) (2003) *Running Pure: The Importance of Forest Protected Areas to Drinking Water*, WWF International and The World Bank, Gland, Switzerland and Washington DC

Dudley, N. and Stolton, S. (2003a) *Biological Diversity, Tree Species Composition and Environmental Protection in Regional FRA-2000*, Geneva Timber and Forest Discussion Paper 33, UNECE and FAO, Geneva and Rome

Dudley, N. and Vallauri, D. (2005) 'Restoration of deadwood as a critical microhabitat in forest landscapes', in Mansourian, S., Dudley, N. and Vallauri, D. (eds) *Forest Restoration in Landscapes: Beyond Planting Trees*, Springer, New York

Dudley, N., Barrett, M. and Baldock, D. (1984) *Acid Rain*, Earth Resources Research, London

Dudley, N., Belokurov, A., Higgins-Zogib, L., Hockings, M., Stolton, S. and Burgess, N. (2007) *Tracking Progress in Managing Protected Areas Around the World*, WWF International, Gland, Switzerland

Dudley, N., Bhagwat, S., Higgins-Zogib, L., Lassen, B., Verschuuren, B. and Wild, R. (2010a) 'Conservation of biodiversity in sacred natural sites in Asia and Africa: A review of the scientific literature', in Verschuuren, B., Wild, R., McNeely, J. and Oviedo, G. (eds) *Sacred Natural Sites: Conserving Nature and Culture*, Earthscan, London

Dudley, N., Higgins-Zogib, L. and Mansourian, S. (2005) *Beyond Belief: Linking Faiths and Protected Areas to Support Biodiversity Conservation*, WWF, Equilibrium and Alliance of Religions and Conservation, Gland, Switzerland, Bristol and Bath, UK

Dudley, N., Jeanrenaud, J. P. and Stolton, S. (1997) *The Year the World Caught Fire*, WWF International, Gland, Switzerland

Dudley, N., Mansourian, S., Stolton, S. and Suksuwan, S. (2008) *Safety Net: Protected Areas and Poverty Reduction*, WWF International, Gland, Switzerland

Dudley, N. and Phillips, A. (2008) 'Names of protected areas', in Dudley, N. and Stolton, S. (eds) *Defining Protected Areas: An International Conference in Almeria, Spain, May 2007*, IUCN, Gland, Switzerland

Dudley, N., Schlaepfer, R., Jackson, W., Jeanrenaud, J. P. and Stolton, S. (2006) *Forest Quality: Assessing Forests at a Landscape Scale*, Earthscan, London

Dudley, N., Stolton, S. and Jeanrenaud, J. P. (eds) (1993) *Towards a New Definition of Forest Quality*, WWF UK, Godalming, UK

Dudley, N. and Stolton, S. (1995) *Air Pollution and Biodiversity*, WWF International, Gland, Switzerland

Dudley, N., Stolton, S., Belokurov, A., Krueger, L. Lopoukhine, N., MacKinnon, K., Sandwith, T. and Sekhran, N. (eds) (2010b) *Natural Solutions: Protected Areas Helping People Cope with Climate Change*, IUCN-WCPA,TNC, UNDP, WCS, The World Bank and WWF, Gland, Switzerland, Washington DC and New York, USA

Dukes, J. S. and Mooney, H. A. (1999) 'Does global change increase the success of biological invaders?', *Trends in Ecology and Evolution*, vo. 14, no 4, pp139–139

Dunlop, M. and Brown, P. R. (2008) *Implications of Climate Change for Australia's National Reserve System: A Preliminary Assessment*. Department of Climate Change, Canberra, Australia

During, H. J. and Willens, J. H. (1986) 'The impoverishment of the bryophyte and lichen fora of the Dutch chalk grassland in the thirty years 1953–1983', *Biological Conservation*, vol 36, pp145–158

Dyurgerov, M.B. and Meier, M.F. (2000) 'Twentieth century climate change: Evidence from small glaciers', *Proceedings of the National Academy of Sciences,* vol 97, no 4, pp1406–1411

Eckholm, E. P. (1975) *The Other Energy Crisis: Firewood*, Worldwatch Paper No 1, Worldwatch Institute, Washington DC

Eckholm, E. P. (1979) *Planting for the Future: Forestry for Human Needs*, Worldwatch Paper No 26. Worldwatch Institue, Washington DC

Edwards, D. P., Hodgson, J. A., Hamer, K. C., Mitchell, S. L., Ahmad, A. H., Cornell, S. J. and Wilcove, D. S. (2010) 'Wildlife-friendly oil palm plantations fail to protect biodiversity effectively', *Conservation Letters*, vol 3, pp236–242

Edwards, M. and Richardson, A. J. (2004) 'Impact of climate change on marine pelagic phenology and trophic mismatch', *Nature*, vol 430, pp881–884

EEA (European Environment Agency) (2004) *High Nature Value Farmland: Characteristics, Trends and Policy Challenges*, Office of Official Publications of the European Communities, Luxembourg

Eeronheimo, O., Ahti, A. and Sahlberg, S. (1997) *Criteria and Indicators for Sustainable Forest Management in Finland*, Ministry of Agriculture and Forestry, Helsinki

Eisenberg, E. (1998) *The Ecology of Eden: Humans, Nature and Human Nature*, Alfred A. Knopf Inc., New York

Elliott, J., Grahn, R., Sriskanthan, G. and Arnold, C. (2002) *Wildlife and Poverty Study*, Department for Environmental Development, London

Elvin, M. (2010) 'Concepts of nature', *New Left Review*, vol 64, July/August 2010, pp65–84

Emerton, L. (ed) (2005) *Values and Rewards: Counting and Capturing Ecosystem Water Services for Sustainable Development*, Water, Nature and Economics Technical Paper No 1, IUCN, Ecosystems and Livelihoods Group Asia

Engblom, E. and Lingdell, P. E. (1991) 'Försurning och bottemfaunaföröndringar i Sverige' (Acidification and changes in benthic fauna in Sweden), *Vatten*, vol 47, no 4, pp348–351

Eriksson, F., Hörnströn, E., Mossberg, P. and Nyberg, P. (1983) 'Ecological effects of lime treatment of acidified lakes and rivers in Sweden', *Hydrobiologia*, vol 101, nos 1–2, pp145–163

Eriksson, M. O. G. (1984) 'Acidification of lakes: Effects on waterbirds in Sweden', *Ambio*, vol 13, no 4, pp260–262

Eriksson, M. O. G. (1985) 'Prey detectability for fish-eating birds in relation to fish density and water transparency', *Ornis Scandinavia*, vol 16, pp1–7

Evans, K. L., Greenwod, J. D. D. and Gaston, K. J. (2007) 'The positive correlation between avian species richness and human population density in Britain is not attributable to sampling bias', *Global Ecology and Biogeography*, vol 16, no 3, pp300–304

Fagan, B. (1999) *Floods, Famines and Emperors: El Niño and the Fate of Civilisations*, Basic Books, Jackson, MS

FAO (2006) *Global Forest Resources Assessment 2005: Towards Sustainable Forest Management*, Food and Agricultural Organization of the United Nations, Rome

Feinberg, J. (1974) 'The rights of animals and unborn generations', in Blackstone, W.T. (ed) *Philosophy and the Environmental Crisis*, University of Georgia Press, Athens, GA

Finlay, R. G. (2008) 'Ecological aspects of mycorrhizal symbiosis: With special emphasis on the functional diversity of interactions involving the extraradical mycelium', *Journal of Experimental Botany*, vol 59, no 5, pp1115–1126

Fitter, R. S. R. (1945) *London's Natural History*, Collins, London

Fitter, R. S. R. (1949) *London's Birds*, Collins, London

Fitzimons, J., Legge, S., Traill, B. and Woinarski, J. (2010) *Into Oblivion*, The Nature Conservancy, Australian Wildlife Conservancy and Pew Environmental Group

Flannery, T. (1994) *The Future Eaters*, Reed New Holland, Sydney

Flannery, T. (2001) *The Eternal Frontier: An Ecological History of North America and Its Peoples*, William Heinemann, London

Flecker, A. S. and Townsend, C. R. (1994) 'Community-wide consequences of trout introductions into New Zealand streams', *Ecological Applications*, vol 4, no 4, pp788–807

Flower, R. J. and Battarbee, R. A. (1983) 'Diatom evidence for recent acidification of two Scottish lochs', *Nature London*, vol 305, pp130–133

Foley, J. A., DeFries, R., Asner, G. P., Barford, C., Bonan, G., Carpenter, S. R., Chapin, F. S., Coe, M. T., Daily, G. C., Gibbs, H.K., Helkowski, J. H., Holloway, E. A., Kucharik, C. J., Monfreda, C., Patz, J. A., Prentice, I. C., Ramankutty, N. and Snyder, P. K. (2005) 'Global consequences of land use', *Science*, vol 309, no 5734, pp570–574

Foltz, R., Denny, F. M. and Baharuddin, A. (2003) *Islam and Ecology: A Bestowed Trust*, Harvard University Press, Cambridge, MA

Forrest, S. C., Strand, H., Haskins, W. H., Freese, C., Proctor, J. and Dinerstein, E. (2004) *Ocean of Grass: A Conservation Assessment for the Northern Great Plains*, Northern Plains Conservation Network and Northern Great Plains Ecoregion, WWF-US, Bozeman, MT

Foster, N. and LeMay, M. H. (1988) *Managing Marine Protected Areas: An Action Plan*. Man and the Biosphere Program, Washington DC

Fowler, C. and Mooney, P. (1990) *The Threatened Gene: Food, Politics, and the Loss of Genetic Diversity*, The Lutterworth Press, Cambridge, UK

Franklin, J. F. and Foreman, R. T. T. (1987) 'Creating landscape patterns by forest cutting: Ecological consequences and principles', *Landscape Ecology*, vol 1, no 1, pp5–18

Fritts, T. H. and Rodda, G. H. (1998) 'The role of introduced species in the degradation of island ecosystems: A case history of Guam', *Annual Review of Ecology, Evolution and Systematics*, vol 29, pp113–140

Fry, G. A. and Cooke, A. S. (1984) *Acid Deposition and its Implications for Nature Conservation in Britain*, Focus on Nature Conservation No 7, Nature Conservancy Council, Peterborough, UK

Fryer, G. (1980) 'Acidity and species diversity in freshwater Crustacea', *Freshwater Biology*, vol 10, pp41–45

Fuller, E. (2003) *The Dodo: Extinction in Paradise*, Bunker Hills Publishing, Charlestown, MA

Gadgil, M. and Guha, R. (1993) *This Fissured Land: An Ecological History of India*, Oxford University Press, Delhi

Gao, X. (1989) *Soul Mountain*, translated by Lee, M., Flamingo, London

Gärdenfors, U. (1989) *Impact of Airborne Pollution on Terrestrial Invertebrates, with Particular Reference to Molluscs*, National Swedish Environment Protection Board Report 3362, Solna, Sweden

Gare, A. E. (1995) *Postmodernism and the Environmental Crisis*, Routledge, London

George, J.L. and Frear, D.E.H. (1966) 'Pesticides in the Antarctic', *Journal of Applied Ecology*, vol 3, supplement, pp155–167

Gesler, W. (1992) 'Therapeutic landscapes: Medical geographic research in light of the new cultural geography', *Social Science & Medicine*, vol 34, pp735–746

Girardot, N., Miller, J. and Xiaogan, L. (eds) (2001) *Daoism and Ecology: Ways within a Cosmic Landscape*, Harvard University Press, Cambridge, MA

Goldberg, E. A., Kirby, K. J., Hall, J. E. and Latham, J. (2007) 'The ancient woodland concept as a practical conservation tool in Great Britain', *Journal of Nature Conservation*, vol 15, pp109–119

Gonzalez, S. (2004) *Biología y conservación de Cérvidos Neotropicales del Uruguay. Informe Final de Proyecto CSIC-UdelaR*, 57pp

González Bernáldez, F. (1992) 'Ecological consequences of the abandonment of traditional land use systems in central Spain', *Options Méditerranéennes*, vol 15, pp23–29

Götmark, F. (1992) 'Naturalness as an evaluation criterion in nature conservation: A response to Anderson', *Conservation Biology*, vol 6, no 3, pp455–458

Grabherr, G., Koch, G. and Kirchmeir, H. (1998) *Bildatlas Naturnhähe Österreichischer Wälder*, Bundesministerium für Land und Forstwirtschaft, Vienna

Green, P. A., Vörösmarty, C. V., Meybeck, M., Galloway, J. N., Peterson, B. J. and Boyer, E. W. (2004) 'Pre-industrial and contemporary fluxes of nitrogen through rivers: A global assessment based on a typology', *Biogeochemistry*, vol 68, pp71–105

Green, R. E., Newton, I., Schultz, S., Cunningham, A. A., Gilbert, M., Pain, D. J. and Prakash, V. (2004) 'Diclofenac poisoning as a cause of vulture population declines across the Indian subcontinent', *Journal of Applied Ecology*, vol 41, pp793–800

Grigg, G. (1989) 'Kangaroo harvesting and the conservation of arid and semi-arid rangelands', *Conservation Biology*, vol 3, no 2, pp194–197

Gross, L. (2005) 'As the Antarctic ice pack recedes, a fragile ecosystem hangs in the balance', *PLoS Biology*, vol 3, no 4, e127, doi:10.1371/journal.pbio.0030127

Grove, A. T. and Rackham, O. (2001) *The Nature of Mediterranean Europe: An Ecological History*, Yale University Press, New Haven and London

Grove, R. (1995) *Green Imperialism: Colonial Expansion, Tropical Island Edens and the Origins of Environmentalism, 1600–1860*, Cambridge University Press, Cambridge UK

Grove, S., Meggs, J. and Goodwin, A. (2002) *A Review of Biodiversity Conservation Issues Relating to Coarse Woody Debris Management in the Wet Eucalypt Production Forests of Tasmania*, Forestry Tasmania, Hobart

Gunderson, L. H. (2000) 'Ecological resilience: In theory and application', *Annual Review of Ecological Systematics*, vol 31, pp425–439

Gurnell, J., Wauters, L. A., Lurz, P. W. W. and Tosi, G. (2004) 'Alien species and interspecific competition: Effects of introduced eastern grey squirrels on red squirrel population dynamics', *Journal of Animal Ecology*, vol 73, pp26–35

Haeussler, S., Bedford, L., Leduc, A., Bergeron, Y. and Kranabetter, J. M. (2002) 'Silvicultural disturbance severity and plant communities of the southern Canadian boreal forest', *Silva Fennica*, vol 36, no 1, pp307–327

Haila, Y. (1997) '"Wilderness" and the multiple layers of environmental thought', *Environment and History*, vol 3, no 2, pp129–147

Hails, S. and Peck, D. (eds) (2007) 'Managing wetlands', *Ramsar Handbook for the Wise Use of Wetlands*, vol 16,, Ramsar Secretariat, Gland, Switzerland

Halpern, B. S. (2003) 'The impact of marine reserves: Do reserves work and does reserve size matter?', *Ecological Applications*, vol 13, pp117–137

Halpern, B. S., Walbridge, S., Selkoe, K. A., Kappel, C. V., Micheli, F., D'Agrosa, C., Bruno, J. F., Casey, K. S., Ebert, C., Fox, H. E., Fujita, R., Heinemann, D., Lenihan, H. S., Madin, E. M. P., Perry, M. T., Selig, E. R., Spaldin, M., Steneck, R. and Watson, R. (2008) 'A global map of human impact on marine ecosystems', *Science*, vol 319, no 2865, pp948–952

Hamilton, L. S., Juvik, J. O. and Scatena, F. N. (1994) *Tropical Montane Cloud Forests*, Ecological Studies Series Vol110, Springer-Verlag, New York

Hamilton, L. with contributions from Dudley, N., Greminger, G., Hassan, N., Lamb, D., Stolton, S. and Tognetti, S. (2008) *Forests and Water*, FAO Forestry Paper 155, Food and Agricultural Organization, Rome

Hannah, L. Lohse, D., Hutchinson, C., Carr, J. L. and Lankerani, A. (1994) 'A preliminary inventory of human disturbance of world ecosystems', *Ambio*, vol 23, nos 4–5, pp246–250

Harmon, D. and Loh, J. (2010) 'The Index of Linguistic Diversity: A new quantitative measure of trends in the status of the world's languages', *Language Documentation and Conservation*, vol 4, pp97–151

Hartzell, H. Jnr (1991) *The Yew Tree: A Thousand Whispers*, Hulogosi, Eugene, OR

Hatfield, R. and Davies, J. (2006) *Global Review of the Economics of Pastoralism*, World Initiative for Sustainable Pastoralism, IUCN, GEF and UNEP

Hawkins, B. (2008) *Plants for Life: Medicinal Plant Conservation and Botanic Gardens*, Botanic Gardens Conservation International, Richmond, UK

Hays, G. C., Richardson, A. J. and Robinson, C. (2005) 'Climate change and marine plankton', *Trends in Ecology and Evolution*, vol 20, no 6, pp337–344

Helle, T. (1995) 'Reindeer husbandry and hunting', in Hytönen, M (ed) *Multiple-use Forestry in the Nordic Countries*, METLA The Finnish Forest Research Institute, Helsinki, pp157–190

Henwood, W. D. (2010) 'Towards a strategy for the conservation and protection of the world's temperate grasslands', *Great Plains Research*, vol 20, pp121–134

Herrmann, J., Degerman, E., Gerhardt, A., Johanssen, C., Lingdell, P. E. and Muniz, I. P. (1993) 'Acid stress effects on stream biology', *Ambio*, vol 22, pp298–307

Hessel, D. T. (1998) 'Christianity and ecology: Wholeness, respect, justice, sustainability', *Earth Ethics*, vol 10, p1

Heywood, V. (1999) *Use and Potential of Wild Plants in Farm Households*, FAO Farm Systems Management Series No 15, Food and Agricultural Organization of the United Nations, Rome

Hickling, R., Roy, D. B., Hill, J. K. and Thomas, C. D. (2005) 'A northward shift of range margins in British Odonata', *Global Change Biology*, vol 11, pp502–506

Higgs, E. S. and Hobbs, R. J. (2010) 'Wild design: Principles to guide interventions in protected areas', in Cole, D. and Yung, L. (eds) *Beyond Naturalness: Rethinking Park and Wilderness Stewardship in an Era of Rapid Change*, Island Press, Washington DC

Hinzman, L. D., Bettez, N. D., Bolton, W. R., Chapin, F. S., Dyurgerov, M. B., Fastie, C. L., Grifith, B., Hollister, R. D., Hope, A., Huntingdon, H. P., Jensen, A. M., Jia, G. J., Jorgenson, T., Kane, D. L., Klein, D. R., Kofinas, G., Lynch, F. E., Oechel, W. C., Osterkamp, T. E., Racine, C. H., Romanovsky, V. E., Stone, R. S., Stow, D. A., Sturm, M., Tweedie, C. E., Vourlitis, G. L., Walker, M. D., Walker, D. A., Webber, P. J., Welker, J. M., Winker, K. S. and Yoshikawa, K. (2005) 'Evidence and implications of recent climate change in northern Alaska and other Arctic regions', *Climatic Change*, vol 72, pp251–298

Hoagland, E. (1985) Introduction to *The Mountains of California* by John Muir, Penguin Books, Harmondsworth, UK

Hobbs, R. J., Cole, D. N., Yung, L., Zavaleta, E. S., Aplet, G. H., Chapin III, F. S., Landres, P. B., Parsons, D. J., Stephenson, N. L., White, P. S., Graber, D. M., Higgs, E. S., Millar, C. I., Randall, J. M., Tonnessen, K. A. and Woodley, S. (2009) 'Guiding concepts for park and wilderness stewardship in an era of global environmental change', *Frontiers in Ecology and the Environment*, doi:10.1890/090089

Hockings, M., James, R., Stolton, S., Dudley, N., Mathur, V., Makombo, J., Courrau, J. and Parrish, J. D. (2008) *Enhancing our Heritage Toolkit: Assessing Management Effectiveness of Natural World Heritage Sites*, World Heritage Papers 23, UNESCO, UN Foundation and IUCN, Paris

Hoegh-Guldberg, O., Mumby, P. J., Hooten, A. J., Steneck, R. S., Greenfield, P., Gomez, E., Harvell, C. D., Sale, P. F., Edwards, A. J., Caldeira, K., Knowlton, N., Eakin, C. M., Iglesias-Prieto, R., Muthiga, N., Bradbury, R. H., Dubi, A. and Hatziolos, M. E. (2007) 'Coral reefs under rapid climate change and ocean acidification', *Science*, vol 318, pp1737–1742

Hoekstra, J. M., Boucher, T. M., Ricketts, T. H. and Roberts, C. (2005) 'Confronting a biome crisis: Global disparities in habitat loss and protection', *Ecology Letters*, vol 8, pp23–29

Hopson, E. (1978) quoted in 'The People of the Whales: A fight for survival', *Indian Affairs*, vol 98, pp7–8

Hourahane, S., Stolton, S., Falzon, C. and Dudley, N. with Phillips, A. and Lee, G. (2008) 'Landscape aesthetics in British national parks', in Mallarach, J. M. (ed) *Protected Landscapes and Cultural and Spiritual Values*, Values of Protected Landscapes and Seascapes, Vol 2, IUCN, Caixa Catalunya, GTZ and Federal Ministry for Economic Cooperation and Development, Germany

Houriet, R. (1971) *Getting Back Together*, Sphere Books, London

Hughes, T. P., Baird, A. H., Bellwood, D. R., Card, M., Connolly, S. R., Folke, C., Grosberg, R., Hoegh-Guldberg, O., Jackson, J. B. C., Kleypas, J., Lough, J. M., Marshall, P., Nystro, M., Palumbi, S. R., Pandolfi, J. M., Rosen, B. and Roughgarden, J. (2003) 'Climate change, human impacts and the resilience of coral reefs', *Science*, vol 301, pp929–933

Hunter, R. (1979) *The Greenpeace Chronicle*, Holt, Rhinehart and Winston, Austin, TX

Hurst, P., Hay, A. and Dudley, N. (1991) *The Pesticide Handbook*, Journeyman, London

Huxley, L. (2003) *The Grey Squirrel Review: Profile of an Alien Invasive Species Grey squirrel* (Sciurus carolinensis), European Squirrel Initiative, Dorset

ICEM (2003) *Lessons Learned in Cambodia, Lao PDR, Thailand and Vietnam*, ICEM, Indooroopilly, Queensland, Australia

International Disaster Reduction Conference (2006) 'IDRC Davos declaration: Participants' self-commitment for action', IDRC, Davos, Switzerland

International Energy Agency (2002) *World Energy Outlook 2002*, International Energy Agency, Paris

IPCC TAR (2001) *Climate Change 2001: Impacts, Adaptation and Vulnerability: IPCC Third Assessment Report*, Cambridge University Press, Cambridge, UK

ISDR (International Strategy for Disaster Reduction) (2004) *Living with Risk: A Global Review of Disaster Reduction Initiatives*, UN/ISDR, Geneva, Switzerland

ITTO (International Tropical Timber Organisation) (1993) *ITTO Guidelines for the Establishment and Sustainable Management of Planted Tropical Forests*, ITTO, Yokahama, Japan

IUCN WCPA (2010) *Next Steps: Convention on Biological Diversity Programme of Work on Protected Areas*, IUCN World Commission on Protected Areas, Gland Switzerland

Jackson, S. and Davis, W. (1994) 'Meeting the goal of biological integrity in water resource programs in the US Environmental Protection Agency', *Journal of the North American Benthological Association*, vol 13, no 4, pp592–597

Janssens, I. A., Freibauer, A., Ciais, P., Smith, P., Nabuurs, G., Folberth, G., Schlamadinger, B., Hutjes, R. W. A., Ceulemans, R., Schulze, E. D., Valentini, R. and Dolman, A. J. (2003) 'Europe's terrestrial biosphere absorbs 7 to 12% of European anthropogenic CO_2 emissions', *Science*, vol 300, pp1538–1542

Jeng, H. and Hong, Y. J. (2005) 'Assessment of a natural wetland for use in wastewater remediation', *Environmental Monitoring and Assessment*, vol 111, pp113–131

Jennings, S., Nussbaum, R., Judd, N. and Evans, T. (2003) *The High Conservation Value Forest Toolkit*, ProForest, Oxford

Jetz, W., Rahbek, C. and Colwell, R. K. (2004) 'The coincidence of rarity and richness and the potential signature in history in centres of endemism', *Ecology Letters*, vol 7, pp1180–1191

Johnson, C. N. and Wroe, S. (2003) 'Causes of extinction of vertebrates during the Holocene of mainland Australia: Arrival of the dingo, or human impact?', *The Holocene*, vol 13, no 6, pp1009–1016

Johnson, K. N., Franklin, J. F., Thomas, J. W. and Gordon, J. (1991) *Alternatives for Management of Late-Successional Forests of the Pacific Northwest*, a Report to the Agriculture Committee and The Merchant Marine and Fisheries Committee of the US House of Representatives by the Scientific Panel on Late-Successional Forest Ecosystems, 8 October 1991

Jokilehto, J. (2006) 'Consideration of authenticity and integrity in World Heritage context', *City and Time*, vol 2, no 1, pp1–16

Jones, D. (1996) *The Botanists and Guides of Snowdonia*, Carreg Gwalch, Llanwrst, Wales

Jones, J. (2001) 'Romancing the stone', *The Guardian*, 5 July 2001

Joppa, L. N., Loarie, S. R. and Pimm, S. L. (2008) 'On the protection of "Protected Areas"', *Proceedings of the National Academy of Sciences*, vol 105, pp6673–6678

Jowitt, D. (1991) *These Hills Are Tapu*, Thames Coast Protection Society, Thames, New Zealand

Juma, C. (1989) *The Gene Hunters: Biotechnology and the Scramble for Seeds*, Zed Press, London

Jungwirth, M., Muhar, S. and Schmutz, S. (2002) 'Re-establishing and assessing ecological integrity in riverine landscapes', *Freshwater Biology*, vol 47, pp867–887

Kaimowitz, D. (2005) *Forests and Human Health: Some Vital Connections*, Swedish CGIAR, Bogor, Indonesia

Kamp, U., Owen, L. A., Crowley, B. J. and Khattak, G. A. (2010) 'Back analysis of landslide susceptibility zonation mapping for the 2005 Kashmir earthquake: An assessment of the reliability of susceptibility zoning maps', *Natural Hazards*, doi:10.1007/s11069-009-9451-7

Kantai, P. (2002) 'Hot and dirty', *EcoForum*, vol 25, no 4, pp16–22

Kapos V., Ravilious, C., Campbell, A., Dickson, B., Gibbs, H. K., Hansen, M. C., Lysenko, I., Miles, L., Price, J., Scharlemann, J. P. W. and Trumper, K. C. (2008) *Carbon and Biodiversity: A Demonstration Atlas*, UNEP-WCMC, Cambridge, UK

Karr, J. R. (1981) 'Assessment of biotic integrity using fish communities', *Fisheries*, vol 6, no 6, pp21–27

Karr, J. R. (1996) 'Ecological integrity and ecological health are not the same', in Schulze, P., Frosch, R. and Risser, P. (eds) *Engineering Within Ecological Constraints*, National Academy of Engineering, Washington DC, pp97–110

Karr, J. R. and Dudley, D. R. (1981) 'Ecological perspective on water quality goals', *Environmental Management*, vol 5, pp55–68

Kathiresan, K. and Rajendran, N. (2005) 'Coastal mangrove forests mitigated tsunami', *Estuarine, Coastal and Shelf Science*, vol 65, no 3, pp601–606

Katz, E. (1992) 'The big lie: Human restoration of nature', *Research in Philosophy and Technology*, vol 12, pp231–241

Kay, C. E. (1994) 'Aboriginal overkills: The role of Native Americans in structuring western ecosystems', *Human Nature*, vol 5, no 4, pp359–398

Kay, C. E. (1997) 'Aboriginal overkill and the biogeography of moose in western North America', *Alces*, vol 35, pp141–164

Kessler, M. (2000) 'Elevational gradients in species richness and endemism of selected plant groups in the central Bolivian Andes', *Plant Ecology*, vol 149, pp181–193

Kettunen, M., Dudley, N., Bruner, A., Pabon, L., Conner, N., Berghofer, A., Vakrou, A., Mulongoy, K. J. and Gidda, S. B. (2011) 'Recognising the value of protected areas', in ten Brink, P. (ed) *The Economics of Ecosystems and Biodiversity in National and International Policy Making*, Earthscan, London

Khenpo, P.T. (2010) 'Sacred mountains and deities of Bhutan', Paper presented at a conference organised by the Government of Bhutan and WWF, Thimphu, Bhutan, May

King, A. and Clifford, S. (1985) *Holding Your Own Ground*, Maurice Temple-Smith, London

King, A. and Clifford, S. (eds) (2000) *The River's Voice: An Anthology of Poetry*, Common Ground, London

Kirby, J. T. (2006) *Mockingbird Song: Ecological Landscapes of the South*, The University of North Carolina Press, Chapel Hill, NC

Kirby, K. (1992) *Woodland and Wildlife*, Whittet Books, London

KNPS (Korea National Parks System) and IUCN (2009) *Korea's Protected Areas: Evaluating the Effectiveness of South Korea's Protected Areas System*, Seoul and Gland, Switzerland

Kormos, C. F. (2008) 'Category Ib', in Dudley, N. and Stolton, S. (eds) *Defining Protected Areas: An International Conference in Almeria, Spain, May 2007*, IUCN, Gland, Switzerland

Kormos, C. F. (2008a) *Handbook of International Wilderness Law and Policy*, Fulcrum Publishing, Golden, Colorado

Kornberg, H. (1979) *Agricultural Pollution*, Seventh Report of the Royal Commission on Environmental Polllution, Her Majesty's Stationary Office, London

Krakauer, J. (1996) *Into the Wild*, Villard Books, New York

Kunwar, R. M., Nepal, B. K., Kshhetri, H. B., Rai, S. K. and Bussmann, R. W. (2006) 'Ethnomedicine in Himalaya: A case study from Dolpa, Humla, Jumla and Mustang districts of Nepal', *Journal of Ethnobiology and Ethnomedicine*, vol 2, doi:10.1186/1746-4269-2-27

Lacerda, L. (1997) 'Global mercury emissions from gold and silver mining', *Water, Air and Soil Pollution*, vol 97, pp209–221

Lal, R. (2004) 'Soil carbon sequestration impacts on global climate change and food security', *Science*, vol 304, pp1623–1627

Landau, R. (2002) 'The Baha'i faith and the environment', in Timmerman, P. (ed) *Encyclopedia of Global Environmental Change. Volume 5: Social and Economic Dimensions of Global Environmental Change*, John Wiley and Sons, London, available at http://bahailibrary.com/articles/landau.environment.html (accessed February 2009).

Landres, P. B., Brunson, M. W., Merigliano, L., Sydoriak, C. and Morton, S. (1999) 'Naturalness and wilderness: The dilemma and irony of managing wilderness', in Cole, D. N., McCool, S. F., Borrie, W. T. and O'Loughlin, J. (eds) (2000) *Wilderness Science in a Time of Change Conference – Volume 5: Wilderness Ecosystems, Threats, and Management; 1999 May 23– 27; Missoula, MT*. Proceedings RMRS-P-15-Vol 5, U.S. Department of Agriculture, Forest Service, Rocky Mountain Research Station, Ogden, UT

Landres, P. B., Morgan, P. and Swanson, F. J. (1999a) 'Overview of the use of natural variability concepts in managing ecological systems', *Ecological Applications*, vol 9, no 4, pp1179–1188

Lantis, M. (1938) 'The Alaskan whale hunt and its affinities', *American Anthropologist*, vol 40, pp438–464

Leach, G. and Mearns, R. (1988) *Beyond the Fuelwood Crisis: People, Land and Trees in Africa*, Earthscan Publications, London

Leatherman, S. P., Chalfont, R., Pendleton, E. C. and McCandless, T. L. (1995) *Vanishing Lands: Sea Level, Society and the Chesapeake Bay*, Laboratory of Coastal Research, University of Maryland, Baltimore, MD

Lee, P. and Cheng, R. (2010 draft) *Canada's Protected Areas Status Report 2010: Area and 'Naturalness'*, Global Forest Watch Canada, Edmonton, Alberta

Lee, P., Aksenov, D., Laestidius, L., Noguerón, R. and Smith, W. (2006) *Canada's Large Intact Forest Landscapes*, Global Forest Watch Canada, Edmonton, Alberta

Leighton, M. and Wirawan, N. (1986) 'Catastrophic drought and fire in Borneo tropical rain forest associated with the 1982–1983 El Niño Southern Oscillation Event', in AAAS Symposium 101, *Tropical Rain Forests and the World Atmosphere*, Westbury Press, Boulder, CO, pp75–102

Leivestadd, H. and Muniz, I. P. (1976) 'Fish kill at low *pH* in a Norwegian river', *Nature London*, vol 259, pp391–393

Lemaire, R. and Stovel, H. (1994) *The Nara Document on Authenticity*, Agency for Cultural Affairs, Japan, UNESCO, ICCROM and ICOMOS, Nara, Japan

Leopold, A. (1949) *A Sand Country Almanac and Sketches Here and There*, Oxford University Press, New York

Leroux, S. J., Krawchuk, M. A., Schmiegelow, F., Cumming, S. G., Lisgo, K., Anderson, L. G. and Petkova, M. (2010) 'Global protected areas and IUCN designations: Do the categories match the conditions?', *Biological Conservation*, vol 143, pp 609–616

Lever, C. (1992) *They Dined on Eland: The Story of the Acclimatisation Societies*, Quiller Press, London

Leverington, F., Hockings, M. and Costa, K. L. (2008) *Management Effectiveness Evaluation in Protected Areas:A Global Study*, University of Queensland, IUCN-WCPA, TNC, WWF, Gatton, Australia

Lewington, A. (2003) *Plants for People* (2nd edn), The Eden Project, London

Lewington, A. and Parker, P. (1999) *Ancient Trees*, Collins and Brown, London

Lewis, S. L., Lopez-Gonzalez, G., Sonké, B., Affum-Baffoe, K., Baker, T. R., Ojo, L. O., Phillips, O. L., Reitsma, J. M., White, L., Comiskey, J. A., Marie-Noel, D., Ewango, C. E. N., Feldpausch, T. R., Hamilton, A. C., Gloor, M., Hart, T., Hladik, A., Lloyd, J., Lovett, J. C., Makana, J. R., Malhi, Y., Mbago, F. M., Ndangalasi, H. J., Peacock, J., Peh, K. S. H., Sheil, D., Sunderland, T., Swaine, M. D., Taplin, J., Taylor, D., Thomas, S. C.,Votere, R. and Woll, H. (2009) 'Increasing carbon storage in intact African tropical forests', *Nature*, vol 457, pp1003–1006

Lindhe, A. and Lindelöw, A. (2004) 'Cut high stumps of spruce, birch, aspen and oak as a breeding substrate for saproxylic beetles', *Forest Ecology and Management*, vol 203, nos 1–3, pp1–20

Llewellyn, O. (1992) 'Desert reclamation and conservation in Islamic law', in Khalid, F. and O'Brien, J. (eds) *Islam and Ecology*, Cassells, London, pp87–98

Locke. H. and Deardon, P. (2005) 'Rethinking protected area categories and the new paradigm', *Environmental Conservation*, vol 32, no 1, pp1–10

Loh, J. and Harmon, D. (2005) 'A global index of biocultural diversity', *Ecological Indicators*, vol 5, pp231–241

Looney, J. H. and James, P. W. (1988) 'Effects on lichens', in Ashmore, M. R., Bell, J. N. B. and Garretty, C. (eds) *Acid Rain and Britain's Natural Ecosystems*, Imperial College Centre for Environmental Technology, London

Lopez, B. (1986) *Arctic Dreams*, Charles Scribner's Sons, New York

Loucks, C., Barber-Meyer, S., Hossain, A. A., Barlow A. and Chowdury, R. M (2010) 'Sea level rise and tigers: Predicted impacts to Bangladesh's Sundarbans mangroves', *Climatic Change*, vol 98, pp291–298

Louv, R. (2005) *Last Child in the Woods: Saving Our Children from Nature Deficit Disorder*, Algonquin Books, Chapel Hill, NC

Lovegrove, R. (2007) *Silent Fields: The Long Decline of a Nation's Wildlife*, Oxford University Press, Oxford

Low, T. (2002) *The New Nature*, Viking Press, Camberwell, Victoria, Australia

Lowenstein, T. (1980) 'Some aspects of sea ice subsistence hunting in Point Hope, Alaska: Report to the North Slope Borough, Coastal Management Plan', NSC, Barrow, Alaska

Luyssaert, S. E., Schulze, D., Börner, A., Knohl, A., Hessenmöller, D., Law, B. E., Ciais, P. and Grace, J. (2008) 'Old-growth forests as global carbon sinks', *Nature*, vol 455, pp213–215

Mabey, R. (1973) *The Unofficial Countryside*, Collins, London

Mabey, R. (1974) *The Pollution Handbook*, Penguin Books, Harmondsworth, UK

Mabey, M. (1980) *The Common Ground*, Hutchinson, London

Mabey, R. (2005) *Fencing Paradise: Reflections on the Myths of Eden*, Eden Project Books, Transworld Publishers, London

Mabey, R. (2010) *Weeds*, Profile Books, London

McCarthy, C. (2006) *The Road*, Alfred A. Knopf, New York

McCarty, J. P. (2001) 'Ecological consequences of recent climate change', *Conservation Biology*, vol 15, no 2, pp320–331

McCloskey, M. J. and Spalding, H. (1989) 'A reconnaissance level inventory of the wilderness remaining in the world', *Ambio*, vol 18, pp221–227

MacKinnon, K. S. (1978) 'Competition between red and grey squirrels', *Mammal Review*, vol 8, no 4, pp185–190

MacKinnon, K. S., Hatta, G., Halim, H. and Mangalik, A. (1997) *The Ecology of Kalimantan*, Oxford University Press, Oxford, UK

McLeod, C. J., Parish, D. M. B. and Robinson, R. A. (2007) 'Niche opportunities and introduced birds: Temporal variation in resource abundance', in Bissonette, J. A. and Storch, I. (eds) *Temporal Dimensions in Landscape Ecology: Wildlife Responses to Variable Resources*, Springer, New York

McNeely, J.A. (ed) (2001) *The Great Reshuffling: Human Dimensions on Alien Invasive Species*, IUCN, Gland, Switzerland

Maffi, L. (2005) 'Linguistic, cultural, and biological diversity', *Annual Review of Anthropology*, vol 34, pp599–617

Maffi, L. and Woodley, E. (2010) *Biocultural Diversity Conservation: A Global Sourcebook*, Earthscan, London

Malcolm, J. R., Liu, C., Neilson, R. P., Hansen, L. and Hannah, L. (2006) 'Global warming and extinction of endemic species from biodiversity hotspots', *Conservation Biology*, vol 20, no 2, pp538–548

Malhi, Y. and Phillips, O. L. (2004) 'Tropical forests and global atmospheric change: A synthesis', *Philosophical Transactions of the Royal Society London B*, vol 359, pp549–555

Mallarach, J. M. (2006) 'Evaluation of the protected areas system of Catalonia, Spain (2002–03)', in Hocking, M., Stolton, S., Dudley, N. and Courrau, J. (eds) *Evaluating Effectiveness: A Framework for Assessing the Management of Protected Areas* (2nd edn), IUCN, Gland, Switzerland and Cambridge, UK

Mallarach, J. M., Morrison, J., Kothari, A., Sarmiento, F., Atauri, J. A. and Wishitemi, B. (2008) 'On defence of protected landscapes: A reply to some criticisms of Category V protected areas and suggestions for improvement', in Dudley, N. and Stolton, S. (eds) *Defining Protected Areas: An International Conference in Almeria, Spain, May 2007*, IUCN World Commission on Protected Areas, Gland, Switzerland

Maller, C., Townsend, M., Pryor, A., Brown, P. and St. Leger, L. (2006) 'Healthy nature – Healthy people: "Contact with nature" as an upstream health promotion intervention for populations', *Health Promotion International*, vol 21, pp45–54

Manning, A. C., Gordon, I. J. and Ripple, W. J. (2009) 'Restoring landscapes of fear with wolves in the Scottish Highlands', *Biological Conservation*, vol 142, pp2314–2321

Mansourian, S., Vallauri, D. and Dudley, N. (eds) (2005) *Forest Restoration in Landscapes: Beyond Planting Trees*, Springer, New York

Margules, C. R. and Pressey, R. L. (2000) 'Systematic conservation planning', *Nature*, vol 405, no 11, pp243–253

Marjokorpi, A. and Ruokolainen, K. (2003) 'The role of traditional forest gardens in the conservation of tree species in West Kalimantan, Indonesia', *Biodiversity and Conservation*, vol 12, pp799–822

Markham, A., Dudley, N. and Stolton, S. (1993) *Some Like it Hot: Climate Change, Biodiversity and the Survival of Species*, WWF International, Gland, Switzerland

Martin, V. (ed) (1982) *Wilderness*, The Findhorn Press, Findhorn, Scotland

Marvier, M., Kareiva, P. and Neubert, M. G. (2004) 'Habitat destruction, fragmentation, and disturbance promote invasion by habitat generalists in a multispecies metapopulation', *Risk Analysis*, vol 24, no 4, pp869–878

Matheson, C. (1932) *Changes in the Fauna of Wales within Historic Times*, National Museum of Wales and the University of Wales, Cardiff

Matthews, E. (ed) (2002) *The State of the Forest: Indonesia*, Global Forest Watch, Forest Watch Indonesia and World Resources Institute, Washington DC

Matthews, E., Payne, R., Rohweder, M. and Murray, S. (2000) *Pilot Analysis of Global Ecosystems: Forest Ecosystems*, World Resources Institute, Washington DC

Matthiessen, P. (1978) *The Snow Leopard*, Chatto and Windus, London

Mazzolli, M. (2010) 'Mosaics of exotic forest plantations and native forests as habitat of pumas', *Environmental Management*, vol 46, pp237–253

MCPFE Liaison Unit and FAO (2003) *State of Europe's Forests 2003: The MCPFE Report on Sustainable Forest Management in Europe*, Ministerial Conference on the Protection of Forests in Europe, Vienna

MCPFE (2007) *Europe's Forests 2007*, Ministerial Conference for the Protection of Forests in Europe Liaison Unit, Warsaw

Medicinal Plant Specialist Group (2007) *International Standard for Sustainable Wild Collection of Medicinal and Aromatic Plants (ISSC-MAP), Version 1.0*, Bundesamt für Naturschutz (BfN), MPSG/SSC/IUCN, WWF Germany, and TRAFFIC, Bonn, Gland, Frankfurt and Cambridge

Meijaard, E., Sheil, D., Nasi, R. and Stanley, S. A. (2006) 'Wildlife conservation in Bornean timber concessions', *Ecology and Society*, vol 11, no 1, art 47, www.ecologyandsociety.org/vol11/iss1/art47/, accessed July 2011

Menzel, A. (2005) 'A 500 year pheno-climatological view on the 2003 heatwave in Europe assessed by grape harvest dates', *Meteorological Zoology*, vol 14, pp75–77

Menzel, A. and Dose, V. (2005) 'Analysis of long-term time-series of beginning of flowering by Bayesian function estimation', *Meteorological Zoology*, vol 14, pp429–434

Merton, T. (1960) *The Wisdom of the Desert: Sayings of the Desert Fathers in the 4th Century*, New Directions Publishers, New York

Merton, T. (translator and interpreter) (1965) *The Way of Chuang Tzu*, Unwin Books, London

Midgley, M. (1983) *Animals and Why They Matter*, University of Georgia Press, Athens, GA

Mill, J. S. (1850–58) *Nature, the Utility of Religion, and Theism*

Millennium Ecosystem Assessment (2005) *Ecosystems and Human Well-being: Synthesis*, Island Press, Washington DC

Milner-Gulland, E. J. and Bennett, E. L. (2003) 'Wild meat: The bigger picture', *Trends in Ecology and Evolution*, vol 18, no 7, pp351–357

Minnemeyer, S., with Walker, T., Collomb, J. G., Cotton, L. and Bryant, D. (2002) *An Analysis of Access into Central Africa's Rainforests*, Global Forest Watch and World Resources Institute, Washington DC

Mitchell, J. H. (2001) *The Wildest Place on Earth: Italian Gardens and the Invention of Wilderness*, Counterpoint, Washington DC

Mithen, S. (2003) *After the Ice: A Global Human History 20,000–5,000 BC*, Harvard University Press, New York

Mittermeier, R. A., Mittermeier, C. G., Brooks, T. M., Pilgrim, J. D., Konstant, W. R., da Fonseca, G. A. B. and Kormos, C. (2003) 'Wilderness and biodiversity conservation', Proceedings of the National Academy of Sciences, vol 100, no 18, pp10309–10313

Montréal Process, The (2007) 'The Montréal Process: Criteria and Indicators for the Conservation and Sustainable Management of Temperate and Boreal Forests: Third edition', Montréal

Moore, N. W. (1962) 'Toxic chemicals and birds: The ecological background to conservation problems', *British Birds*, vol 55, pp428–435

Mote, P. W., Hamlet, A. F., Clark, M. P. and Lettermaier, D. P. (2005) 'Declining mountain snowpack in western North America', *American Meteorological Society*, January 2005, pp39–45

Muir, J. (1894) *The Mountains of California*, The Century Company, New York

Muriuki, J. (2006) 'Forests as pharmacopoeia: Identifying new plant-based treatments for malaria', *Unasylva*, vol 57, pp24–25

Mwamgomo, E., Stolton, S. and Dudley, N. (2005) 'Ecological integrity: A draft assessment measured against key management targets for Serengeti National Park', Enhancing our Heritage Project, University of Queensland, Brisbane

Myers, N. (1984) *The Primary Source: Tropical Forests and Our Future*, W. W. Norton, London and New York

Nabuurs, G. J., Masera, O., Andrasko, K., Benitez-Ponce, P., Boer, R., Dutschke, M., Elsiddig, E., Ford-Robertson, J., Frumhoff, P., Karjalainen, T., Krankina, O., Kurz, W. A., Matsumoto, M., Oyhantcabal, W., Ravindranath, N. H., Sanz Sanchez, M. J. and Zhang, X. (2007) 'Forestry', in Metz, B., Davidson, O. R., Bosch, P. R., Dave, R., Meyer, L. A. (eds) *Climate Change 2007: Mitigation. Contribution of Working Group III to the Fourth Assessment Report of the Intergovernmental Panel on Climate Change*, Cambridge University Press, Cambridge, UK and New York

Nagendra, H. (2008) 'Do parks work? Impact of protected areas on land cover clearing', *Ambio*, vol 37, pp330–337

Narayanan, V. (2001) 'Water, wood, and wisdom: Ecological perspectives from the Hindu traditions', *Daedalus* (American Academy of Arts and Science), vol 130, no 4, pp179–206

Nash, R. F. (ed) (1989) *American Environmentalism: Readings in Conservation History*, McGraw Hill, New York

Nash, R. F. (2001) *Wilderness and the American Mind* (4th edn), Yale University Press, New Haven, CT

Nasi, R., Brown, D., Wilkie, D., Bennett, E., Tutin, C., van Tol, G. and Christophersen, T. (2008) *Conservation and Use of Wildlife Based Resources: The Bushmeat Crisis,*

CBD Technical Series No 33, Secretariat of the Convention on Biological Diversity, Montreal

National Research Council (1989) *Lost Crops of the Incas: Little-Known Plants of the Andes with Promise for Worldwide Cultivation*, Ad Hoc Panel of the Advisory Committee on Technology Innovation, Board on Science and Technology for International Development, Office of International Affairs, Washington DC

Naylor, R. L., Goldburg, R. J., Primavera, J. H., Kautsky, N., Beveridge, M. C. M., Clay, J., Folke, C., Lubchenco, J., Mooney, H. and Troell, M. (2000) 'Effect of aquaculture on world fish supplies', *Nature*, vol 405, pp1017–1024

Negussie, G. (1997) 'Use of traditional values in the search for conservation goals: The kaya forests of the Kenyan coast', Paper presented at the African Rainforests and the Conservation of Biodiversity Conference, Limbe Botanical Garden, 17–24 January 1997

Neira, E., Verscheure, H. and Revenga, C. (2002) *Chile's Frontier Forests: Conserving a Global Treasure*, Global Forest Watch, World Resources Institute, Washington DC

Nelson, A. and Chomitz, K. (2009) *Protected Area Effectiveness in Reducing Tropical Deforestation*, The World Bank, Washington DC

Nelson, J. and Hossack, L. (eds) (2003) *Indigenous Peoples and Protected Areas in Africa*, Forest Peoples Programme, Moreton-in-Marsh, UK

Newman, D. J., Gordon, C. M. and Snader, K. M. (2003) 'Natural products as sources of new drugs over the period 1981–2002', *Journal of Natural Products*, vol 66, pp1022–1037

Newman, J. R., Novakova, E. and McClave, J. T. (1985) 'The influence of industrial air emissions on the nesting ecology of the house martin *Delichon urbica* in Czechoslovakia', *Biological Conservation*, vol 31, pp229–248

Newmark, W. D. (1995) 'Extinction of mammal populations in western North American national parks', *Conservation Biology*, vol 9, pp512–526

Nielsen, C., Ravn, H. P., Nentwig, W. and Wade, M. (eds) (2005) *The Giant Hogweed Best Practice Manual: Guidelines for the Management and Control of an Invasive Weed in Europe*, Forest & Landscape Denmark, Hoersholm

Noguerón, R., with Bryant, D. A., Stritholt, J. and Kool, J. (2002) *Low Access Forests and Their Level of Protection in North America*, Global Forest Watch and World Resources Institute, Washington DC

Norton-Griffiths, M. (1979) 'The influence of grazing, browsing, and fire on the vegetation dynamics of the Serengeti', in Sinclair, A. R. E and Norton-Griffiths, M. (eds) *Serengeti: Dynamics of an Ecosystem*, The University of Chicago Press, Chicago, IL

Ntiamoa-Baidu, Y. (1997) *Wildlife and Food Security in Africa*, FAO Conservation Guide, no 33, FAO, Rome

Occhipinti-Ambrogi, A. (2007) 'Global change and marine communities: Alien species and climate change', *Marine Pollution Bulletin*, vol 55, pp342–352

Oelschlaeger, M. (1991) *The Idea of Wilderness*, Yale University Press, New Haven and London

Oerlemans, J. (2005) 'Extracting a climate signal from 169 glacier records', *Science*, vol 308, pp675–677

Ogle, B. (1996) 'People's dependency on forests for food security', in Ruiz Pérez, M. and Arnold, J. E. M. (eds) *Current Issues in Non-Timber Forest Products Research*, Center for International Forestry Research, Bogor, Indonesia, pp219–241

Oglethorpe, J., Honzak, C. and Margoluis, C. (2008) *Healthy People, Healthy Ecosystems: A Manual for Integrating Health and Family Planning into Conservation Projects*, World Wildlife Fund, Washington DC

Ohlson, M., Söderström, L., Hörnberg, G., Zackrisson, O. and Hermansson, J. (1996) 'Habitat qualities versus long-term continuity as determinants of biodiversity in boreal old-growth swamp forests', *Biological Conservation*, vol 81, no 3, pp221–231

Økland, J. (1992) 'Effects of acidic water on freshwater snails: Results of a study of 1000 lakes throughout Norway', *Environmental Pollution*, vol 78, nos 1–3, pp127–130

Oliver, C. O. and Larson, B. C. (1990) *Forest Stand Dynamics*, McGraw-Hill, New York

Oliver, I., Smith, P. L., Lunt, I. and Parkes, D. (2002) 'Pre-1750 vegetation, naturalness and vegetation condition: What are the implications for biodiversity conservation?', *Ecological Management and Restoration*, vol 3, no 3, pp176–178

Omar, S. (1991) 'Dynamics of range plants following 10 years of protection in arid rangelands of Kuwait', *Journal of Arid Land Environments*, vol 21, pp99–111

Omar, S., Bhat, N. R., Shahid, S. A. and Assem, A. (2005) 'Land and vegetation degradation in war-affected areas of the Sabah Al-Ahmad Nature Reserve of Kuwait: A case study of Umm. Ar. Riman', *Journal of Arid Environments*, vol 62, pp475–490

Ormerod, S. J., Tyler, S. J. and Lewis, J. M. S. (1985) 'Is the breeding distribution of dippers influenced by stream acidity?', *Bird Study*, vol 32, pp32–39

Orr, Y. and Spanier, Y. (1992) 'Traditional Jewish attitudes towards plant and animal conservation', in Rose, A. (ed) *Judaism and Ecology*, Cassell, London

Overrein, L. N., Seip, H. M. and Tollan, A. (1980) *Acid Precipitation: Effects on Forests and Fish: Final Report of the SNF Project 1972–1980*, Research Report FR 19/80, SNF Project, Oslo

Pabon-Zamora, L., Bezaury, J., Leon, F., Gill, L., Stolton, S., Grover, A., Mitchell, S. and Dudley, N. (2008) *Nature's Values: Assessing Protected Area Benefits*, Quick Guide Series, The Nature Conservancy, Arlington VA

Pagiola, S., Bishop, J. and Landell-Mills, N. (eds) (2002) *Selling Forest Environmental Services*, Earthscan, London

Palheta, D. and Taylor, A. (1995) 'Mercury in environmental and biological samples from a gold mining area in the Amazon region of Brazil', *The Science of the Total Environment*, vol 168, pp63–69

Palmer, M. and Finlay, V. (2003) *Faith in Conservation*, The World Bank, Washington DC

Pamuk, O. (2001) *My Name is Red*, trans. Göknar, E. M., Faber and Faber, London

Panario, D. and Bidegain, M. (1997) 'Climate change effects on grasslands in Uruguay', *Climate Research*, vol 9, nos 1–2, pp37–40

Park, G. (1995) *Ngā Uruora – The Groves of Life: Ecology and History in a New Zealand Landscape*, Victoria University Press, Wellington

Parish, F., Sirin, A., Charman, D., Jooster, H., Minayeva, T. and Silvius, M. (eds) (2007) *Assessment on Peatlands, Biodiversity and Climate Change*, Global Environment Centre, Kuala Lumpur and Wetlands International, Wageningen, Netherlands

Parmesan, C. (1996) 'Climate and species' range', *Nature*, vol 382, pp765–766

Parmesan, C. (2006) 'Ecological and evolutionary responses to recent climate change', *Annual Review of Ecology, Evolution and Systematics*, vol 37, pp637–669

Parmesan, C. and Yohe, G. (2003) 'A globally coherent fingerprint of climate change impacts across natural systems', *Nature*, vol 421, pp37–42

Parmesan, C., Ryrholm, N., Stefanescu, C., Hill, J. K., Thomas, C. D., Descimon, H., Huntley, B., Laila, L., Kullberg, J., Tammaru, T., Tennent, W. J., Thomas, J. A. and

Warren, M. (1999) 'Poleward shifts in geographical ranges of butterfly species associated with regional warming', *Nature*, vol 399, pp579–583

Parody, J. M., Cuthbert, F. J. and Decker, E. H. (2001) 'The effect of 50 years of landscape change on species richness and community composition', *Global Ecology and Biogeography*, vol 10, no 3, pp305–313

Parr, S. J. (1991) 'Occupation of new conifer plantations in Wales', *Bird Study*, vol 38, no 2, pp103–111

Parr, S. J. (1994) 'Changes in the population size and nest sites of merlins (*Falco columbarius*) in Wales between 1970 and 1991', *Bird Study*, vol 41, no 1, pp42–47

Parviainen, J. (1995) 'The impact of fire on Finnish forests in the past and today', IBFRA Conference 30 July–5 August 1995, Joensuu, Finland

Parviainen, J. (2005) 'Virgin and natural forest in the temperate zone of Europe', *Forest, Snow and Landscape Research*, vol 79, nos 1–2, pp9–18

Pathak, N. (ed) (2009) *Community Conserved Areas in India: A Directory*, Kalpavriksh, Pune, India

Pattanayak, S. K., Corey, C. G., Lau, Y. F. and Kramer, R. A. (2003) *Forest Malaria: A Microeconomic Study of Forest Protection and Child Malaria in Flores, Indonesia*, Duke University, Durham, NC, available at: www.env.duke.edu/solutions/documents/forest-malaria.pdf, accessed 1 August 2009

Pauli, H., Gottfried, M. and Grabherr, G. (1986) 'Effects of climate change on mountain ecosystems: Upward shifts in Alpine plants', *World Resources Review*, vol 8, no 3, pp382–390

Paulson, D. R. (2001) 'Recent odonata records from southern Florida: Effects of global warming?', *International Journal of Odonatology*, vol 4, pp57–69

Pauly, D., Watson, R. and Alder, J. (2005) 'Global trends in world fisheries: impacts on marine ecosystems and food security', *Philosophical Transactions of the Royal Society B*, vol 360, pp5–12

Pedersen, L. B. and Bille-Larsen, J. (1999) 'A comparison of litterfall and element fluxes in even aged Norway spruce, sitka spruce and beech stands in Denmark', *Forest Ecology and Management*, vol 114, no, 8, pp55–70

Persson, J. and Manus, S. (1990) *A Richer Forest*, The National Board of Forestry, Jönköping, Sweden, translated C. Stock, English language version 1992

Perry, A. L., Low, P. J., Ellis, J. R. and Reynolds, J. D. (2005) 'Climate change and distribution shifts in marine fishes', *Science*, vol 308, pp1912–1915

Peterken, G. (2002) *Reversing the Habitat Fragmentation of British Woodlands*, WWF UK, Godalming

Peterson, G., Allen, C. R. and Holling, C. S. (1998) 'Ecological resilience, biodiversity and scale', *Ecosystems*, vol 1, pp6–18

Phillips, B. L., Brown, G. P. and Shine, R. (2003) 'Assessing the potential impact of cane toads on Australian snakes', *Conservation Biology*, vol 17, no 6, pp1738–1747

Philips, S. J. and Comus, P. W. (2000) *A Natural History of the Sonoran Desert*, Arizona-Sonora Desert Museum and University of California Press, Tucson, AZ, and Berkley, CA

Pilgrim, S. E., Cullen, L. C., Smith, D. J. and Pretty, J. (2008) 'Ecological knowledge is lost in wealthier communities and countries', *Environmental Science and Technology*, vol 42, no 4, pp1004–1009

Pimentel, D., Zuniga, R. and Morrison, D. (2005) 'Update on the environmental and economic costs associated with alien-invasive species in the United States', *Ecological Economics*, vol 52, pp273– 288

Pimm, S. L., Moulton, M. P. and Justice, J. L. (1994) 'Bird extinctions in the Central Pacific', *Philosophical Transaction of the Royal Society London B*, vol 344, pp27–33

Pino, J., Rodà, F., Ribas, F. and Pons, X. (2000) 'Landscape structure and bird species richness: Implications for conservation in rural areas between natural parks', *Landscape and Urban Planning*, vol 49, pp35–48

Poff, N. L., Allen, J. D., Bain, M. B., Karr, J. R., Prestegaard, K. L., Richter, B. D., Sparks, R. E. and Stromberg, J. C. (1997) 'The natural flow regime: A paradigm for river conservation and restoration', *Bioscience*, vol 47, no 11, pp769–784

Pope John Paul II (1990) 'The ecological crisis: A common responsibility peace with God The Creator, peace with all of creation. Message of Blessed John Paul II for the celebration of the World Day of Peace, 1 January', Catholic Conservation Center, New York, available from http://conservation.catholic.org/ecologicalcrisis.htm, accessed 26 July 2011

Potapov, P., Yaroshenko, A., Turubanova, S., Dubinin, M., Laestadius, L., Thies, C., Aksenov, D., Egorov, A., Yesipova, Y., Glushkov, I., Karpachevskiy, M., Kostikova, A., Manisha, A., Tsybikova, E. and Zhuravleva, I. (2008) 'Mapping the world's intact forest landscapes by remote sensing', *Ecology and Society*, vol 13, no 2, 51pp [online], available at www.ecologyandsociety.org/vol13/iss2/art51/, accessed July 2011

Pounds, J. A., Bustamente, M. R., Coloma, L. A., Consuegra, J. A., Fogden, M. P. L., Fister, P. N., La Marca, E., Masters, K. L., Merino-Viteri, A., Puschendorf, R., Ron, S. R., Sánchez-Azofeifa, G. A., Still, C. J. and Young, B. E. (2006) 'Widespread amphibian extinctions from epidemic disease driven by global warming', *Nature*, vol 439, pp161–167

Pounds, J. A., Fogden, M. P. L. and Campbell, J. H. (1999) 'Biological responses to climate change on a tropical mountain', *Nature*, vol 398, pp611–615

Prasad Oli, K. (2010) 'Kailash Sacred Landscape Conservation Initiative', International Centre for Integrated Mountain Development, Kathmandu

Prebble, J. (1963) *The Highland Clearances*, Secker and Warburg, London

Pretty, J. (2004) 'How nature contributes to mental and physical health', *Spirituality and Health International*, vol 5, no 2, pp68–78

Pretty, J., Adams, B., Berkes, F., Ferreira de Athayde, S., Dudley, N., Hunn, E., Maffi, L., Milton, K., Rapport, D., Robbins, P., Sterling, E., Stolton, S., Tsing, A., Vintinner, E. and Pilgrim, S. (2009) 'The intersections of biological and cultural diversity: Towards integration', *Conservation and Society*, vol 7, no 2, pp100–112

Putz, F., Synnott, T., Peña-Claros, M., Pinard, M. Sheil, D., Vanclay, J., Sist, P., Gourlet-Fleury, S., Griscom, B., Palmer, J. and Zagt, R. In review. 'Sustaining tropical forest goods and services with selective logging'

Pyke, C. R. (2004) 'Habitat loss confounds climate change impacts', *Frontiers of Ecology and the Environment*, vol 2, no 4, pp178–182

Raatikainen, M. (1988) 'Estimates of wild berry yields in Finland', in Vänninn, I. and Raatikainen, M. (eds) *Proceedings of the Finnish-Soviet Symposium on Non-Timber Forest Resources in Jyväskylä, Finland, 25–29 August 1986: Acta Bottanica Fennica*, vol 136, pp9–10

Rackham, O. (2006) *Woodlands*, Collins, London

Ramsar Secretariat (2002) 'Climate change and wetlands: Impacts, adaptation and mitigation', COP8 Information Paper DOC 11

Ramsar Scientific & Technical Review Panel and Biodiversity Convention Secretariat (2007) 'Water, wetlands, biodiversity and climate change: Report on outcomes of an expert meeting, 23–24 March 2007', Gland, Switzerland

Redford, K.R. (1992) 'The empty forest'. *Bioscience*, vol. 42, no. 6, pp 42–53

Redford, K. R. (2000) 'Natural areas, hunting and nature conservation in the neotropics', *Wild Earth*, Fall 2000, pp41–48

Rees, I. B. (1992) *The Mountains of Wales: An Anthology in Verse and Prose*, University of Wales Press, Cardiff

Republica Oriental del Uruguay, OEA, and BID (1992) *Estudio Ambiental Nacional: Plan de Accion Ambiental*, Organizacion de los Estados Americanos, Washington DC

Rescia, A., Schmitz, M. F., Martín de Agar, P., de Pablo, C. L., Atauri, J. A. and Pineda, F. D. (1994) 'Influence of landscape complexity and land management on woody plant diversity in Northern Spain', *Journal of Vegetation Science*, vol 5, pp505–516

Revenga, C., Brunner, J., Henninger, N., Kassem, K. and Payne, R. (2000) *Pilot Analysis of Global Ecosystems: Freshwater Systems*, World Resources Institute, Washington DC

Revenga, C., Murray, S., Abramovitz, J. and Hammond, A. (1998) *Watersheds of the World: Ecological Value and Vulnerability*, World Resources Institute and World-watch Institute, Washington DC

Rice, R. E., Gullison, R. E. and Reid, J. W. (1997) 'Can sustainable forest management save tropical forests?', *Scientific American*, vol 276, pp34–39

Rice, R., Sugal, C., Frumhoff, P. C., Losos, E. and Gullison, R. (2001) 'Options for conserving biodiversity in the context of logging in tropical forests', in Bowles, I. A. and Prickett, G. T. (eds) *Footprints in the Jungle: Natural Resource Industries, Infrastructure and Biodiversity Conservation*, Oxford University Press, Oxford, pp168–179

Richter, B. D., Baumgartner, J. M., Powell, J. and Braun, D. P. (1996) 'A method for assessing hydrologic alteration within ecosystems', *Conservation Biology*, vol 10, no 4, pp1163–1174

Ricketts, T. H., Daily, G. C., Erlich, P. R. and Michener, C. D. (2004) 'Economic value of tropical forests to coffee production', Proceedings of the National Academy of Sciences, vol 101, no 34, pp12579–12582

Ricketts, T. H., Soares-Filho, B., da Fonseca, G. A. B., Nepstad, D., Pfaff, A., Petsonk, A., Anderson, A., Boucher, D., Cattaneo, A., Conte, M., Creighton, K., Linden, L., Maretti, C., Moutinho, P., Ullman, R. and Victurne, R. (2010) 'Indigenous lands, protected areas, and slowing climate change', *PLoS Biology*, vol 8, no 3, doi:10.1371/journal.pbio.1000331

Rietbergen-McCracken, J., Maginnis, S. and Sarre, A. (eds) (2008) *The Forest Landscape Restoration Handbook*, Earthscan, London

Riebesell, U., Zondervan, I., Rost, B., Tortell, P. D., Zeebe, R. E. and More, F. M. M. (2000) 'Reduced calcification of marine plankton in response to atmospheric CO_2', *Nature*, vol 407, pp364–367

Rixon, C. A. M., Duggan, I. C., Bergeron, N. M. N., Ricciardi, A. and MacIsaac, H. J. (2005) 'Invasion risks posed by the aquarium trade and live fish markets on the Laurentian Great Lakes', *Biodiversity and Conservation*, vol 14, pp1365–1381

Roberts, C. M., Andelman, S., Branch, G., Bustamante, R. H., Castilla, J. C., Dugan, J., Halpern, B. S., Lafferty, K. D., Leslie, H., Lubchenko, J., McCardle, D., Possingham, H. P., Ruckelhaus, M. and Warne, R. R. (2003) 'Ecological criteria for evaluating candidate sites for marine reserves', *Ecological Applications*, vol 13, no 1 (supplement), ppS199–S214

Roberts, D. L. and Solow, A. R. (2003) 'When did the dodo become extinct?', *Nature*, vol 426, p245

Roberts, K. (1983) *Man and the Natural World: Changing Attitudes in England 1500– 1800*, Allen Lane, Harmondsworth, UK

Roe, D., Mulliken, T., Milledge, S., Mremi, J., Mosha, S. and Grieg-Gran, M. (2002) *Making a Killing or Making a Living? Wildlife Trade, Trade Controls and Rural Livelihoods*, IIED and TRAFFIC, London

Rolston, H. III (1989) *Environmental Ethics: Duties and Values to the Natural World*, Temple University Press, Philadelphia, PA

Rolston, H. III (1995) 'Duties to endangered species', in Elliot, R. (ed) *Environmental Ethics*, Oxford University Press, Oxford, pp60–75

Rose, D. B. (2008) 'What do we mean by wild?', in Dudley, N. and Stolton, S. (eds) *Defining Protected Areas: An International Conference in Almeria, Spain, May 2007*, IUCN, Gland, Switzerland

Rose, F. and James, P. W. (1974) 'Regional studies of the British flora: 1 The corticolous and lignicolous species of the New Forest, Hampshire', *The Lichenologist*, vol 6, pp1–72

Rose, F. and Wallace, E. C. (1974) 'Changes in the bryophyte flora of Britain', in Hawksworth, D. L. (ed) *The Changing Flora and Fauna of Britain*, Academic Press, London, pp27–46

Rousseau, J. J. (1754) *Discourse on the Origins of Inequality among Men*

Rowell, A., Marriott, J. and Stockman, L. (2005) *The Next Gulf: London, Washington and Oil Conflict in the Gulf*, Constable, London

Ruitenbeek, J. H. (1990) *Economic Analysis of Tropical Forest Conservation Initiatives; Examples from West Africa*. WWF UK, Godalming, UK

Russel, K. C. (2000) 'Exploring how the wilderness therapy process relates to outcomes', *The Journal of Experimental Education*, vol 23, no 3, pp170–176

Sabbagh, K. (1999) *A Rum Affair: A True Story of Botanical Fraud*, Allen Lane, The Penguin Press, London

Sagoff, M. (1984) 'Animal liberation and environmental ethics: Bad marriage quick divorce', *Osgoode Hall Law Journal*, vol 22, pp297–307

Salo, K. (1995) 'Non-timber forest products and their utilisation', in Hytönen, M. (ed) *Multiple Use Forestry in the Nordic Countries*, METLA The Finnish Forest Research Institute, Helsinki

Sandars, N. K. (1960) *The Epic of Gilgamesh*, Penguin Books, Harmondsworth, UK

Sanderson, E. W., Jaiteh, M., Levy, M. A., Redford, K. H., Wannebo, A. V. and Woolmer, G. (2002) 'The human footprint and the last of the wild', *Bioscience*, vol 52, no 10, pp891–904

Santos, M. J. and Thorne, J. H. (2010) 'Comparing culture and ecology: Conservation planning of oak woodlands in Mediterranean landscapes of Portugal and California', *Environmental Conservation*, doi:10.1017/S0376892910000238

Savidge, J. A. (1987) 'Extinction of an island forest avifauna by an introduced snake', *Ecology*, vol 68, pp660–668

SCBD (2004) *Akwé Kon Voluntary Guidelines for the Conduct of Cultural, Environmental and Social Impact Assessment regarding Developments Proposed to Take Place on, or which are Likely to Impact on, Sacred Sites and on Lands and Waters Traditionally Occupied or Used by Indigenous and Local Communities*, Secretariat of the Convention on Biological Diversity, Montreal

Schaberg, P. G., DeHayes, D. H., Hawley, G. J. and Nijensohn, S. E. (2008) 'Anthropogenic alterations of genetic diversity within tree populations: Implications for forest ecosystem resilience', Forest Ecology and Management, vol 256, pp855–862

Schama, S. (1995) *Landscape and Memory*, Alfred A. Knopf, New York

Schnitzler, A., Génot, J. C., Wintz, M. and Hale, B. W. (2008) 'Naturalness and conservation in France', *Journal of Agricultural and Environmental Ethics*, vol 21, pp423–436

Schroder, A., Persson, L. and de Roos, A. M. (2005) 'Direct experimental evidence for alternative stable states: A review', *Oikos*, vol 110, pp3–19

Schuman, G. E., Janzen, H. H. and Herrick, J. E. (2002) 'Soil carbon dynamics and potential carbon sequestration by rangelands', *Environmental Pollution*, vol 116, pp391–396

Schwarz, U., Bratrich, C., Hulea, O., Moroz, S., Pumputyte, S., Rast, G., Bern, M. R., Siposs, V. (2006) *2006 Floods in the Danube River Basin: Flood Risk Mitigation for People Living along the Danube: The Potential for Floodplain Protection and Restoration*, WWF Danube-Carpathian Programme, Vienna

Scoones, I., Melnyk, M. and Pretty, J. N. (1992) *The Hidden Harvest. Wild Foods and Agricultural Systems: A Literature Review and Annotated Bibliography*, International Institute for Environment and Development, London

SENAPA (2005) 'Serengeti National Park General Management Plan: 2006–2016', Tanzania National Parks

Senior, J. (2010) 'Parks Victoria: Healthy parks, healthy people', in Stolton, S. and Dudley, N. (eds) *Vital Sites*, WWF and Equilibrium Research, Gland, Switzerland

Shaankar, R. U., Ganeshaiah, K. N., Krishnan, S., Ramya, R., Meera, C., Aravind, N. A., Kumar, A., Rao, D., Vanaraj, G., Ramachandra, J., Gauthier, R., Ghazoul, J., Poole, N. and Chinnappa Reddy, B. V. (2004) 'Livelihood gains and ecological costs of non-timber forest product dependence: Assessing the roles of dependence, ecological knowledge and market structure in three contrasting human and ecological settings in South India', *Environmental Conservation*, vol 31, no 3, pp242–253

Shepheard, P. (1997) *The Cultivated Wilderness: Or, What Is Landscape?*, The MIT Press, Cambridge, MA

Shepherd, P. (1998) *The Plants of Nottingham: A City Flora*, Wildtrack Publishing, Sheffield

Shiva, V. (2002) *Water Wars: Privatization, Pollution and Profit*, Pluto Press, London

Shultis, J. (1999) 'The duality of wilderness', *Society and Natural Resources*, vol 12, no 5, pp1–16

Shultz, S., Baral, H. M., Charman, S., Cunningham, A. A., Das, D., Ghalsasi, G. R., Goudar, M. S., Green, R. E., Jones, A., Nighot, P., Pain, D. J. and Prakash, V. (2004) 'Diclofenac poisoning is widespread in declining vulture populations across the Indian subcontinent', *Proceedings of the Royal Society London B*, vol 271, ppS458–S460

Sinclair, A. R. E. and Arcese, P. (eds) (1995) *Serengeti II: Dynamics, Management and Conservation of an Ecosystem*, Chicago University Press, Chicago, IL, pp71–90

Sinclair, A. R. E and Norton-Griffiths, M. (eds) (1979) *Serengeti: Dynamics of an Ecosystem*, Chicago University Press, Chicago, IL

Sinclair, A. R. E., Packer, C., Mduma, S. A. R. and Fryxell, J. M. (eds) (2008) *Serengeti III: Human Impacts on Ecosystem Dynamics*, Chicago University Press, Chicago IL

Sinclair, I. (2010) 'Life on the margins', *The Guardian*, 29 May 2010

Singer, P. (1975) *Animal Liberation*, Pimlico, London

Singhvi, L. M. (1990) 'The Jain declaration on nature', Jainism Global Resource Center, Alpharetta, GA, available at www.jainworld.com/jainbooks/Books/Jaindecl.htm (accessed May 2008)

Sloan, N. A. (2002) 'History and application of the wilderness concept in marine conservation', *Conservation Biology*, vol 16, no 2, pp294–305

Smith, R. I. L. (1994) 'Vascular plants as bioindicators of regional warming in Antarctica', *Oecologia*, vol 99, pp322–28

Smith, S. D., Huxman, T. E., Zitzer, S. F., Charlet, T. N., Housman, D. C., Coleman, J. S., Fenstermaker, L. K., Seemann, J. R. and Nowak, R. S. (2000) 'Elevated CO_2 increases productivity and invasive species success in an arid ecosystem', *Nature*, vol 408, pp79–82

Sparks, T. H. and Menzel, A. (2002) 'Observed changes in seasons: An overview', *International Journal of Climatology*, vol 22, pp1715–1725

Spooner, D. S., McLean, K., Ramsay, G., Waugh, R. and Bryan, G. J. (2005) 'A single domestication for potato based on multilocus amplified fragment length polymorphism genotyping', *Proceedings of the National Academy of Sciences of the United States of America*, vol 102, no 41, pp14694–14699

Soulé, M. (1985) 'What is conservation biology?', *Bioscience*, vol 35, no 11, pp727–734

Stattersfield, A. J., Crosby, M. J., Long, A. J. and Wege, D. C. (1998) *Endemic Bird Areas of the World: Priorities for Biodiversity Conservation*, Birdlife Conservation Series No 7, Birdlife International, Cambridge

Steinbeck, J. (1939) *The Grapes of Wrath*, William Heinemann Ltd, London

Steinbeck, J. (1945) *Cannery Row*, William Heinemann Ltd, London

Stephens, S. S. and Wagner, M. R. (2007) 'Forest plantations and biodiversity: A fresh perspective', *Journal of Forestry*, vol 105, no 6, pp307–313

Stirling, I., Lunn, N. J. and Iacozza, J. (1999) 'Long-term trends in the population ecology of polar bears in Western Hudson Bay in relation to climate change', *Arctic*, vol 53, no 3, pp294–306

Stocks, B. J., Fosberg, M. A., Lynham, T. J., Mearns, L., Wotton, B. M., Yang, Q., Jin, J. Z., Lawrence, K., Hartley, G. R., Mason, J. A., and McKenney, D. W. (1998) 'Climate change and forest fire potential in Russian and Canadian boreal forests', *Climatic Change*, vol 38, pp1–13

Stoddard, J. L., Jeffries, D. S., Lükewille, A., Claire, T. A., Dillon, P. J., Driscoll, C. T., Forsius, M., Johannessen, M., Kahl, J. S., Kellog, J. H., Kemp, A., Mannio, J., Monteith, D. T., Murdocj, P. H., Patrick, S., Rebsdorf, A., Skjelkvåle, B. L., Stainton, M. P., Traaen, T., van Dam, H., Webster, K. E., Wieting, J. and Wilander, A. (1999) 'Regional trends in aquatic recovery from acidification in North America and Europe', *Nature*, vol 401, pp575–578

Stolton, S. and Dudley, N. (eds) (2010a) *Arguments for Protected Areas: Multiple Benefits for Conservation and Use*, Earthscan, London

Stolton, S. and Dudley, N. (2010b) *Vital Sites: The Contribution of Protected Areas to Human Health*, WWF and Equilibrium Research, Gland, Switzerland

Stolton, S., Boucher, T., Dudley, N., Hoekstra, J., Maxted, N. and Kell, S. (2008) 'Ecoregions with crop wild relatives are less well protected', *Biodiversity*, vol 9, pp52–55

Stolton, S., Geier, B. and McNeely, J. A. (eds) (2000) *The Relationship between Nature Conservation, Biodiversity and Organic Agriculture*, IFOAM, IUCN and WWF, Tholey-Theley, Germany

Stone, L., Gabric, A. and Berman, T. (1996) 'Ecosystem resilience, stability, and productivity: Seeking a relationship', *American Naturalist*, vol 148, pp892–903

Stout, G.E. (1982) 'Effects of coyote reduction on white-tailed deer production on Fort Sill, Oklahoma', *Wildlife Society Bulletin*, vol. 10, pp329–332

Strauss, S. Y. and Irwin, R. E. (2004) 'Ecological and evolutionary consequences of multi-species plant-animal interactions', *Annual Review of Ecology and Evolutionary Systematics*, vol 35, pp435–466

Strindberg, A. (trans. Sandbach, M.) (1987) *By the Open Sea*, Penguin, Harmondsworth, UK (original title *I Havsbandet*, published 1890)

Strittholt, J., Noguerón, R., Berquist, J. and Alvarez, M. (2006) *Mapping Undisturbed Landscapes of Alaska*, World Resources Institute, Conservation Biology Institute and Global Forest Watch, Washington DC

Stroeve, J., Holland, M. M., Meier, W., Scambos, T. and Serreze, M. (2007) 'Arctic sea ice decline: Faster than forecast', *Geophysical Research Letters*, vol 34, L09501, doi:10.1029/2007/GL029703

Sub-Committee on Acid Rain (1981) *Still Waters: The Chilling Reality of Acid Rain*, House of Commons, Canada, Ottawa

Sukopp, H. (1981) 'Veränderungen von Flora und Vegetation', in Sonderh, F. N. (ed) *Beachtung ökologischer Grezen bei der Landbewirtschaftung*, vol 197, S255–264. Quoted in Baldock, D. (1990) *Agriculture and Habitat Loss in Europe*, WWF International CAP Discussion Paper No 3, WWF International, Gland, Switzerland

Sulayem, M. and Joubert, E. (1994) 'Management of protected areas in the kingdom of Saudi Arabia', *Unasylva*, no 176, UN Food and Agricultural Organization, Rome

Sullivan, T. P., Lautenschlager, R. A. and Wagner, R. G. (1999) 'Clearcutting and burning of northern spruce-fir forests: Implications for small mammal communities', *Journal of Applied Ecology*, vol 36, no 3, pp327–344

Swearer, D. K. (1998) 'Buddhism and ecology: Challenge and promise', *Earth Ethics*, vol 10, no 1, pp19–22

Sylven, M., Wijnberg, B. and Schepers, F. (undated) *Rewilding Europe*, WWF, ARK and Wild Wonders of Europe, Nijmegen, The Netherlands

Taylor, F., Mateke, S. and Butterworth, K. (1996) 'A holistic approach to the domestication and commercialization of non-timber forest products', in Leakey, R., Temu, A., Melnyk, M. and Vantomme, P. (eds) *International Conference on Domestication and Commercialization of Non-Timber Forest Products*, Agroforestry Systems, Non-Wood Forest Products, No 9, Food and Agriculture Organization of the United Nations, Rome, pp75–85

TEEB (2009) *The Economics of Ecosystems and Biodiversity for National and International Policy Makers*

TEEB (2010) *The Economics of Ecosystems and Biodiversity: Ecological and Economic Foundations*, edited by Pushpam Kumar; an output of TEEB: The Economics of Ecosystems and Biodiversity, Earthscan, London

TEEB (2011a) *The Economics of Ecosystems and Biodiversity in National and International Policy Making*, edited By Patrick ten Brink, an output of TEEB: The Economics of Ecosystems and Biodiversity. Earthscan, London

TEEB (2011b) *The Economics of Ecosystems and Biodiversity in Local and Regional Policy and Management*, edited by Heidi Wittmer and Haripriya Gundimeda, an output of TEEB: The Economics of Ecosystems and Biodiversity, Earthscan, London

TEEB (2011c) *The Economics of Ecosystems in Business and Enterprise*, edited by Josh Bishop, an out put of TEEB: The Economics of Ecosystems and Biodiversity, Earthscan, London

ten Kate, K. and Laird, S. A. (1999) *The Commercial Use of Biodiversity: Access to Genetic Resources and Benefit Sharing*, Earthscan, London

Terborgh, J. (1992) *Diversity and the Tropical Rain Forest*, Scientific American Library, New York

Thoreau, H. D. (1849) *On the Duty of Civil Disobedience* (original title 'Resistance to Civil Government'), in Peabody, E. P. (ed) *Aesthetic Papers*, Boston, MA

Thoreau, H. D. (1854) *Walden or Life in the Woods*, Ticknor and Field, Boston, MA

Thorpe, V. and Dudley, N. (1985) *Pall of Poison: The Spray Drift Story*, The Soil Association, Haughley, UK

Tickle, A., with Fergusson, M. and Drucker, G. (1995) *Acid Rain and Nature Conservation in Europe: A Preliminary Study of Areas at Risk from Acidification*, WWF International, Gland, Switzerland

Thompson, I., Mackey, B., McNulty, S. and Mosseler, A. (2009) *Forest Resilience, Biodiversity, and Climate Change: A Synthesis of the Biodiversity/Resilience/Stability Relationship in Forest Ecosystems*, CBD Technical Series No 43, Secretariat of the Convention on Biological Diversity, Montreal

Tinner, W., Hubschmid, P., Wehrli, M., Ammann, B. and Conedera, M. (1999) 'Long-term forest fire ecology and dynamics in southern Switzerland', *Journal of Ecology*, vol 87, pp273–289

Tompkins, D. M., Sainsbury, A. W., Nettleton, P., Buxton, D. and Gurnell, J. (2002) 'Parapoxvirus causes a deleterious disease in red squirrels associated with UK population declines', *Proceedings of the Royal Society London*, vol 269, pp529–533

Tompkins, S. (1986) *The Theft of the Hills: Afforestation in Scotland*, The Ramblers Association and WWF, London

TRAFFIC (1998) *Europe's Medicinal and Aromatic Plants: Their Use, Trade and Conservation: A Species in Danger Report*, Cambridge, UK

Trumper, K., Bertzky, M., Dickson, B., van der Heijden, G., Jenkins, M. and Manning P. (2009) *The Natural Fix? The Role of Ecosystems in Climate Mitigation*, UNEP rapid response assessment, United Nations Environment Programme, UNEPWCMC, Cambridge, UK

Tryzna, T. (ed) (2005) *The Urban Imperitive: Urban Outreach Strategies for Protected Area Agencies*, IUCN, Gland, Switzerland

Tucker, M. E. and Williams, D. R. (eds) (1998) *Buddhism and Ecology: The Interconnection of Dharma and Deeds*, Harvard University Press, Cambridge, MA

Turk, R. and Wirth, V. (1975) 'The pH dependence of SO_2 damage to lichens', *Oecologia*, vol 19, pp285–291

Turpie, J., Clark, B. and Hutchings, K. (2006) *The Economic Value of Marine Protected Areas along the Garden Route Coast, South Africa, and Implications of Changes in Size and Management*, WWF South Africa, Stellenbosch

Ulrich, S. C. and Ward, J. C. (1997) *Indicators of Natural Character of Freshwater: Generic Approaches to Management*, Information Paper No 57, Lincoln Environmental/Centre for Resource Management, Lincoln University, New Zealand

UNECE (2000) *Forest Resources of Europe, CIS, North America, Australia, Japan and New Zealand – Main Report*, United Nations Economic Commission for Europe and United Nations Food and Agriculture Organization, New York and Geneva

UNEP-WCMC (2008) *State of the World's Protected Areas: An Annual Review of Global Conservation Progress*, UNEP-WCMC, Cambridge

UNEP and WHRC (2007) *Reactive Nitrogen in the Environment: Too Much or Too Little of a Good Thing*, United Nations Environment Programme, Paris

UNESCO (2005) *Operational Guidelines for the Implementation of the World Heritage Convention*, World Heritage Committee and World Heritage Centre, Paris

UNESCO Website, http://whc.unesco.org/en/list/946, accessed 13 September 2010

UNHSP (United Nations Human Settlement Programme) (2003) *Water and Sanitation in the World's Cities: Local Action for Global Goals*, Earthscan, London

Ura, K. (2004) 'The herdsman's dilemma', *Journal of Bhutan Studies*, vol 11, pp1–43

Urban, M. C., Phillips, B. L., Skelly, D. K. and Shine, R. (2007) 'The cane toad's (*Chaunus [Bufo] marinus*) increasing ability to invade Australia is revealed by a dynamically updated range model', *Proceedings of the Royal Society B*, vol 274, pp1413–1419

Utting, P. (1991) *The Social Origins and Impact of Deforestation in Central America*, United Nations Research Institute for Social Development, Discussion Paper 24, UNRISD, Geneva, pp23–25

Vale, T. R. (1998) 'The myth of the humanized landscape: An example from Yosemite National Park', *Natural Areas Journal*, vol 18, no 3, pp231–236

Vallauri, D. and Poncet, L. (2002) *Etat de la protection des forêts en France: Indicateurs 2002*, WWF, Paris, www.wwf.fr/content/download/694/3365/version/2/file/Fiche13.pdf, accessed 23 January 2011

Vallauri, D., Aronson, J. and Dudley, N. (2005) 'An attempt to develop a framework for restoration planning', in Mansourian, S., Vallauri, D. and Dudley, N. (eds) *Forest Restoration in Landscapes: Beyond Planting Trees*, Springer, New York, pp65–72

van Auken, O. W. (2000) 'Scrub invasion of North American semiarid grassland', *Annual Review of Ecology and Systematics*, vol 31, pp197–215

van der Heijden, M. G. A., Klironomos, J. N., Streitwolf-Engel, R., Boller, T., Wiemken, A. and Sanders, I. R. (1998) 'Mycorrhizal fungal diversity determines plant biodiversity, ecosystem variability and productivity', *Nature*, vol 396, no 5, pp69–72

van Dobben, H. F., de Wit, T. and van Dam, D. (1983) 'Effects of acid deposition on vegetation in the Netherlands', *VDI-Berichte* number 500

van Herk, C. M., Aptroot, A., van Dobben, H. F. (2002) 'Long-term monitoring in the Netherlands suggests that lichens respond to global warming', *Lichenologist*, vol, 34, pp141–154

van Zalinge, N. (2003) 'Data requirements for the fishery management in Tonle Sap', in FAO and MRC, *New Approches for the Improvement of Inland Fishery Capture Statistics for the Mekong Basin*, Food and Agricultural Organisation, Bangkok, pp67–74

Vancura, V., Kun, Z. and van der Donk, M. (2008) 'Pan Parks perspectives for a wilder Europe', *International Journal of Wilderness*, vol 14, no 1, pp38–42

Vedeld, P., Angelsen, A., Sjaastad, E. and Berg, G. K. (2004) *Counting on the Environment: Forest Incomes and the Rural Poor*, Environmental Economics Series Paper No 98, World Bank, Washington DC

Vermes, G. (1962) *The Complete Dead Sea Scrolls in English*, Pelican Books, Harmondsworth, UK

Vissier, M. E. and Both, C. (2005) 'Shifts in phenology due to global climate change: The need for a yardstick', *Proceedings of the Royal Society*, vol 272, pp2561–2569

Vittor, A. Y., Pan, W., Gilman, R. H., Tielsch, J., Glass, G., Shields, T., Sánchez-Lozano, W., Pinedo, V. V., Salas-Cobos, E., Flores, S. and Patz, J. A. (2009) 'Linking deforestation to malaria in the Amazon: Characterization of the breeding habitat of the principal malaria vector, *Anopheles darling*', *American Journal of Tropical Medicine and Hygiene*, vol 81, pp5–12

Vogel, D. (1999) *How Green is Judaism?*, University of Berkeley, Berkeley, CA

Vors, L. S. and Boyce, M. S. (2009) 'Global decline of caribou and reindeer', *Global Change Biology*, vol 15, no 11, pp2626–2633

Vos, C. C., Berry, P., Opdam, P., Baveco, H., Nijhof, B., O'Hanley, J., Bell, C. and Kuipers, H. (2008) 'Adapting landscapes to climate change: Examples of climate-proof ecosystem networks and priority adaptation zones', *Journal of Applied Ecology*, vol 45, pp1722–1731

Wakenham-Dawson, A. and Aebischer, N. B. (1998) 'Factors determining winter densities of birds on Environmentally Sensitive Area arable reversion grassland in southern England, with special reference to skylarks (*Alauda arvensis*)', *Agriculure, Ecosystems and Environment*, vol 70, pp189–201

Walker, B., Holling, C. S., Carpenter, S. R., and Kinzig, A. (2004) 'Resilience, adaptability and transformability in social–ecological systems', *Ecology and Society*, vol 9, no 2 [online], www.ecologyandsociety.org/vol9/iss2/art5, accessed 19 December 2010

Walston, J., Robinson, J. G., Bennett, E. L., Breitenmoser, U., da Fonseca, G. A. B., Goodrich, J., Gumal, M., Hunter, L., Johnson, A., Karanth, K. U., Leader-Williams, N., MacKinnon, K., Miquelle, D., Pattanavibool, A., Poole, C., Rabinowitz, A., Smith, J. L. D., Stokes, E. J., Stuart, S. N., Vongkhamheng, C. and Wibiscono, H. (2010) 'Bringing the tiger back from the brink: The six percent solution', *PLoS Biology*, vol 8, no 9

Walther, G. R., Post, E., Convey, P., Menzel, A., Parmesan, C., Beebee, T. J. C., Fromentin, J. M., Hoegh-Guldberg, O. and Bairlein, F. (2002) 'Ecological responses to recent climate change', *Nature*, vol 416, pp389–395

Watson, A., Alessa, L. and Glaspell, B. (2003) 'The relationship between traditional ecological knowledge, evolving cultures, and wilderness protection in the circumpolar North', *Conservation Ecology*, vol 8, no 1

Weber, T. (1988) *Hugging the Trees: The Story of the Chipko Movement*, Viking, London

White, G. (1789) *The Natural History and Antiquities of Selborne*, Thames and Hudson, London

White, L. (1967) 'The historic roots of our ecologic crisis', *Science*, vol 155, no 3767, pp1203–1207

White, R., Murray, S. and Rohweder, M. (2000) *Pilot Analysis of Global Ecosystems: Grassland Ecosystems*, World Resources Institute, Washington DC

Whittaker, J. B. (1994) 'Interactions between insects and air pollutants', in Alscher, R. G. and Wellburn, A. R. (eds) *Responses to the Gaseous Environment: Molecular, Metabolic and Physiological Aspects*, Chapman and Hall, London, Glasgow, New York

WHO (2002) *WHO Traditional Medicine Strategy 2002–2005*, World Health Organization, Geneva

WHO (2005) *Ecosystems and Human Well-being: Health Synthesis*, World Health Organisation, Geneva, Switzerland

Wild, R. and McLeod, C. (eds) (2008) *Sacred Natural Sites: Guidelines for Protected Area Managers*, IUCN, Gland, Switzerland

Wild, R. G. and Mutebi, J. (1997) 'Bwindi Impenetrable Forest Uganda: Conservation through collaborative management', *Nature and Resources*, vol 33, nos 3 and 4, pp33–51

Wiles, G. F., Bart, J., Beck, R. E. Jr. and Aguon, C. F. (2003) 'Impacts of the brown tree snake: Patterns of decline and species persistence in Guam's avifauna', *Conservation Biology*, vol 17, no 5, pp1350–1360

Willis, K. J. and Birks, H. J. B. (2006) 'What is natural? The need for a long-term perspective in biodiversity conservation', *Science*, vol 314, pp1261–1265,

Williamson, H. (1927) *Tarka the Otter*, G. P. Putnam's Sons, London

Wilson, E. O. (1988) *Biodiversity*, National Academy Press, Washington DC

Wood, S., Sebastian, K. and Scherr, S. J. (2000) *Pilot Analysis of Global Ecosystems: Agroecosystems*, International Food Policy Research Institute and World Resources Institute, Washington DC

Woodley, S. (2010) 'Ecological integrity: A framework for ecosystem-based management', in Cole, D. and Yung, L. (eds) *Beyond Naturalness: Rethinking Park and Wilderness Stewardship in an Era of Rapid Change*, Island Press, Washington DC, pp106–124

Woodley, S., Kay, J. and Francis, G. (1993) *Ecological Integrity and the Management of Ecosystems*, St Lucie Press, Ottawa, Canada

Woodward, L., Stolton, S. and Dudley, N. (eds) (1990) *Food Quality: Concepts and Methodology: Proceedings of a Colloquium Organised by Elm Farm Research Centre in Association with the University of Kassel*, Elm Farm Research Centre, Newbury, UK

Worboys, G. L., Francis, W. L. and Lockwood, M. (eds) (2010) *Connectivity Conservation Management: A Global Guide*, Earthscan, London

World Bank (2004) *Saving Fish and Fishers: Toward Sustainable and Equitable Governance of the Global Fishing Sector*, Report No 29090-GLB, Agriculture and Rural Development Department, World Bank, Washington DC

World Water Council (2000) *World Water Vision*, Earthscan, London

Worm, B., Hilborn, R., Baum, J. K., Branch, T. A., Collie, J. S., Costello, C., Fogarty, M. J., Fulton, E. A., Hutchings, J. A., Jennings, S., Jensen, O. P., Lotze, H. K., Mace, P. M., McClanahan, T. R., Minto, C., Palumbi, S. R., Parma, A., Ricard, D., Rosenberg, A. A., Watson, R. and Zeller, D. (2009) 'Rebuilding global fisheries', *Science*, vol 325, pp578–585

Wright, R. F., Dale, T., Gjessing, E. T., Hendrey, G. R., Henkiksen, A., Johannssen, M. and Muniz, I. P. (1976) 'Impact of acid precipitation on freshwater ecosystems in Norway', *Water, Air and Soil Pollution*, vol 6, pp483–499

Wroe, S., Field, J., Fullagar, R. and Jermin, L. S. (2004) 'Megafaunal extinction in the late Quaternary and the global overkill hypothesis', *Alcheringa: An Australasian Journal of Palaeontology*, vol 28, no 1, pp291—331

WWF (undated) *Free-Flowing Rivers: Economic Luxury or Ecological Necessity?*, WWF, Zeist, Netherlands

Yalden, D. W. (1988) 'Feral wallabies in the Peak District', *Journal of Zoology*, vol 215, no 2, pp369–374

Yaroshenko, A. Y., Potapov, P. V. and Turubanova, S. A. (2001) *The Last Intact Forest Landscapes of Northern European Russia*, Greenpeace Russia and Global Forest Watch, Moscow and Washington DC

Zakrzewski, P. A. (2002) 'Bioprospecting or biopiracy? The pharmaceutical industry's use of indigenous medicinal plants as a source of potential drug candidates', *University of Toronto Medical Journal*, vol 79, pp252–254

Index